ST. MARY'S COLLEGE OF MARYLAND
ST. MARY'S CITY, MARYLAND

W9-BWI-764

HERR EUGEN DÜHRING'S
REVOLUTION IN SCIENCE

[ANTI-DÜHRING]

48395

Herr Eugen Dühring's

Revolution in Science

(*Anti-Dühring*)

BY FREDERICK ENGELS

INTERNATIONAL PUBLISHERS, NEW YORK

Translated by EMILE BURNS

Edited by C. P. DUTT

Library of Congress Catalog Card Number: 66-21950

New Printing, 1966

COPYRIGHT, 1939

INTERNATIONAL PUBLISHERS CO., INC.

———

PRINTED IN THE U. S. A.

CONTENTS

v

PART II. POLITICAL ECONOMY

PART III. SOCIALISM

HERR EUGEN DÜHRING'S
REVOLUTION IN SCIENCE
[*ANTI-DÜHRING*]

PREFACES TO THE THREE EDITIONS

I

The following work is by no means the fruit of any "inner urge." On the contrary.

When three years ago Herr Dühring, as an adept and at the same time a reformer of socialism, suddenly issued his challenge to his age, friends in Germany repeatedly urged on me their desire that I should write a critical examination of this new socialist theory for the central organ of the Social-Democratic Party, at that time the *Volksstaat*. They thought this absolutely necessary in order to prevent a new occasion for sectarian divisions and confusion from developing within the Party, which was still so young and had but just achieved definite unity. They were in a better position than I was to judge the situation in Germany, and I was therefore compelled to accept their view. Moreover, it became apparent that the new convert was being welcomed by a section of the socialist press with a warmth which it is true was only extended to Herr Dühring's good will, but which at the same time also indicated that in this section of the Party press, there existed good will, precisely on account of Herr Dühring's good will, to take also without examination Herr Dühring's doctrine into the bargain. There were also people who were already beginning to spread this doctrine in a popularised form among the workers. And finally Herr Dühring and his little sect were using all the arts of advertisement and intrigue to force the *Volksstaat* to take a definite stand in relation to the new doctrine which had come forward with such mighty pretensions.

Nevertheless it was a year before I could make up my mind to neglect other work and get my teeth into this sour apple. It was the kind of apple that, once bitten into, had to be completely devoured;

and it was not only very sour, but also very large. The new socialist theory was presented as the ultimate practical fruit of a new philosophical system. It was therefore necessary to examine it in connection with this system, and in doing so to examine the system itself; it was necessary to follow Herr Dühring into that vast territory in which he dealt with all things under the sun and then a few more. This was the origin of a series of articles which appeared in the Leipzig *Vorwärts*, the successor of the *Volksstaat*, from the beginning of 1877 on and is here presented as a connected whole.

It was thus the nature of the object itself which forced the criticism to assume a length entirely out of proportion to the scientific content of his object, that is to say, of Dühring's writings. But there are also two other considerations which may excuse this length of treatment. On the one hand it gave me, in connection with the very diverse subjects touched on in this book, the opportunity to develop in a positive form my views on questions which are today of wide scientific or practical interest. This has been done in every single chapter, and although this work cannot in any way aim at presenting another system as an alternative to Herr Dühring's "system," yet it is to be hoped that the reader will not fail to observe the internal coherence underlying the views which I have advanced. I have already had proof enough that in this respect my work has not been entirely fruitless.

On the other hand, the "system-creating" Herr Dühring is by no means an isolated phenomenon in contemporary Germany. For some time now in Germany systems of cosmogony, of natural philosophy in general, of politics, of economics, etc., have been shooting up by dozens overnight, like mushrooms. The most insignificant doctor of philosophy and even the student will not go in for anything less than a complete "system." Just as in the modern state it is presumed that every citizen is competent to pass judgment on all the issues upon which he has to vote; and as in economics it is assumed that every consumer is a real specialist on all the commodities which he has occasion to buy for his maintenance—so similar assumptions are now to be made in science. Freedom of science is taken to mean that people write on every subject which they have not studied, and put this forward as the only strictly scientific method. Herr **Dühring**, however, is one of the most characteristic types of this noisy pseudo-science which in Germany nowadays is forcing its way to the front everywhere and is drowning everything with its booming—sublime nonsense. Sublime nonsense in poetry, in philosophy, in politics, in economics, in the writing of history; sublime nonsense in the lecture-room and on the platform, sublime nonsense everywhere; sublime nonsense which lays claim to a superiority and depth of thought distinguishing it from the simple, commonplace nonsense of other nations; sublime nonsense the most characteristic mass-product of Germany's intellectual industry, cheap but bad—just like other German products, along with which unfortunately it was not exhibited at Philadelphia. Even German socialism, particularly since Herr Dühring's good example, has lately gone in for a considerable amount of sublime nonsense, producing one person after another who gives himself airs about "science," of which he "really never learnt a word." This is an infantile sickness which marks the first phase of, and is inseparable from, the conversion of the German student to social-democracy, but will rapidly be thrown off in view of the remarkably healthy instincts of our working class.

It was not my fault that I had to follow Herr Dühring into realms where at best I can only claim to be a dilettante. In such cases I have for the most part limited myself to putting forward the correct, uncontested facts in opposition to my adversary's false or distorted assertions. This applies to jurisprudence and in many instances also to natural science. In other cases it has been a question of general views connected with the theory of natural science—that is to say, a field where even the professional scientific investigator is compelled to pass beyond his own specialty and encroach on neighbouring territory—territory on which his knowledge is, therefore, as Herr Virchow has admitted, just as superficial as any of ours. I hope that in respect of minor inexactitudes and clumsiness of expression, I shall be granted the same indulgence as is shown to each other by writers in this domain.

Just as I was completing this preface I received a publisher's notice composed by Herr Dühring, of a new "authoritative" work of Herr Dühring's: *New Basic Principles for a Rational Physics and Chemis-*

try. Conscious as I am of the inadequacy of my knowledge of physics and chemistry, I nevertheless believe that I know my Herr Dühring, and therefore, without having seen the work itself, think that I am entitled to say in advance that the principles of physics and chemistry put forward in it will be worthy to take their place, according to their erroneousness or platitudinousness, among the principles of economics, world schematism, etc., which were discovered earlier by Herr Dühring and are examined in this book of mine; and also that the rhigometer, or instrument constructed by Herr Dühring for measuring extremely low temperatures, will serve as a measure not of temperatures either high or low but simply and solely of the ignorant arrogance of Herr Dühring.

London, June 11, 1878.

II

I had not expected that a second edition of this book would have to be published. The subject matter of its criticism is now practically forgotten; the work itself has not only been available to many thousands of readers in the form of a series of articles published in the Leipzig *Vorwärts* in the course of 1877 and 1878, but has also appeared in its entirety as a separate book, of which a large edition was printed. How then can anyone still be interested in what I had to say about Herr Dühring several years ago?

I think that I owe this in the first place to the fact that this book, as in general almost all my other works that were still current at the time, was prohibited within the German Empire as soon as the Anti-Socialist Law came into force. To anyone whose brain has not been ossified by the hereditary bureaucratic prejudices of the countries of the Holy Alliance, the effect of this measure must have been self-evident: a doubled and trebled sale of the prohibited books, and the exposure of the impotence of the gentlemen in Berlin who issue prohibitions and are unable to enforce them. Indeed the kindness of the Imperial Government has brought me more new editions of my minor works that I can hold myself responsible for; I have had no time to make a proper revision of the text, and have been obliged as a rule simply to allow it to be reprinted as it stood.

But there was also another factor. The "system" of Herr Dühring which is criticised in this book ranges over a very wide theoretical domain; and I was compelled to follow him wherever he went and to oppose my conceptions to his. In the process of carrying this out my negative criticism became positive; the polemic was transformed into a more or less connected exposition of the dialectical method and of the communist world outlook represented by Marx and myself—an exposition covering a fairly comprehensive range of subjects. After its first public formulation in Marx's *Poverty of Philosophy* and in the *Communist Manifesto,* this theory of ours passed through an incubation period of fully twenty years before the publication of *Capital.* Since then its influence has been more and more rapidly extending among ever-widening circles, and it now finds recognition and support far beyond the boundaries of Europe, in every country which contains on the one hand proletarians and on the other consistent scientific theoreticians. It seems therefore that there is a public whose interest in the subject is great enough for them to take into the bargain the polemics against the Dühring statements, in spite of the fact that these have now largely lost their point, for the sake of the positive conceptions developed alongside of the polemics.

I may note in passing that inasmuch as the genesis and development of the mode of outlook expounded in this book were due in far greater measure to Marx, and only in a very small degree to myself, it was of course self-understood between us that this exposition of mine should not be issued without his knowledge. I read the whole manuscript to him before it was printed, and the tenth chapter of the section on economics ('From the *Critical History*') was written by Marx, and my part in it was only to shorten it slightly, to my regret, for purely external reasons. As a matter of fact, we had always been accustomed to help each other out in special subjects.

With the exception of one chapter, the present new edition is an unaltered reprint of the former edition. I had no time for a thoroughgoing revision, although there was much in the form of presentation that I should have liked to alter. But I am under the obligation to prepare for the press the manuscripts which Marx has left, and this is much more important than anything else. Then again, my

conscience is opposed to making any alterations. The book is a
polemic, and I think that I owe it to my adversary not to improve
anything in my work when he is not in a position to improve his.
I could only claim the right to make a rejoinder to Herr Dühring's
reply. But I have not read, and will not read unless there is some
special reason to do so, what Herr Dühring has written in connection
with my attack; I have finished with him so far as his theories are
concerned. Besides, I must observe the rules of decency in literary
warfare all the more strictly in his regard, because of the despicable
injustice that has since been done him by the University of Berlin.
It is true that the University has not gone unpunished. A University
which so abases itself as to deprive Herr Dühring, in circumstances
which everyone knows, of the right to teach, cannot be surprised
to find Herr Schweninger forced on it in circumstances which are
equally well-known to everyone.

The only chapter in which I have allowed myself some additional
elucidation is the second of the third section: *Theory*. This chapter
deals simply and solely with the exposition of one central point in
the world outlook for which I stand, and my adversary cannot
therefore complain if I attempt to state it in a more popular form
and to make it more complete. And there was in fact a special reason
for doing this. I had revised three chapters of the book (the first
chapter of the introduction and the first and second of the third
section) of my friend Lafargue with a view to their translation into
French and publication as a separate pamphlet; and after the French
edition had served as the basis for Italian and Polish editions, a
German edition was issued under the title: *The Development of
Socialism from Utopia to Science*. This ran through three editions
within a few months, and also appeared in Russian and Danish
translations. In all these editions it was only the chapter in question
which had been amplified, and it would have been pedantic, in the
new edition of the original work, to have tied myself down to its
original form instead of the later form which had become known
internationally.

Passages which I should otherwise have liked to alter are those
covering in the main two points. The first was the history of primitive society, the key to which was provided by Morgan only in

1877. But as I have since then had the opportunity, in my work: *The Origin of the Family, Private Property and the State* (Zurich, 1884), to work up the material which in the meantime had become available to me, a reference to this later work meets the case.

The second point concerns the section dealing with theoretical natural science. There is much that is clumsy in my exposition of this question and much of it could be expressed today in a clearer and more definite form. Inasmuch as I have not allowed myself the right to amend this section, I am just for that reason under an obligation, as an alternative to amending it, to criticise myself here.

Marx and I were pretty well the only people to rescue conscious dialectics from German idealist philosophy and apply it in the materialist conception of nature and history. But a knowledge of mathematics and natural science is essential to a conception of nature which is dialectical and at the same time materialist. Marx was well versed in mathematics, but we could only partially, intermittently and sporadically keep up with the natural sciences. For this reason, when I retired from business and transferred my home to London, thus enabling myself to give the necessary time to it, I went through as complete as possible a "moulting," as Liebig calls it, in mathematics and the natural sciences, and spent the best part of eight years on it. I was right in the middle of this "moulting" process when I had occasion to turn my attention to Herr Dühring's so-called natural philosophy. It is therefore only too natural that in dealing with this subject I was often unable to find the correct technical expression, and in general moved with a certain clumsiness in the field of theoretical natural science. On the other hand, my knowledge that I was still insecure in this field made me cautious, and I cannot be charged with real blunders in relation to the facts known at that time or with the incorrect presentations of recognised theories. In this connection there was only one unrecognised genius of a mathematician who complained in a letter to Marx that I had made a wanton attack upon the honour of $\sqrt{-1}$.

It goes without saying that my recapitulation of mathematics and the natural sciences was undertaken in order to convince myself in detail—of which in general I was not in doubt—that amid the welter of innumerable changes taking place in nature, the same dialectical laws of motion are in operation as those which in history govern the apparent fortuitousness of events; the same laws as those which similarly form the thread running through the history of the development of human thought and gradually rise to consciousness in the mind of man; the laws which Hegel first developed in all-embracing but mystical form, and which we made it our aim to strip of this mystic form and to bring clearly before the mind in their complete simplicity and universality. It went without saying that the old natural philosophy—in spite of its real value and the many fruitful seeds it contains—was unable to satisfy us.*

---

* It is much easier, along with the unthinking mob à la Karl Vogt, to assail the old natural philosophy than to appreciate its historical significance. It contains a great deal of nonsense and phantasy, but not more than the contemporary unphilosophical theories of the empirical natural scientists and that there was also in it much that was sensible and rational is beginning to be perceived now that the theory of evolution is becoming widespread. Haeckel, for example, was fully justified in recognising the merits of Treviranus and Oken. In his primordial slime and primordial vesicle Oken put forward as biological postulates what were in fact subsequently discovered as protoplasm and cell. As far as Hegel is concerned, in many respects he is head and shoulders above his empiricist contemporaries, who thought that they had explained all unexplained phenomena when they had endowed them with some power—the power of gravity, the power of buoyancy, the power of electrical contact, etc., or where this would not do, with some unknown substance: the substance of light, of warmth, of electricity, etc. The imaginary substances have now been pretty well discarded, but the power humbug against which Hegel fought still pops up gaily, for example, as lately as 1869 in Helmholtz's Innsbruck lecture (Helmholtz, Popular Lectures, Vol. 2, 1871, German edition, p. 190). In opposition to the deification of Newton which was handed down from the French of the eighteenth century, and the English heaping of honours and wealth on Newton, Hegel brought out the fact that Kepler, whom Germany allowed to starve, was the real founder of the modern mechanics of the celestial bodies, and that the Newtonian law of gravity was already contained in all three of Kepler's laws, in the third law even explicitly. What Hegel proves by a few simple equations in his Natural Philosophy §270 and Notes (Hegel's Works, German edition, 1842, Vol. VII, p. 98 and 113-15), appears again as the outcome of the most recent mathematical mechanics in Gustav Kirchhoff's Lectures on Mathematical Physics, second German edition, Leipzig, 1877, p. 10, and in essentially the same simple mathematical form as had first been developed by Hegel. The natural philosophers stand in the same relation to consciously

As is more fully brought out in this book, natural philosophy, particularly in the Hegelian form, was lacking in that it did not recognise any development of nature in time, any "succession," but only "juxtaposition." This was on the one hand grounded in the Hegelian system itself, which ascribed historical evolution only to the "spirit," but on the other hand was also due to the whole state of the natural sciences at that period. In this Hegel fell far behind Kant, whose nebular theory had already indicated the origin of the solar system, and whose discovery of the retardation of the earth's rotation by the tides had already also proclaimed its extinction. And finally, to me there could be no question of building the laws of dialectics into Nature, but of discovering them in it and evolving them from it.

But to do this systematically and in each separate department is a gigantic task. Not only is the domain to be mastered almost limitless; over the whole of this domain natural science itself is also in such a mighty process of being revolutionised that even people who can devote the whole of their spare time to it can hardly keep pace. Since Karl Marx's death, however, my time has been requisitioned for more urgent duties, and I have therefore been compelled to lay aside my work. For the present I must content myself with the indications given in this book, and must wait to find some later opportunity to put together and publish the results which I have arrived at, perhaps in conjunction with the extremely important mathematical manuscripts left by Marx.

It may be, however, that the advance of theoretical natural science will make my work to a great extent or even altogether superfluous. For the revolution which is being forced on theoretical natural science by the mere need to set in order the purely empirical discoveries, great masses of which are now being piled up, is of such a kind that it must bring the dialectical character of natural events more and more to the consciousness even of those empiricists who are most opposed to it. The old rigid antitheses, the sharp, impassable dividing lines are more and more disappearing. Since even the last "pure" gases have been liquefied, and since it has been proved that

dialectical natural science as the utopians to modern communism. [*Note by F. Engels.*]

a body can be brought into a condition in which the liquid and the gaseous forms cannot be distinguished from each other, the physical states have lost the last relics of their former absolute character. With the thesis of the kinetic theory of gases, that in perfect gases at equal temperature the squares of the speeds with which the individual gas molecules move are in inverse ratio to their molecular weight, heat also takes its place directly among the forms of motion which can be immediately measured as such. Although ten years ago the great basic law of motion, then recently discovered, was as yet conceived merely as a law of the *conservation* of energy, as the mere expression of the indestructibility and uncreatability of motion, that is, merely in its quantitative aspect, this narrow, negative conception is being more and more supplanted by the positive idea of the *transformation* of energy, in which for the first time the qualitative content of the process comes into its own, and the last vestige of a creator external to the world is obliterated. That the quantity of motion (so-called energy) remains unaltered when it is transformed from kinetic energy (so-called mechanical force) into electricity, heat, potential energy, etc., and *vice versa,* no longer needs to be preached as something new; it serves as the already secured basis for the investigation, which is now of much greater significance, into the process of transformation itself, the great basic process, knowledge of which comprises all knowledge of Nature. And since biology has been pursued in the light of the theory of evolution, in the domain of organic nature one fixed boundary line of classification after another has been swept away. The almost unclassifiable intermediate links are growing daily more numerous; closer investigation throws organisms out of one class into another, and distinguishing characteristics which had become almost articles of faith are losing their absolute validity; we now have mammals that lay eggs, and if the report is confirmed, also birds that walk on all-fours. Years ago Virchow was compelled, following on the discovery of the cell, to dissolve the unity of the individual animal being into a federation of cell-states—a theory which was progressive rather than scientific and dialectical—and now the conception of animal (therefore also human) individuality is becoming far more complex owing to the discovery of the amœba-like white blood corpuscles which creep about within the bodies of the higher animals. It is however precisely the polar antagonisms put forward as irreconcilable and insoluble, the forcibly fixed lines of demarcation and distinctions between classes, which have given modern theoretical natural science its restricted and metaphysical character. The recognition that these antagonisms and distinctions are in fact to be found in nature, but only with relative validity, and that on the other hand their imagined rigidity and absoluteness have been introduced into nature only by our minds—this recognition is the kernel of the dialectical conception of nature. It is possible to reach this standpoint because the accumulating facts of natural science compel us to do so; but we reach it more easily if we approach the dialectical character of these facts equipped with the consciousness of the laws of dialectical thought. In any case natural science has now advanced so far that it can no longer escape the dialectical synthesis. But it will make this process easier for itself if it does not lose sight of the fact that the results in which its experiences are summarized are concepts; but that the art of working with concepts is not inborn and also is not given with ordinary everyday consciousness, but requires real thought, and that this thought similarly has a long empirical history, not more and not less than empirical natural science. Only by learning to assimilate the results of the development of philosophy during the past two and a half thousand years will it be able to rid itself on the one hand of any isolated natural philosophy standing apart from it, outside it and above it, and on the other hand also of its own limited method of thought, which was its inheritance from English empiricism.

London, September 23, 1885.

III

The following new edition is a reprint of the former edition, except for a few very unimportant stylistic changes. It is only in one chapter—the tenth of Part II: 'From the *Critical History*'—that I have allowed myself to make substantial additions to the text, on the following grounds.

As already stated in the preface to the second edition, this chapter was in all essentials the work of Marx. I was forced to make considerable cuts in Marx's manuscript, which in its first form had been intended as an article for a journal; and I cut precisely those parts of it in which the critique of Dühring's statements was overshadowed by his own treatment of developments in the history of economics. But this is just the section of the manuscript which is even today of the greatest and most permanent interest. I consider myself under an obligation to give in as full and faithful a form as possible the passages in which Marx assigns to people like Petty, North, Locke and Hume their appropriate place in the genesis of classical political economy; and even more his explanation of Quesnay's *Economic Tableau*, which has remained an insoluble riddle of the sphinx for all modern economists. On the other hand, wherever the thread of the argument makes this possible, I have omitted passages which refer exclusively to Herr Dühring's writings.

For the rest I may well be perfectly satisfied with the degree to which, since the previous edition of this book was issued, the views expounded in it have penetrated into the general consciousness of science and of the working class in every civilised country of the world.

F. ENGELS.

London, May 23, 1894.

INTRODUCTION

I. GENERAL

Modern socialism is, in its content, primarily the product of the perception on the one hand of the class antagonisms existing in modern society, between possessors and non-possessors, wage workers and bourgeois; and on the other hand, of the anarchy ruling in production. In its theoretical form, however, it originally appears as a further and ostensibly more consistent extension of the principles established by the great French philosophers of the eighteenth century. Like every new theory, it had at first to link itself on to the intellectual material which lay ready to its hand, however deep its roots lay in economic facts.

The great men who in France were clearing the minds of men for the coming revolution themselves acted in an extremely revolutionary fashion. They recognised no external authority of any kind. Religion, conceptions of nature, society, political systems, everything was subjected to the most merciless criticism; everything had to justify its existence at the bar of reason or renounce all claim to existence. The reasoning intellect was applied to everything as the sole measure. It was the time when, as Hegel says, the world was stood upon its head; first, in the sense that the human head and the principles arrived at by its thought claimed to be the basis of all human action and association; and then later on also in the wider sense, that the reality which was in contradiction with these principles was in fact turned upside down from top to bottom. All previous forms of society and government, all the old ideas handed down by tradition, were flung into the lumber-room as irrational; the world had hitherto allowed itself to be guided solely by prejudices; everything in the past deserved only pity and contempt. Now for the first time appeared the light of day; henceforth, superstition, injustice, privilege and oppression were to be superseded by eternal truth, eternal justice, equality grounded in Nature and the inalienable rights of man.

We know today that this kingdom of reason was nothing more than the idealised kingdom of the bourgeoisie; that eternal justice found its realisation in bourgeois justice; that equality reduced itself to bourgeois equality before the law; that bourgeois property was proclaimed as one of the essential rights of man; and that the government of reason, the Social Contract of Rousseau, came into existence and could only come into existence as a bourgeois democratic republic. No more than their predecessors could the great thinkers of the eighteenth century pass beyond the limits imposed on them by their own epoch.

But side by side with the antagonism between the feudal nobility and the bourgeoisie was the general antagonism between the exploiters and the exploited, the rich idlers and the toiling poor. And it was precisely this circumstance that enabled the representatives of the bourgeoisie to put themselves forward as the representatives not of a special class but of the whole of suffering humanity. Still more; from its origin the bourgeoisie had been saddled with its antithesis: that capitalists cannot exist without wage workers, and in the same degree as the mediæval burgher of the guild developed into the modern bourgeois, so the guild journeyman and the day labourer outside the guilds developed into the proletarian. And although, on the whole, the bourgeoisie in their struggle with the nobility could claim to represent at the same time the interests of the different sections of workers of that period, yet in every great bourgeois movement there were independent outbursts of that class which was the more or less developed forerunner of the modern proletariat. For example, the Thomas Münzer tendency in the period of the reformation and peasant war in Germany; the Levellers in the great English revolution; in the great French revolution, Babeuf. Alongside of these revolutionary armed uprisings of a class which was as yet undeveloped, the corresponding theoretical manifestations made their appearance; in the sixteenth and seventeenth centuries, utopian portrayals of ideal social conditions; in the eighteenth century, actual communistic theories (Morelly and Mably). The demand for equality was no longer limited to political rights, but was extended also to the social conditions of individuals; it was not merely class privileges that were to be abolished, but class distinctions themselves.

An ascetic communism, linked to Spartan conceptions, was the first form in which the new doctrine made its appearance. Then came the three great utopians: Saint Simon, with whom bourgeois tendencies still had a certain influence, side by side with proletarian; Fourier, and Owen, who, in the country where capitalist production was most developed, and under the influence of the antagonisms begotten of this, worked out his schemes for the removal of class distinctions systematically and in direct relation to French materialism.

It is common to all three of these that they do not come forward as representatives of the interests of the proletariat which in the meantime history has brought into being. Like the philosophers of the Enlightenment they aim at the emancipation not of a definite class but of all humanity. Like them, they wish to establish the kingdom of reason and eternal justice; but their kingdom is spheres apart from that of the French philosophers. To them the bourgeois world based on the principles of these philosophers is also irrational and unjust, and therefore finds its way to the rubbish bin just as readily as feudalism and all earlier forms of society. If pure reason and justice have not hitherto ruled the world, this has been due only to the fact that until now men have not rightly understood them. What was lacking was just the individual man of genius, who has now arisen and has recognised the truth; the fact that he has now arisen, that the truth has been recognised precisely at this moment, is not an inevitable event, following of necessity in the chain of historical development, but a mere happy accident. He might just as well have been born five hundred years earlier, and would then have saved humanity five hundred years of error, strife and suffering.

This mode of outlook is essentially that of all English and French and of the first German Socialists, including Weitling. To all these socialism is the expression of absolute truth, reason and justice, and needs only to be discovered to conquer the world by virtue of its own power; as absolute truth is independent of time and space and of the historical development of man, it is a mere accident when and where it is discovered. At the same time, absolute truth, reason and justice are different for the founder of each different school; and as each one's special kind of absolute truth, reason and justice is in turn conditioned by his subjective understanding, his conditions of existence, the measure of his knowledge and intellectual training, so the only solution possible in this conflict of absolute truths is that they should grind each other down. And from this nothing could emerge but a kind of eclectic average socialism, such as in fact dominated the minds of most socialist workers in France and England up to the present time; a mixture, admitting of the most manifold shades, of such of the critical observations, economic doctrines and delineations of future society made by the various founders of sects as excite the least opposition; a mixture which is the more easily produced the more its individual constituents have the sharp edges of precision rubbed off in the stream of debate, as pebbles are rounded in a brook. In order to make socialism into a science it had first to be placed upon a real basis.

Meanwhile, along with and after the French philosophy of the eighteenth century, the newer German philosophy had arisen, culminating in Hegel. Its greatest merit was the re-adoption of dialectics as the highest form of thinking. The old Greek philosophers were all natural born dialecticians, and Aristotle, the most encyclopædic intellect of them, had even already analysed the most essential forms of dialectic thought. The newer philosophy, on the other hand, although it too included brilliant exponents of dialectics (e.g., Descartes and Spinoza), had become especially under English influence, more and more rigidly fixed in the so-called metaphysical mode of reasoning, by which also the French of the eighteenth century, at all events in their special philosophical works, were almost exclusively dominated. But outside philosophy in the restricted sense, the French were nevertheless able to produce masterpieces of dialectic; we need only recall Diderot's Le Neveu de Rameau and Rousseau's Discourse on the Origin of Inequality among Men. We give here, in brief, the essential character of these two modes of thought; we shall have to return to them later in greater detail.

When we reflect on Nature, or the history of mankind, or our own intellectual activity, the first picture presented to us is of an endless maze of relations and interactions, in which nothing remains what, where and as it was, but everything moves, changes, comes into being and passes out of existence. This primitive, naïve, yet intrinsically correct conception of the world was that of ancient Greek philosophy, and was first clearly formulated by Heraclitus: everything is and also is not, for everything is in *flux,* is constantly changing, constantly coming into being and passing away. But this conception, correctly as it covers the general character of the picture of phenomena as a whole, is yet inadequate to explain the details of which this total picture is composed; and so long as we do not understand these, we also have no clear idea of the picture as a whole. In order to understand these details, we must detach them from their natural or historical connections, and examine each one separately, as to its nature, its special causes and effects, etc. This is primarily the task of natural science and historical research; branches of science which the Greeks of the classical period, on very good grounds, relegated to a merely subordinate position, because they had first of all to collect materials for these sciences to work upon. The beginnings of the exact investigation of nature were first developed by the Greeks of the Alexandrian period, and later on, in the Middle Ages, were further developed by the Arabs. Real natural science, however, dates only from the second half of the fifteenth century, and from then on it has advanced with constantly increasing rapidity.

The analysis of Nature into its individual parts, the grouping of the different natural processes and natural objects in definite classes, the study of the internal anatomy of organic bodies in their manifold forms—these were the fundamental conditions of the gigantic strides in our knowledge of Nature which have been made during the last four hundred years. But this method of investigation has also left us as a legacy the habit of observing natural objects and natural processes in their isolation, detached from the whole vast interconnection of things; and therefore not in their motion, but in their repose; not as essentially changing, but as fixed constants; not in their life, but in their death. And when, as was the case with Bacon and Locke, this way of looking at things was transferred from natural science to philosophy, it produced the specific narrow-mindedness of the last centuries, the metaphysical mode of thought.

To the metaphysician, things and their mental images, ideas, are isolated, to be considered one after the other apart from each other, rigid, fixed objects of investigation given once for all. He thinks in absolutely discontinuous antitheses. His communication is: "Yea, yea, Nay, nay, for whatsoever is more than these cometh of evil." For him a thing either exists, or it does not exist; it is equally impossible for a thing to be itself and at the same time something else. Positive and negative absolutely exclude one another; cause and effect stand in an equally rigid antithesis one to the other. At first sight this mode of thought seems to us extremely plausible, because it is the mode of thought of so-called sound common sense. But sound common sense, respectable fellow as he is within the homely precincts of his own four walls, has most wonderful adventures as soon as he ventures out into the wide world of scientific research. Here the metaphysical mode of outlook, justifiable and even necessary as it is in domains whose extent varies according to the nature of the object under investigation, nevertheless sooner or later always reaches a limit beyond which it becomes one-sided, limited, abstract, and loses its way in insoluble contradictions. And this is so because in considering individual things it loses sight of their connections; in contemplating their existence it forgets their coming into being and passing away; in looking at them at rest it leaves their motion out of account; because it cannot see the wood for the trees. For everyday purposes we know, for example, and can say with certainty whether an animal is alive or not; but when we look more closely we find that this is often an extremely complex question, as jurists know very well. They have cudgelled their brains in vain to discover some rational limit beyond which the killing of a child in its mother's womb is murder; and it is equally impossible to determine the moment of death, as physiology has established that death is not a sudden, instantaneous event, but a very protracted process. In the same way every organic being is at each moment the same and not the same; at each moment it is assimilating matter drawn from without, and excreting other matter; at each moment the cells of its body are dying and new ones are being formed; in fact, within a longer or shorter period the matter of its body is completely renewed and is replaced by other atoms of matter, so that every organic being is at all times itself and yet something other than itself. Closer investigation also shows us that the two poles of an antithesis, like positive and negative, are just as inseparable from each other as they are opposed, and that despite all their opposition they mutually penetrate each other. It is just the same with cause and effect; these are conceptions which only have validity in their application to a particular case as such, but when we consider the particular case in its general connection with the world as a whole they merge and dissolve in the conception of universal action and interaction, in which causes and effects are constantly changing places, and what is now or here an effect becomes there or then a cause, and *vice versa.*

None of these processes and methods of thought fit into the frame of metaphysical thinking. But for dialectics, which grasps things and their images, ideas, essentially in their interconnection, in their sequence, their movement, their birth and death, such processes as those mentioned above are so many corroborations of its own method of treatment. Nature is the test of dialectics, and it must be said for modern natural science that it has furnished extremely rich and daily increasing materials for this test, and has thus proved that in the last analysis Nature's process is dialectical and not metaphysical. But the scientists who have learnt to think dialectically are still few and far between, and hence the conflict between the discoveries made and the old traditional mode of thought is the explanation of the boundless confusion which now reigns in theoretical natural science and reduces both teachers and students, writers and readers to despair.

An exact representation of the universe, of its evolution and that of mankind, as well as of the reflection of this evolution in the human mind, can therefore only be built up in a dialectical way, taking constantly into account the general actions and reactions of becoming and ceasing to be, of progressive or retrogressive changes. And the more recent German philosophy worked with this standpoint from the first. Kant began his career by resolving the stable solar system of Newton and its eternal permanence—after the famous initial impulse had once been given—into a historical process: the formation of the sun and of all the planets out of a rotating nebulous mass. Together with this he already drew the conclusion that given this origin of the solar system, its ultimate dissolution was also inevitable. Half a century later his views were given a mathematical basis by Laplace, and another fifty years later the spectroscope proved the existence in space of such incandescent masses of gas in various stages of condensation.

This newer German philosophy culminated in the Hegelian system, in which for the first time—and this is its great merit—the whole natural, historical and spiritual world was presented as a process, that is, as in constant motion, change, transformation and development; and the attempt was made to show the internal interconnections in this motion and development. From this standpoint the history of mankind no longer appeared as a confused whirl of senseless deeds of violence, all equally condemnable before the judgment seat of the now matured philosophic reason, and best forgotten as quickly as possible, but as the process of development of humanity itself. It now became the task of thought to follow the gradual stages of this process through all its devious ways, and to trace out the inner regularities running through all its apparently fortuitous phenomena.

That Hegel did not succeed in this task is here immaterial. His epoch-making service was that he propounded it. It is indeed a task which no individual will ever be able to solve. Although Hegel— with Saint-Simon—was the most encyclopædic mind of his age, yet he was limited, in the first place, by the necessarily restricted compass of his own knowledge, and, secondly, by the similarly restricted scope and depth of the knowledge and ideas of his age. But there was also a third factor. Hegel was an idealist, that is to say, the thoughts within his mind were to him not the more or less abstract images of real things and processes, but, on the contrary, things and their development were to him only the images made real of the "Idea" existing somewhere or other already before the world existed. This mode of thought placed everything on its head, and completely reversed the real connections of things in the world. And although Hegel grasped correctly and with insight many individual interconnections, yet, for the reasons just given, there is also much that in point of detail also is botched, artificial, laboured, in a word, wrong. The Hegelian system as such was a colossal miscarriage—but it was also the last of its kind. It suffered, in fact, from an internal and insoluble contradiction. On the one hand, its basic assumption was the historical outlook, that human history is a process of evolution, which by its very nature cannot find intellectual finality in the discovery of any so-called absolute truth; but on the other hand, it laid claim to being the very sum-total of precisely this absolute truth. A system of natural and historical knowledge which is all-embracing and final for all time is in contradiction to the fundamental laws of dialectical thinking; which however, far from excluding, on the contrary includes, the idea that the systematic knowledge of the external universe can make giant strides from generation to generation.

The realisation of the entire incorrectness of previous German idealism led necessarily to materialism, but, it must be noted, not to the simple metaphysical and exclusively mechanical materialism of the eighteenth century. Instead of the simple and naïvely revolutionary rejection of all previous history, modern materialism sees history as the process of the evolution of humanity, and its own problem as the discovery of laws of motion of this process. The conception was prevalent among the French of the eighteenth century, as well as with Hegel, of Nature as a whole, moving in narrow circles and remaining immutable, with its eternal celestial bodies, as Newton taught, and unalterable species of organic beings, as Linnæus taught. In opposition to this conception, modern materialism embraces the more recent advances of natural science, according to which Nature also has its history in time, the celestial bodies, like the organic species which under favourable circumstances people them, coming into being and passing away, and the recurrent circles, in so far as they are in any way admissible, assuming infinitely vaster dimensions. In both cases modern materialism is essentially dialectical, and no longer needs any philosophy standing above the other sciences. As soon as each separate science is required to get clarity as to its position in the great totality of things and of our knowledge of things, a special science dealing with this totality is superfluous. What still independently survives of all former philosophy is the science of thought and its laws—formal logic and dialectics. Everything else is merged in the positive science of Nature and history.

While, however, the revolution in the conception of Nature could only be carried through to the extent that research furnished the corresponding positive materials of knowledge, already much earlier certain historical facts had occurred which led to a decisive change in the conception of history. In 1831, the first working-class rising had taken place in Lyons; between 1838 and 1842 the first national workers' movement, that of the English Chartists, reached its height. The class struggle between proletariat and bourgeoisie came to the front in the history of the most advanced European countries, in proportion to the development there, on the one hand, of large-scale industry, and on the other, of the newly-won political domination of the bourgeoisie. Facts more and more forcibly stamped as lies the teachings of bourgeois economics as to the identity of the interests of capital and labour, as to the universal harmony and universal prosperity that free competition brings. All these things could no longer be ignored, any more than the French and English socialism which was their theoretical, even though extremely imperfect, expression. But the old idealist conception of history, which was not yet displaced, knew nothing of class struggles based on material interests, in fact knew nothing at all of material interests; production and all economic relations appeared in it only incidentally, as subordinate elements in the "history of civilisation." The new facts made imperative a new examination of all past history, and then it was seen that *all* past history was the history of class struggles, that these warring classes of society are always the product of the conditions of production and exchange, in a word, of the *economic* conditions of their time; that therefore the economic structure of society always forms the real basis from which, in the last analysis, is to be explained the whole superstructure of legal and political institutions, as well as of the religious, philosophical, and other conceptions of each historical period. Now idealism was driven from its last refuge, the philosophy of history; now a materialist conception of history was propounded, and the way found to explain man's consciousness by his being, instead of, as heretofore, his being by his consciousness.

But the socialism of earlier days was just as incompatible with this materialist conception of history as the French materialist conception of Nature was with dialectics and modern natural science.

It is true that the earlier socialism criticised the existing capitalist mode of production and its consequences, but it could not explain them, and so also could not get the mastery over them; it could only simply reject them as evil. But what had to be done was to show this capitalist mode of production on the one hand in its historical sequence and in its inevitability for a definite historical period, and therefore also the inevitability of its downfall, and on the other hand also to lay bare its essential character, which was still hidden, as its critics had hitherto attacked its evil consequences rather than the process of the thing itself. This was done by the discovery of *surplus value*. It was shown that the appropriation of unpaid labour is the basic form of the capitalist mode of production and of the exploitation of the worker effected through it; that even if the capitalist buys the labour power of his labourer at its full value as a commodity on the market, he yet extracts more value from it than he paid for; and that in the ultimate analysis this surplus value forms those sums of value from which are heaped up the constantly increasing masses of capital in the hands of the possessing classes. The process both of capitalist production and of the production of capital was explained.

These two great discoveries, the materialist conception of history and the revelation of the secret of capitalist production by means of surplus value, we owe to *Marx*. With these discoveries socialism became a science, which had in the first place to be developed in all its details and relations.

This was how things stood in the fields of theoretical socialism and extinct philosophy, when Herr Eugen Dühring, not without considerable din, sprang on to the stage and announced that he had accomplished a complete and total revolution of philosophy, political economy and socialism.

Let us see what Herr Dühring promises us and—how he fulfils his promises.

II. WHAT HERR DÜHRING PROMISES

The writings of Herr Dühring with which we are here primarily concerned are his *Cursus der Philosophie* [*Course of Philosophy*], his *Cursus der National- und Sozial-ökonomie* [*Course of Political and Social Economy*] and his *Kritische Geschichte der National-ökonomie und des Sozialismus* [*Critical History of Political Economy and Socialism*]. The first named is the one which particularly claims our attention here.

On the very opening page Herr Dühring introduces himself as "the man who *claims to represent* this power (of philosophy) in his age and for its immediately foreseeable future development." He thus proclaims himself to be the only real philosopher of today and of the "foreseeable" future. Whoever differs from him differs from truth. Many people, even before Herr Dühring, have *thought* something of this kind about themselves, but—except for Richard Wagner—he is probably the first who has calmly blurted it out. And the truth to which he refers is "a final and ultimate truth."

Herr Dühring's philosophy is "the *natural* system or the *philosophy of reality* . . . in it reality is so conceived as to *exclude any tendency* to a visionary and subjectively limited conception of the world." This philosophy is therefore of such a nature that it lifts Herr Dühring far above the bounds set by what he himself can hardly deny are his personal and subjective limitations. And this is in fact necessary if he is to be in a position to lay down final and ultimate truths, although so far we do not yet see how this miracle is to come to pass.

This "natural system of knowledge which in itself is of value to the mind" has, "without in any way compromising the profundity of thought, *securely established* the basic forms of being." From its "really critical standpoint" it provides the elements of a philosophy which is real and therefore directed to the reality of Nature and of life, a philosophy which cannot allow the validity of any merely apparent horizon, but in *its mighty revolutionising sweep involves all earths and heavens of external and inward Nature;* it is a "new mode of thought," and its results are "from the foundation upwards original conclusions and views ... system-creating ideas ... established truths." In it we have before us "a work which must find its strength in concentrated initiative"—whatever that may mean; an "investigation *going to the roots* ... a *deep-rooted* science ... *a strictly scientific* conception of things and of men ... an all-round penetrating work of thought ... a *creative* scheme of hypotheses and deductions controllable by thought ... the *absolute fundamental basis.*" In the economic and political sphere he gives us not only "historical and systematically comprehensive works," of which the historical works are, to boot, notable for "*my* historical treatment *in the grand style,*" while those dealing with economics have brought about "creative changes"; but he even finishes with a fully worked out socialist plan of his own for the society of the future, which is the "practical fruit of *a clear theory going to the ultimate roots of things*" and, like the Dühring philosophy, is consequently infallible and is the only way to salvation. For "only in that socialist structure which I have sketched in my *Course of Political and Social Economy* can a true ownership take the place of the ownership which is merely illusory and transitory or even based cn violence." And the future has to follow these directions.

This bouquet of glorifications of Herr Dühring by Herr Dühring could easily be multiplied tenfold. It may already have created some doubt in the mind of the reader as to whether it is really a philosopher with whom he is dealing, or a—but we must beg the reader to reserve judgment until he has got to know the above-mentioned "going to the roots of things" at closer quarters. We have given the above bouquet only for the purpose of showing that we have before us not any ordinary philosopher and Socialist, who merely expresses his ideas and leaves it to the future course of events to judge their worth, but quite an extraordinary creature, who claims to be not less infallible than the Pope, and whose doctrine is the one way of salvation and must just be accepted by anyone who does not want to fall into the most reprehensible heresy. What we are here confronted with is certainly not one of those works in which all socialist literature, recently even German, has abounded—works in which people of various calibres, in the most straightforward way in the world, try to clear up questions the solution of which requires material that to a greater or lesser extent perhaps is not at their disposal; works in which, whatever their scientific and literary shortcomings, the social-ist goodwill is always deserving of recognition. On the contrary, Herr Dühring offers us principles which he declares are final and ulti-mate truths, and therefore any views conflicting with these are false from the outset; he is in possession not only of the exclusive truth but also of the sole strictly scientific method of investigation, in con-trast with which all others are unscientific. Either he is right—and in this case we have before us the greatest genius of all time, the first superhuman, because infallible, human being. Or he is wrong, and in that case, whatever judgment we may form about him, benevo-lent consideration for any good intentions he may possibly have had would nevertheless be the most deadly insult to Herr Dühring.

When a man is in possession of the final and ultimate truth and of the only strictly scientific approach, it is only natural that he should have a certain contempt for the rest of erring and unscien-tific humanity. We must therefore not be surprised that Herr Dühring should speak of his predecessors with the most extreme disdain, and that there are only a few exceptional cases, admitted by him to be great men, who find mercy at the bar of his deep-rooted principles.

Let us hear first what he has to say about the philosophers: "Leib-nitz, devoid of any better sentiments, that best of all possible courtier-philosophers." He goes so far as even to tolerate Kant; but after Kant everything got into a muddle: there followed the "aridities and equally childish and windy stupidities of the degenerate successors of the great man, namely, a Fichte and a Schelling...monstrous caricatures of ignorant natural philosophising...the monstrosities that came after Kant" and "the delirious phantasies" crowned by "a Hegel." The last-named used a "Hegel jargon" and spread the "Hegel pestilence" by means of his "moreover even in form un-scientific method" and his "crudities."

The natural scientists come off no better, but, as only Darwin is cited by name we must confine ourselves to him: "Darwinian semi-poetry and dexterity in metamorphosis, with its gross-minded nar-

rowness of comprehension and blunted sense of differentiation....
In our view what is specific to Darwinism, from which of course
the Lamarckian elements must be excluded, is *a piece of brutality
directed against humanity.*"

But the Socialists come off worst of all. With the exception at any
rate of Louis Blanc—the most insignificant of them all—they are
all sinners together and fall short of the reputation which they
should have before (or behind) Herr Dühring. And not only in
regard to truth and scientific approach—no, also in regard to their
character. Except for Babeuf and a few Communards of 1871 they
are all of them not "men." The three utopians are called "social
alchemists." Of these three, a certain indulgence is shown in the
treatment of Saint-Simon, in so far as he is merely charged with
"exaltation of mind," and there is a compassionate indication that
he suffered from religious mania. With Fourier, however, Herr
Dühring completely loses patience. For Fourier "revealed every
element of delirium... ideas which one would normally have most
expected to find in mad-houses... the wildest dreams... products of
delirium... the unspeakably silly Fourier," "this childish mind,"
this "idiot," is withal not even a Socialist; his *Phalanstère* is absolutely not a piece of rational socialism, but "a caricature constructed
on the model of everyday commerce." And finally, "Anyone who
does not find this remark (of Fourier's, about Newton) sufficient to
convince himself that in Fourier's name and in the whole of Fourier-
ism it is only the first syllable (*fou* = crazy) that has any truth in
it, should *himself be classed under some category of idiots.*" Finally,
Robert Owen "had feeble and paltry ideas... his reasoning, so crude
in its ethics... a few commonplaces distorted into perversions...
nonsensical and crude ways of looking at things... Owen's range of
ideas is hardly worth subjecting to more serious criticism... his
vanity"—and so on. Herr Dühring extremely wittily characterises the
utopians by references to their names as follows: Saint-Simon—
saint (holy); Fourier—*fou* (crazy); Enfantin—*enfant* (childish);
he only needs to add: Owen—o woe! and a whole important period
in the history of socialism has in four words been simply condemned,
and anyone who has any doubts about it "should himself be classed
under some category of idiots."

As for Dühring's opinions on the later Socialists, for the sake of brevity we will only cite those on Lassalle and Marx:

Lassalle: "Pedantic, hair-splitting efforts to popularise ... rampant scholasticism ... a monstrous hash of general theories and paltry trash ... Hegel-superstition, senseless and formless ... a horrifying example ... peculiarly limited ... pompousness combined with the most petifogging paltriness ... our Jewish hero ... pamphleteer ... common ... fundamental instability in his view of life and of the world."

Marx: "narrowness of conception ... his works and achievements in and by themselves, that is, regarded from a purely theoretical standpoint, are without any permanent significance in our domain (the critical history of socialism), and in the general history of intellectual tendencies they can take their place at most as symptoms of the influence of one branch of modern sectarian scholastics ... impotence of the faculties of concentration and logical arrangement ... deformity of thought and style, degrading manner of language ... Anglicized vanity ... duping ... barren conceptions, which in fact are only bastards of historical and logical phantasy ... deceptive twisting ... personal vanity ... vile mannerisms ... insolent ... buffoonery pretending to be witty ... Chinese erudition ... philosophical and scientific backwardness."

And so on, and so forth—for this too is only a little superficial bouquet out of the Dühring rose garden. It must be understood that, at the moment, we are not in the least concerned as to whether these amiable expressions of abuse—which, if he had any education, should forbid Herr Dühring from finding *anything* vile and insolent —are also final and absolute truths. And—for the moment—we will guard against expressing any doubt as to their deep-rootedness, as we might otherwise be prohibited even from trying to find the category of fools to which we belong. We only thought it was our duty to give, on the one hand, an example of what Herr Dühring calls "the select language of the considered and, in the real sense of the word, moderate mode of expression"; and on the other hand, to make it clear that to Herr Dühring the worthlessness of his predecessors is no less established a fact than his own infallibility. Whereupon we sink to the ground in deepest reverence before the mightiest genius of all time—if that is how things really stand.

PART I

PHILOSOPHY

III. CLASSIFICATION. APRIORISM

Philosophy, according to Herr Dühring, is the development of the highest form of consciousness of the world and of life, and in a wider sense embraces the *principles* of all knowledge and volition. Wherever a series of cognitions or stimuli or a group of forms of being come to be examined by human consciousness, the *principles* underlying these of necessity become the object of philosophy. These principles are the simple, or until now assumed to be simple, constituents of complex knowledge and volition. Like the chemical composition of bodies, the general conception of things can also be reduced to basic forms and basic elements. These ultimate constituents or principles, when they have once been discovered, are valid not only for the immediately known and accessible world, but also for the world which to us is unknown and inaccessible. Philosophical principles consequently provide the final completing link required by the sciences in order to make of them a uniform system by which Nature and human life can be explained. Apart from the fundamental forms of all being, philosophy has only two special subjects for investigation—Nature and the world of man. Thus we find our material *quite spontaneously* arranged in three groups, namely, the general scheme of the universe, the science of the principles of Nature, and finally the science of mankind. This succession at the same time contains *an inner logical sequence*, for the formal principles which are valid for all existence take precedence, and the objective realms to which they are *to be applied* then follow in the degree of their subordination. So far Herr Dühring, and almost entirely word for word.

What he is dealing with are therefore *principles*, formal principles derived from *thought* and not from the external world, which are to be applied to Nature and the realm of man, and to which therefore Nature and the realm of man have to conform. But whence does thought obtain these principles? From itself? No, for Herr Dühring himself says: the realm of pure thought is limited to logical schemata

41

and mathematical forms (the latter, moreover, as we shall see, is wrong). Logical schemata can only relate to *forms of thought;* but what we are dealing with here are only forms of *being,* of the external world, and these forms can never be created and derived by thought out of itself, but only from the external world. But with this the whole relationship is inverted: the principles are not the starting point of the investigation, but its final result; they are not applied to Nature and human history, but abstracted from them; it is not Nature and the realm of humanity which conform to these principles, but the principles are only valid in so far as they are in conformity with Nature and history. That is the only materialistic conception of the matter, and Herr Dühring's contrary conception is idealistic, makes things stand completely on their heads, and fashions the real world out of ideas, out of schemata, schemes or categories existing somewhere before the world, from eternity—just like a *Hegel.*

In fact, let us compare Hegel's *Encyclopædia* and all its delirious phantasies with Herr Dühring's final and absolute truths. With Herr Dühring we have in the first place general world schematism, which Hegel calls Logic. Then with both of them we have the application of these schemata or logical categories to Nature: the Philosophy of Nature; and finally their application to the realm of man, which Hegel calls the Philosophy of Mind. The "inner logical sequence" of the Dühring succession therefore leads us "quite spontaneously" back to Hegel's *Encyclopædia,* from which it has been taken with a loyalty which would move that wandering Jew of the Hegelian school, Professor Michelet of Berlin, to tears.

Such a result comes of accepting in quite a naturalistic way "consciousness," "thought," as something given, something from the outset in contrast to being, to Nature. If this were so, it must seem extremely remarkable that consciousness and Nature, thinking and being, the laws of thought and the laws of Nature, should be so closely in correspondence. But if the further question is raised: what then are thought and consciousness, and whence they come, it becomes apparent that they are products of the human brain and that man himself is a product of Nature, which has been developed in and along with its environment; whence it is self-evident that the products of the human brain, being in the last analysis also products

of Nature, do not contradict the rest of Nature but are in correspondence with it.

But Herr Dühring cannot permit himself such a simple treatment
of the subject. He thinks not only in the name of humanity—in itself
no small achievement—but in the name of the conscious and reasoning beings on all celestial bodies. It would in fact be "a degradation
of the basic forms of consciousness and knowledge to attempt to
rule out or even to put under suspicion their sovereign validity and
their unconditional claim to truth, by applying the epithet 'human'
to them." So in order that no suspicion may arise that on some celestial body or other twice two may make five, Herr Dühring cannot
treat thought as a human characteristic, and so he has to cut it off
from the only real foundation on which we find it, namely, mankind
and Nature; and with that he tumbles hopelessly into an ideology
which reveals him as the epigone of the "epigone," Hegel. In passing
we may note that we shall often meet Herr Dühring again on other
celestial bodies.

It goes without saying that no materialistic doctrine can be founded
on such an ideological basis. Later on we shall see that Herr
Dühring is forced more than once to endow Nature surreptitiously
with conscious activity—that is to say, therefore, with what in plain
language is called: God.

But our philosopher of reality had also other motives for shifting
the basis of all reality from the real world to the world of thought.
The science of this general world schematism, of these formal underlying principles of being, is indeed precisely the foundation of Herr
Dühring's philosophy. If we deduce world schematism not from our
minds, but only *through* our minds from the real world, deducing
the basic principles of being from what is, we need no philosophy
for this purpose, but positive knowledge of the world and of what
happens in it; and what this yields is also not philosophy, but positive science. In that case, however, Herr Dühring's whole volume
would be nothing but love's labour lost.

Further: if no philosophy as such is any longer required, then
also there is no more need of any system, not even of any natural
system of philosophy. The perception that all the phenomena of
Nature are systematically interconnected drives science on to prove

this systematic interconnection throughout, both in general and in detail. But an adequate, exhaustive scientific statement of this interconnection, the formulation in thought of an exact picture of the world system in which we live, is impossible for us, and will always remain impossible. If at any time in the evolution of mankind such a final, conclusive system of the interconnections within the world— physical as well as mental and historical—were brought to completion, this would mean that human knowledge had reached its limit, and, from the moment when society had been brought into accord with that system, further historical evolution would be cut short— which would be an absurd idea, pure nonsense. Mankind therefore finds itself faced with a contradiction: on the one hand, it has to gain an exhaustive knowledge of the world system in all its interrelations; and on the other hand, because of the nature both of man and of the world system, this task can never be completely fulfilled. But this contradiction lies not only in the nature of the two factors—the world, and man—it is also the main lever of all intellectual advance, and finds its solution continuously, day by day, in the endless progressive evolution of humanity, just as for example mathematical problems find their solution in an infinite series or continued fractions. Each mental image of the world system is and remains in actual fact limited, objectively through the historical stage and subjectively through the physical and mental constitution of its maker. But Herr Dühring explains in advance that his mode of reasoning is of such a kind that it entirely excludes any tendency to a subjectively limited view of the world. We saw above that he was omnipresent—on all possible celestial bodies. We now see that he is also omniscient. He has solved the ultimate problems of science and so nailed boards across the future of all knowledge.

As with the basic forms of being, so also Herr Dühring thinks that he can produce ready-made the whole of pure mathematics *a priori*, that is, without making use of the experiences offered us by the external world. In pure mathematics, in his view, the mind deals "with its own free creations and imaginations"; the concepts of number and form are "its adequate object, which it can create of itself," and they even have "a validity which is independent of *particular* experience and of the real content of the world."

That pure mathematics has a validity which is independent of the *particular* experience of each individual is, for that matter, correct, and this is true of all established facts in every science, and indeed of all facts whatsoever. The magnetic poles, the fact that water is composed of hydrogen and oxygen, the fact that Hegel is dead and that Herr Dühring is alive, hold good independently of my own experience or that of any other individuals, and even independently of Herr Dühring's experience, when he begins to sleep the sleep of the just. But it is not at all true that in pure mathematics the mind deals only with its own creations and imaginations. The concepts of number and form have not been derived from any source other than the world of reality. The ten fingers on which men learnt to count, that is, to carry out the first arithmetical operation, may be anything else, but they are certainly not a free creation of the mind. Counting requires not only objects that can be counted, but also the ability to exclude all properties of the objects considered other than their number—and this ability is the product of a long historical evolution based on experience. Like the idea of number, so the idea of form is derived exclusively from the external world, and does not arise in the mind as a product of pure thought. There must be things which have shape and whose shapes are compared before anyone can arrive at the idea of form. Pure mathematics deals with the space forms and quantity relations of the real world—that is, with material which is very real indeed. The fact that this material appears in an extremely abstract form can only superficially conceal its origin in the external world. But in order to make it possible to investigate these forms and relations in their pure state, it is necessary to abstract them entirely from their content, to put the content aside as irrelevant; hence we get the point without dimensions, lines without breadth and thickness, a and b and x and y, constants and variables; and only at the very end of all these do we reach for the first time the free creations and imaginations of the mind, that is to say, imaginary magnitudes. Even the apparent derivation of mathematical magnitudes from each other does not prove their *a priori* origin, but only their rational interconnection. Before it was possible to arrive at the idea of deducing the *form* of a cylinder from the rotation of a rectangle about one of its sides, a number of real rectangles and cylinders, in however imperfect a form, must have been examined. Like all other sciences, mathematics arose out of the *needs* of men; from the measurement of land and of the content of vessels, from the computation of time and mechanics. But, as in every department of thought, at a certain stage of development the laws abstracted from the real world become divorced from the real world, and are set over against it as something independent, as laws coming from outside, to which the world has to conform. This took place in society and in the state, and in this way, and not otherwise, *pure* mathematics is subsequently *applied* to the world, although it is borrowed from this same world and only represents one section of its forms of interconnection—and it is only just precisely because of this that it can be applied at all.

But just as Herr Dühring imagines that, out of the axioms of mathematics, "which moreover, in accordance with the pure logical concept, neither require nor are capable of proof," he can deduce the whole of pure mathematics without any kind of empirical ingredients whatsoever, and then apply it to the world, so he likewise imagines that he can produce out of his head, in the first place, the basic forms of being, the simple elements of all knowledge, the axioms of philosophy; then that he can deduce from these the whole of philosophy or world schematism, and then, by sovereign decree, impose this conception of his on Nature and humanity. Unfortunately Nature is not at all, and humanity only to an infinitesimal degree, composed of the Prussia of Manteuffel of 1850.

Mathematical axioms are expressions of the most trivial thought content, which mathematics is obliged to borrow from logic. They can be reduced to two.

1) The whole is greater than the part. This statement is pure tautology, as the quantitatively conceived idea "part" is of itself definitely related to the idea "whole," and in fact in such a way that "part" states, without further ceremony, that the quantitative "whole" consists of several quantitative "parts." In stating this expressly, the so-called axiom does not take us a step further. This tautology can even in a way be *proved* by saying: a whole is that which consists of many parts; a part is that of which many make a whole; therefore

the part is less than the whole—in which the futility of repetition brings out even more clearly its emptiness of content.

2) If two magnitudes are equal to a third, then they are equal to one another. This statement, as Hegel has already shown, is a conclusion, the correctness of which is guaranteed by logic, and which is therefore proved, although outside of pure mathematics. The remaining axioms relating to equality and inequality are merely logical extensions of this conclusion.

These meagre principles could not cut much ice, either in mathematics or anywhere else. In order to get any further, we are obliged to import real relations, relations and space forms which are taken from real bodies. The ideas of lines, planes, angles, polygons, cubes, spheres, etc., are all taken from reality, and it requires a pretty good portion of naïve ideology to believe the mathematicians—that the first line came into existence through the movement of a point in space, the first plane through the movement of a line, the first solid through the movement of a plane, and so on. Even language rebels against such a conception. A mathematical figure of three dimensions is called a solid body, *corpus solidum*, hence even in Latin a tangible object; it therefore has a name derived from sturdy reality and by no means from the free imagination of the mind.

But why all this prolixity? After Herr Dühring, on pages 42 and 43, has enthusiastically sung the independence of pure mathematics from the world of experience, its apriorism, its preoccupation with its own free creations and imaginations of the mind, he says on page 63: "It is, of course, easy to overlook that these mathematical elements (number, magnitude, time, space and geometric progression) are *ideal only in their form . . . absolute magnitudes* are therefore something completely *empirical,* no matter to what species they belong," but "mathematical conceptions are capable of definition which is adequate even though *divorced* from actual experience." This last sentence is more or less true of *every* abstraction, but does not by any means prove that it is not an abstraction from reality. In Dühring's world schematism pure mathematics arose out of pure thought—in his philosophy of nature it is something completely empirical, taken from the external world and then divorced from it. Which are we to believe?

IV. WORLD SCHEMATISM

"All-embracing being is *one*. In its self-sufficiency it has nothing alongside of it or over it. To associate a second being with it would be to make it something that it is not, namely, a part or constituent of a more comprehensive whole. We extend, as it were, our *unified* thought like a framework, and nothing that should be comprised in this concept of *unity* can contain a duality within itself. Nor again can anything escape being subject to this concept of unity.... The essence of all thought consists in the synthesis of the elements of consciousness into a unity.... It is the unified synthesis which gave rise to the *indivisible idea of the world*, and the universe, as the name itself implies, is apprehended as something in which everything is united into a *unity*."

Thus far Herr Dühring. This is the first example of the application of the mathematical method: "Every question can be decided *axiomatically* in accordance with simple basic forms, as if simple ... basic principle of mathematics were concerned."

"All-embracing being is one." If tautology, the simple repetition in the predicate of what is already expressed in the subject—if that makes an axiom, then we have here one of the purest water. Herr Dühring tells us in the subject that being embraces everything, and in the predicate he intrepidly declares that in that case there is nothing outside it. What colossal "system-creating thought"!

This is indeed system-creating! Within the space of six lines further on, Herr Dühring has transformed the *oneness* of being, by means of our unified thought, into its *unity*. As the essence of all thought consists in bringing things together into a unity, so being, as soon as it is conceived, is thought of as unified, the idea of the world as indivisible; and because being as conceived, the *idea of the world*, is unified, therefore real being, the real universe, is also an indivisible unity. And with that "there is no longer any room for

48

things beyond, once the mind has learnt to conceive being in its homogeneous universality."

That is a campaign which puts Austerlitz and Jena, Königgrätz, and Sedan completely in the shade. In a few sentences, hardly a page after we have set the first axiom to work, we have already done away with, put aside, destroyed, everything beyond the world—God and the heavenly hosts, heaven, hell and purgatory, along with the immortality of the soul.

How do we get from the oneness of being to its unity? Because it is in our minds that we conceive it at all. In so far as we spread our idea of unity around being like a frame, its oneness becomes a unity, a thought-unity; for the essence of *all* thought consists in bringing together the elements of consciousness into a unity.

This last statement is simply untrue. In the first place, thought consists just as much in the analysis of objects of consciousness into their elements as in the synthesis of related elements into a unity. Without analysis, no synthesis. Secondly, without committing blunders thought can only bring together into a unity those elements of consciousness in which or in whose real prototypes this unity *already exists*. If I include a shoe brush in the unity of mammals, this does not help it to get lacteal glands. The unity of being, that is, the question of whether its conception as a unity is correct, is therefore precisely what was to be proved, and when Herr Dühring assures us that he conceives being as a unity and not as twofold, he tells us nothing more than his own unauthoritative opinion.

If we try to state his process of thought without irrelevancies, we get the following: "I begin with being. I therefore think what being is. The thought of being is a unity. But thinking and being must be in agreement, they are in conformity with each other, they 'coincide.' Therefore being is a unity also in reality. Therefore there cannot be anything 'beyond.' " But if Herr Dühring had spoken openly in this way, instead of treating us to the above-cited oracular passages, the ideology would have been clearly visible. To attempt to prove the reality of any product of thought by the identity of thinking and being, that was indeed one of the most ridiculous delirious phantasies of—a Hegel.

Even if his whole method of proof had been correct, Herr Dühring would still not have won an inch of ground from the spiritualists. The latter would reply briefly: to us also the universe *is* simple; the division into this world and the world beyond exists only from our specifically earthly, sinful standpoint; in itself, that is, in God, all being is a unity. And they would accompany Herr Dühring to his other beloved celestial bodies and show him one or many on which there had been no original sin, where therefore no opposition exists between this world and the beyond, and where the unity of the universe is a postulate of faith.

The most comical part of the business is that Herr Dühring, in order to prove the non-existence of God from the idea of being, uses the ontological proof for the existence of God. This runs: when we think of God, we conceive him as the sum total of all perfections. But the sum total of all perfections necessarily includes existence, since a non-existent being is necessarily imperfect. We must therefore include existence among the perfections of God. Therefore God must exist. Herr Dühring reasons in exactly the same way: if we think of being, we conceive it as *one* idea. Whatever is included in *one* idea is a unity. Being would not correspond to the idea of being, if it were not a unity. Therefore it must be a unity. Therefore there is no God, and so on.

When we speak of *being*, and solely of *being*, unity can only consist in that all the objects to which we are referring—*are*, exist. They are included in the unity of this being, and in no other unity, and the general statement that they all *are* not only cannot give them any additional qualities, whether common to them all or not, but provisionally excludes all such qualities from consideration. For as soon as we stray even a millimetre from the simple basic fact that being is common to all these things, then the *differences* between these things begin to emerge—and whether these differences consist in the fact that some are white, and others black, that some are animate, and others inanimate, that some are of this world and others beyond, could not be decided by us from the fact that mere existence is equally an attribute of them all.

The unity of the world does not consist in its being, although its being is a pre-condition of its unity, as it must certainly first *be*, before it can be *one*. Being, indeed, is always an open question beyond the point where our sphere of observation ends. The real unity of the world consists in its materiality, and this is proved not by a few juggling phrases, but by a long and protracted development of philosophy and natural science.

To return to the text. The *being* which Herr Dühring is telling us about is "not that pure being which is identical, lacking all special determinants, and in fact representing only the antithesis to the idea of *nothing* or the absence of idea." But we shall see very soon that Herr Dühring's universe in fact starts with a being which lacks all inner differentiation, all motion and change, and is therefore in fact only an antithesis to the idea of nothing, and therefore really nothing. Out of this *being-nothing* develops the present differentiated, changing universe, which represents a development, a *becoming*; and it is only after we have grasped this that we are able to "maintain the conception of universal being which is identical" in spite of this perpetual change. We have now, therefore, the idea of being on a higher plane, where it includes within itself both stability and change, being and becoming. Having reached this point, we find that "genus and species, general and particular, are the simplest forms of differentiation, without which the constitution of things cannot be understood." But these are means of differentiation of *qualities*; and after these have been dealt with, we proceed: "In opposition to genus stands the idea of magnitude, as of an identity in which no further differences of kind exist"; and so from *quality* we pass to *quantity*, and this is always *"measurable."*

Let us now compare this "penetrating analysis of the general scheme of phenomena" and its "really critical standpoint" with the crudities, aridities and delirious phantasies of a Hegel. We find that Hegel's *Logic* starts from *being*—as with Herr Dühring; that being turns out to be *nothing*, just as in Herr Dühring's argument; that from this being-nothing there is a transition to *becoming*; the result of which is determinate being, *i.e.*, a higher, more realised form of being—just the same as with Herr Dühring. Determinate being leads on to *quality*, and quality on to *quantity*—just the same as with Herr Dühring. And so that no essential feature may be missing, Herr Dühring tells us on another occasion: "From the realm of nonperception man enters that of perception, in spite of all quantitative gradations, only through a *qualitative leap,* of which we ... can say that it is infinitely different from the mere gradations of one and the same quality." This is precisely the Hegelian nodal line of measure relations, in which, at certain definite nodal points, the purely quantitative increase or decrease gives rise to a *qualitative leap;* for example, in the case of water which is heated or cooled, where boiling-point and freezing-point are the nodes at which—under normal pressure—the transition to a new form of aggregate takes place, and where consequently quantity becomes transformed into quality.

Our investigation has likewise tried to reach down to the roots, and it finds, as the roots of the deep-rooted basic scheme of Herr Dühring, the "delirious phantasies" of a Hegel, the categories of Hegelian *Logic,* Part I, the Theory of Being, in strictly Old-Hegelian "succession" and with hardly any attempt to cloak the plagiarism!

And not content with pilfering from his worst-slandered predecessor the latter's whole scheme of being, Herr Dühring, after himself giving the above-quoted example of the sudden leap from quantity into quality, has the effrontery to say of Marx: "How ridiculous, for example, is the reference (made by Marx) to the Hegelian *confused nebulous idea* that *quantity becomes transformed into quality!*"

Confused, nebulous idea! Who has become transformed here? And who is ridiculous here, Herr Dühring?

All these pretty little things are therefore not only not "axiomatically decided" in accordance with the rules, but are merely imported from outside, that is to say, from Hegel's *Logic.* And in fact in such a form that in the whole chapter there is not a single trace of any internal coherence except in so far as it too is borrowed from Hegel, and the whole question finally trickles out in a meaningless subtilising about space and time, stability and change.

From existence Hegel passes to essence, to dialectics. Here he is dealing with the determinations of thought, their internal *antagonisms* and contradictions, as for example, positive and negative; he then comes to *causality* or the relation of cause and effect and ends with *necessity.* Not otherwise Herr Dühring. What Hegel calls the theory of essence Herr Dühring translates into "logical properties of being." These, however, consist above all of the "antagonism of forces," of *opposites*. Contradiction, however, Herr Dühring absolutely denies; we will return to this point later. Then he passes over to *causality*, and from this to necessity. So that when Herr Dühring says of himself: "We, who do not philosophise *out of a cage*," he apparently means that he philosophises *in a cage*, namely, the cage of the Hegelian scheme of categories.

V. NATURAL PHILOSOPHY. TIME AND SPACE

We come now to *natural philosophy*. Here again Herr Dühring has every cause for dissatisfaction with his predecessors. Natural philosophy "sank so low that it became an arid, spurious doggerel founded on ignorance," and "fell to the prostituted philosophistics of a Schelling and his like, rigging themselves out in the priesthood of the Absolute and hoodwinking the public." Weariness has saved us from these "deformities"; but up to now they have only given place to "lack of principle"; "and as far as concerns the public at large, it is well known that the disappearance of a great charlatan is often only the opportunity for a lesser but more commercially experienced successor to put out again, under another signboard, the products of his predecessor." Scientific investigators themselves feel little "inclination to make excursions into the realm of world-encompassing ideas," and consequently jump to "wild and hasty" conclusions in the theoretical sphere. The need for deliverance is therefore urgent, and by a stroke of good luck Herr Dühring is at hand.

In order to appreciate correctly the revelations which now follow, on the development of the world in time and its limitations in space, we must now turn back again to certain passages in the *World Schematism*.

Infinity—which Hegel calls *bad* infinity—is attributed to being, also in accordance with Hegel (*Encyclopædia* § 93), and then this infinity is investigated. "The clearest form of an infinity which can be conceived *without contradiction* is the unlimited accumulation of numbers in a numerical series. ... As we can add yet another unit to each number, without ever exhausting the possibility of further numbers, so also to every state of being a further state succeeds, and infinity consists in the unlimited begetting of this series of states. This *exactly conceived* infinity has consequently also one single basic form with one single direction. For although it is equally possible for our thought to conceive an opposite direction in the accumulation of states of being, this retrogressive infinity is nevertheless only a rashly conceived image of thought. For, because it must run through reality in a *reverse* direction, in each of its states it would have an infinite succession behind itself. But this would involve the impermissible contradiction of an infinite series which has been counted, and so it is clearly contrary to reason to postulate any second direction in infinity."

The first conclusion drawn from this conception of infinity is that the chain of causes and effects in the world must at some time have had a beginning; "an infinite number of causes which must already have succeeded one another is inconceivable, just because it presupposes that the uncountable has been counted." And thus a *final cause* is proved.

The second conclusion is "the law of definite number: the accumulation of identities of any actual species of separate things is only conceivable as forming a definite number." Not only must the number of celestial bodies existing at any point of time be in itself finite, but also the total number of all the tiniest independent particles of matter existing in the world. The fact that this is necessary is the real reason why no composite body can be conceived except as composed of atoms. All actual subdivision has always a definite limit, and must have it if the contradiction of the counted uncountable is to be avoided. For the same reason, not only must the number of the earth's revolutions round the sun up to the present time be a finite number, even though it cannot be stated, but all periodical processes of Nature must have had some beginning, and all the different forms, all the complex phenomena of Nature which appear in succession must have their roots in one *identical state*. This identical state may, without involving a contradiction, have existed from eternity; but even this idea would be excluded if time in itself was composed of real parts and was not merely arbitrarily divided up by our minds owing to the variety of the possibilities which we can conceive. The case is quite different with the real, differentiated content of time; this time, filled with realisation of the actual facts of distinct categories and the forms of being of this sphere, belongs, precisely because of their differentiation, to the sphere of the enumerable. If we imagine a state in which no change occurs and in whose identity no differences of any kind provide a succession, the more specialised idea of time is merged into the more general idea of being. What the accumulation of empty duration would mean is quite unimaginable.

Thus far Herr Dühring, and he is not a little edified at the significance of these revelations. At first he hopes that they will "at least not be regarded as insignificant truths"; but later we find: "Remember the *extremely simple* formulations by means of which we helped forward the ideas of infinity and their critique to a *hitherto unknown import* ... the elements of the universal conception of space and time, so *simply* developed by means of the sharpening and deepening now effected."

We helped forward! The deepening and sharpening now effected! Who are we, and when is this now? Who is deepening and sharpening?

"Thesis. The world has a beginning in time, and is limited also with regard to space.

"Proof. For if we assumed that the world had no beginning in time, then an eternity must have elapsed up to every given point of time, and therefore an infinite series of successive states of things must have passed in the world. The infinity of a series, however, consists in this, that it never can be completed by means of a successive synthesis. Hence an infinite past series of worlds is impossible, and the beginning of the world a necessary condition of its existence. This was what had to be proved first.

"With regard to the second, let us assume again the opposite. In that case the world would be given as an infinite whole of co-existing things. Now we cannot conceive in any way the extension of a quantum, which is not given within certain limits to every intuition, except through the synthesis of its parts, nor the totality of such a quantum in any way, except through a completed synthesis, or by the repeated addition of unity to itself. In order therefore to conceive the world, which fills all space, as a whole, the successive synthesis of the parts of an infinite world would have to be looked upon as completed; that is, an infinite time would have to be looked upon as elapsed, during the enumeration of all co-existing things. This is impossible. Hence an infinite aggregate of real things cannot be regarded as a given whole, nor, therefore, as given at the same time.

Hence it follows that the world is not infinite, as regards extension in space, but enclosed in limits. This was the second that had to be proved." *

These sentences are copied word for word from a well-known book which first appeared in 1781 and is called: *The Critique of Pure Reason*, by *Immanuel Kant*, where everybody can read them, in Part I, Section II, Book II, Division II, second paragraph: The First Antinomy of Pure Reason. So that Herr Dühring's fame rests only on his having tacked on the name—Law of Definite Number—to an idea expressed by Kant, and on having made the discovery that there was once a time when as yet there was no time, though there was a world. As regards all the rest, that is, anything in Herr Dühring's exposition which has some meaning, "we"—is Immanuel Kant, and the "now" is only ninety-five years ago. Certainly "extremely simple"! Remarkable "hitherto unknown import"!

Kant, however, does not at all claim that the above statements are established by his proof. On the contrary; on the opposite page he states and proves the opposite: that the world can have no beginning in time and no end in space; and it is precisely in this that he finds the antinomy, the insoluble contradiction, that the one is just as demonstrable as the other. People of smaller calibre might perhaps feel a little doubt where "a Kant" found an insoluble difficulty. But not so our valiant fabricator of "absolutely original conclusions and views"; he cheerfully copies down such of Kant's antinomy as suits his purpose, and throws the rest aside.

The problem itself has a very simple solution. Eternity in time, infinity in space, mean from the start, and in the simple meaning of the words, that there is no end in *any* direction, neither forwards nor backwards, upwards or downwards, to the right or to the left. This infinity is something quite different from that of an infinite series, for the latter always starts out from one, with one first term. The inapplicability of this idea of series to our object becomes clear directly we apply it to space. The infinite series, transferred to the sphere of space, is the line drawn in a definite direction to infinity. Is the infinity of space expressed in this even in the most remote way?

* Kant: *Critique of Pure Reason.* English translation by Max Müller, second edition, pp. 344 and 346.—*Ed.*

On the contrary, the idea of spatial dimensions involves six lines drawn from this one point in three opposite directions, and consequently we would have six of these dimensions. Kant saw this so clearly that he only transferred his numerical series indirectly, in a roundabout way, to the space relations of the world. Herr Dühring, on the other hand, compels us to accept six dimensions in space, and immediately afterwards can find no words to express his indignation at the mathematical mysticism of Gauss, who could not rest content with the usual three dimensions of space.

As applied to time, the infinite line or series of units in both directions has a certain figurative meaning. But if we think of time as something counted from *one* forward, or as a line starting from a definite *point,* we imply in advance that time has a beginning: we put forward as a presupposition precisely what we are to prove. We give the infinity of time a one-sided, halved character; but a one-sided, a halved infinity is also a contradiction in itself, the exact opposite of an "infinity conceived without contradiction." We can only get past this contradiction if we assume that the *one* from which we begin to count the series, the point from which we proceed to measure the line—that this is any one within the series, that it is any one of the points within the line, so that where we place the starting point does not make any difference to the line or to the series.

But what of the contradiction of "the infinite series which has been counted?" We shall be in a position to examine this more closely as soon as Herr Dühring has performed for us the clever trick of *counting the series.* When he has completed the task of counting from — ∞ (minus infinity) to 0, then let him come again. It is certainly obvious that, at whatever point he begins to count, he will leave behind him an infinite series and, with it, the task which he was to fulfil. Let him just reserve his own infinite series $1+2+3+4 \ldots$ and try to count from the infinite end back to 1; it would obviously be the attempt of a man who has not the faintest understanding of what the problem is. And again: if Herr Dühring states that the infinite series of elapsed moments of time has been counted, he is thereby stating that time has a beginning; for otherwise he would not have been able to start "counting" at all. Once again, therefore, he puts into the argument, as a presupposition, the thing that he has to prove. The idea of an infinite series which has been counted, in other words, the world-encompassing Dühringian law of definite number, is therefore a *contradictio in adjecto*, contains within itself a contradiction, and in fact an *absurd* contradiction.

It is clear that the infinity which has an end but no beginning is neither more nor less infinite than that which has a beginning but no end. The slightest dialectical insight should have told Herr Dühring that beginning and end necessarily belong together, like the North Pole and the South Pole, and that if the end is left out, the beginning just becomes the end—the *one* end which the series has; and vice versa. The whole fraud would be impossible but for the mathematical usage of working with infinite series. Because in mathematics it is necessary to start from definite, finite terms in order to reach the indefinite, the infinite, all mathematical series, positive or negative, must start from 1, or they cannot be used for calculation. The abstract requirements of a mathematician are, however, very far from being a compulsory law for the world of reality.

But for that matter Herr Dühring will never succeed in conceiving real infinity without contradiction. Infinity is a contradiction, and is full of contradictions. From the outset it is a contradiction that an infinity is composed of nothing but finites, and yet this is the case. The finiteness of the material world leads no less to contradictions than its infiniteness, and every attempt to get over these contradictions leads, as we have seen, to new and worse contradictions. It is just *because* infinity is a contradiction that it is an infinite process, unrolling endlessly in time and in space. The removal of the contradiction would be the end of infinity. Hegel saw this quite correctly, and for that reason, treated with well-merited contempt the gentlemen who subtilise over this contradiction.

Let us pass on. So time had a beginning. What was there before this beginning? The universe, which was then in an identical, unchanging state. And as in this state no changes succeeded one another, so also the more specialised idea of time changes into the more general idea of *being*. In the first place, we are here not in the least concerned as to what ideas change in Herr Dühring's head. The subject at issue is not the *idea of time* but *real* time, which Herr Dühring cannot rid himself of so cheaply. In the second place,

however much the idea of time may merge in the more general idea
of being, this does not take us one step further. For the basic forms
of all being are space and time, and existence out of time is just as
gross an absurdity as existence out of space. The Hegelian "time-
lessly unrolled being" and the neo-Schelling "unpreconceivable
being" are rational ideas compared with this being out of time.
And for this reason Herr Dühring sets to work very cautiously; in
fact it was probably time, but of such a kind as cannot really be
called time; time, indeed, in itself does not consist of real parts, and
is only divided up at will by our mind—only an actual filling up of
time with distinguishable facts is susceptible of being counted—
what the accumulation of empty duration means is quite unimaginable. What this accumulation means is here beside the point; the
question is, whether the world, in the state here assumed has duration,
passes through a duration in time? We have long known that we
can get nothing by measuring such a duration without content, just
as we can get nothing by measuring without aim or purpose in empty
space; and Hegel, just because of the pointlessness of such an effort,
calls such an infinity *bad*. According to Herr Dühring time exists
only through change, not change in and through time. Just because
time is different from change, is independent of it, is it possible to
measure it by change, for measuring always implies something
different from the thing to be measured. And time in which no recognisable changes occur is very far removed from *not* being time;
it is rather *pure* time, unaffected by any foreign admixtures, that is,
real time, time *as such*. In fact, if we want to grasp the idea of time
in all its purity, divorced from all external and irrelevant admixtures,
we are compelled to put on one side, as not being relevant in this
connection, all the various events which occur simultaneously and
one after another in time, and in this way to form the idea of a time
in which nothing happens. In doing this, therefore, we have not let
the idea of time be submerged in the general idea of being, but have
thereby for the first time arrived at the pure idea of time.

But all these contradictions and impossibilities are only mere
child's play compared with the confusion into which Herr Dühring
falls with his identical original state of the world. If the world had
ever been in a state in which no change whatever was taking place,

how could it pass from this state to a changing state? The absolutely unchanging, especially when it has been in this state from eternity, cannot possibly get out of such a state by itself and pass over into the state of motion and change. A first impulse must therefore have come in from outside, from outside the universe, an impulse which set it in motion. But as everyone knows, the "first impulse" is only another expression for God. God and the beyond, which in his world schematism Herr Dühring pretended to have so beautifully unrigged, are both brought up by him again, here, sharpened and deepened, in his natural philosophy.

Further, Herr Dühring says: "Where magnitude is attributed to a constant element of being, this magnitude will remain absolute and unalterable. This holds good ... of matter and mechanical force." The first sentence, it may be noted in passing, is a precious example of Herr Dühring's axiomatic-tautological grandiloquence: where magnitude does not change, it remains the same. Therefore the amount of mechanical force which at any time exists in the world remains the same for all eternity. We will overlook the fact that, in so far as this is correct, Descartes already knew and said it in the philosophy of nearly three hundred years ago; that in natural science the theory of the conservation of energy has ruled for the last twenty years; and that Herr Dühring, in limiting it to *mechanical* force, does not in any way improve on it. But where was the mechanical force at the time of the unchanging state of the world? Herr Dühring obstinately refuses to give us any answer to this question.

Where, Herr Dühring, was the eternally constant mechanical force at that time, and what was it doing? The reply: "The original state of the universe, or to put it more plainly, of an unchanging existence of matter which had within it no accumulation of changes in time, is an idea which can only be rejected by a mind which sees the apex of wisdom in the self-mutilation of its own creative powers"—Therefore: either you accept without examination my unchanging original state, or I, the creative genius Eugen Dühring, certify you as intellectual eunuchs. That may, of course, terrify a good many people. We, who have already seen some examples of Herr Dühring's creative power, can permit ourselves to leave this genteel abuse unanswered for the moment, and ask once again: But, Herr Dühring, if you please, what about that mechanical force?

Herr Dühring at once grows embarrassed. In actual fact, he stammers: "The absolute identity of that original border state does not in itself provide any principle of transition. But we must remember that at bottom the position is similar with every new link, however small, in the chain of existence with which we are familiar. So that whoever tries to raise difficulties in the fundamental case now under consideration, must take care that he does not allow himself to accept them on less obvious occasions. Moreover, the possibility exists of interposing successively graduated intermediate stages, and this keeps open the bridge of continuity by which it is possible to move backwards and reach the end of the process of change. It is true that from a purely conceptual standpoint this continuity does not help us past the main difficulty, but it is the basic form of all law and of every known form of transition, so that we are entitled to use it also as a bridge between that first equilibrium and the disturbance of it. But if we had conceived the so-to-speak (!) motionless equilibrium on the model of the ideas which are accepted without any particular reluctance (!) in our present-day mechanics, then there would be no way of explaining how matter could have reached the process of change." Apart from the mechanics of masses there is, however, also a transformation of mass movement into the movement of extremely small particles, but as to how this takes place—"for this up to the present we have no general principle at our disposal and consequently we should not be surprised if these processes take place somewhat *in the dark.*"

That is all Herr Dühring has to say. And in fact, we would have to see the acme of wisdom not only in the self-mutilation of our creative power, but also in blindly implicit faith, if we allowed ourselves to be put off with these really pitiable subterfuges and circumlocutions. Herr Dühring admits that absolute identity cannot of its own initiative make the transition to change. It contains within itself no means whereby absolute equilibrium can pass into motion. What is there, then? Three false, bad arguments.

First: it is just as difficult to show the transition from each link, however small, in the chain of existence, with which we are familiar, to the next one.—Herr Dühring seems to think his readers are sucklings. The establishment of individual transitions and connections between the tiniest links in the chain of existence is precisely the content of natural science, and when it finds itself stuck at some point in its work no one, not even Herr Dühring, thinks of explaining the motion which has taken place by nothing, but always only by the transfer, transformation or propagation of some previous motion. But here the issue is avowedly of accepting motion as having arisen out of immobility, that is, *out of nothing*.

In the second place, we have the "bridge of continuity." This, it is admitted, from the standpoint of pure reasoning does not help us over the difficulty, but all the same we are entitled to *use* it as a transition between immobility and motion. Unfortunately the continuity of immobility consists in *not* moving; how therefore it is to produce motion remains more mysterious than ever. And however infinitely small the parts into which Herr Dühring minces his transition from non-motion to motion, and however long the duration he assigns to this process, we have not got a ten-thousandth part of a millimetre further. Without an act of creation we could never get from nothing to something, even if the something was as small as a mathematical differential. The bridge of continuity is therefore not even an asses' bridge; it is only passable for Herr Dühring.

Thirdly: so long as present-day mechanics holds good—and this, according to Herr Dühring, is one of the most essential levers for the formation of thought—it cannot be explained how it is possible to pass from immobility to motion. But the mechanical theory of heat shows us that the movement of masses under certain conditions changes into molecular movement (although even here motion takes place as the result of another motion, but never as the result of immobility); and this, Herr Dühring shyly suggests, may possibly furnish a bridge between the strictly static (in equilibrium) and dynamic (in motion). But these processes take place "somewhat in the dark." And it is in the dark that Herr Dühring leaves us sitting.

This is the point we have reached with all his deepening and sharpening—that we have perpetually gone deeper into ever sharper nonsense, and finally land up where of necessity we had to land up —"in the dark." But this does not worry Herr Dühring much. Right on the next page he has the effrontery to declare that he has "been able to provide a real content for the idea of identical stability, directly from the behaviour of matter *and mechanical forces*." And this man describes other people as "charlatans"!

Fortunately, in spite of all this helpless wandering and confusion "in the dark," we are left with one consolation, and this is certainly elevating to the soul: "The mathematics of the inhabitants of other celestial bodies can rest on no other axioms than our own!"

VI. NATURAL PHILOSOPHY. COSMOGONY, PHYSICS, CHEMISTRY

Passing on, we come now to the theories of the mode and manner in which the present world came into existence. A state of universal dispersion of matter is said to have been the conception with which the Ionic philosophers began, but particularly from the time of Kant the assumption of primordial nebular mass had played a new role, in which gravitation and the radiation of heat led to the gradual formation of the separate solid celestial bodies. The contemporary mechanical theory of heat makes it possible to deduce the earlier states of the universe in a far more definite form. However, "the state of gaseous dispersion can only be a starting point for serious deductions when it is possible to characterise more closely the mechanical system then existing in it. Otherwise not only does the idea in fact remain extremely nebulous, but the original fog also really becomes, as the deductions make progress, ever thicker and more impenetrable; ... meanwhile it all still remains in the vagueness and formlessness of an idea of diffusion that cannot be more closely determined," and so "this gaseous universe" provides us with "only an extremely airy conception."

The Kantian theory of the origin of all existing celestial bodies from rotating nebular masses was the greatest advance made by astronomy since Copernicus. For the first time the conception that Nature had no history in time began to be shaken. Until then the celestial bodies were believed to have been constant from their very beginning, always in the same state and always following the same courses; and even though individual organisms on the various celestial bodies died out, nevertheless genus and species were held to be immutable. It is true that Nature was apparently in constant motion, but this motion appeared as the incessant repetition of the same processes. Kant made the first breach in this conception, which corresponded exactly to the metaphysical mode of thought, and indeed he did it in such a scientific way that most of the proofs used by him still hold good today. At the same time, the Kantian theory is still, strictly considered, only a hypothesis. But the Copernican world system too is still no more than this, and since the spectroscopic proof, breaking down all denials, of the existence of such red-hot gaseous masses in the starry heavens, the scientific opposition to Kant's theory has been silenced. Even Herr Dühring cannot complete his construction of the world without such a nebular stage, but takes his revenge for this by demanding to be shown the mechanical system existing in this nebular stage, and because no one can show him this, he applies all kinds of depreciatory epithets to this nebular stage of the universe. Contemporary science unfortunately cannot describe this system to Herr Dühring's satisfaction. Just as little is it able to answer many other questions. To the question: Why do toads have no tails?—up to now it has only been able to answer: because they have lost them. But if anyone likes to fly into a temper, and say that this is to leave the whole question in the vagueness and formlessness of an idea of loss which cannot be more closely determined, and that it is an extremely airy conception, such an application of moral indignation to natural science does not take us a step further forward. Such expressions of dislike and bad temper can be used always and everywhere, and just for that reason they are never any use anywhere. Who is hindering Herr Dühring from himself discovering the mechanical system of the original nebula?

Fortunately we now learn that the Kantian nebular mass "is far from coinciding with a completely identical state of the world medium, or, to put it another way, with an identical state of matter." It was really fortunate for Kant that he was able to content himself with going back from the existing celestial bodies to the nebular ball, and did not even dream of the identical state of matter! It may be remarked in passing that when contemporary natural science describes the Kantian nebular ball as the primordial nebula, it is self-evident that this is only to be understood in a relative sense. It is the primordial nebula, on the one hand, in that it is the origin of the existing celestial bodies, and on the other hand because it is the earliest form of matter which we have up to now been able to work back to. This certainly does not exclude, but rather implies, the supposition that before the nebular stage matter had passed through an infinite series of other forms.

Herr Dühring sees his advantage here. Where we, with science, stand still for the time being at a provisional primordial nebula, his science of science helps him much further back to that "state of the world medium which cannot be understood either as purely static in the present meaning of the idea, or as dynamic"—which therefore cannot be understood at all. "The unity of matter and mechanical force which we call the world medium is what might be termed a logical-real formula through which we can present the identical state of matter as the pre-condition of all enumerable stages of evolution."

We are clearly not by a long way rid of the primordial identical state of matter. Here it is spoken of as the unity of matter and mechanical force, and this as a logical-real formula, etc. As soon as the unity of matter and mechanical force comes to an end, motion begins.

The logical-real formula is nothing but a lame attempt to make the Hegelian categories of "in itself" and "for itself" usable in the philosophy of reality. With Hegel, "in itself" covers the original identity of the hidden, undeveloped contradictions within a thing, a process or an idea; and "for itself" brings in the distinction and separation of these latent elements and is the starting point of their conflict. We should therefore think of the motionless original state as the unity of matter and mechanical force, and of the transition to movement as their separation and opposition. What we have gained by this is not any proof of the reality of that fantastic original state, but only the fact that it is possible to conceive it under the Hegelian category of "in itself," and its equally fantastic termination under the category of "for itself." Hegel help us!

Matter, Herr Dühring says, is the bearer of all reality: on which basis there cannot be any mechanical force apart from matter. Mechanical force is moreover a state of matter. But in the original state, when nothing happened, matter and its state, mechanical force, were one. Afterwards, when something began to happen, this state must apparently have become different from matter. So we are to let ourselves be put off with these mystical phrases and with the assurance that the identical state is neither static nor dynamic, neither in equilibrium nor in motion. We still do not know where mechanical force was in that state of the universe, or how we are to get from absolute immobility to motion without an impulse from outside, that is, without God.

The materialists before Herr Dühring spoke of matter and motion. He reduces motion to mechanical force as its supposed basic form, and thereby makes it impossible for himself to understand the real connection between matter and motion, which in fact was also unclear to all former materialists. And yet it is simple enough. *Motion is the mode of existence of matter.* Never anywhere has there been matter without motion, nor can there be. Motion in cosmic space, mechanical motion of smaller masses on the various celestial bodies, the motion of molecules as heat or as electrical or magnetic currents, chemical decomposition and combination, organic life—at each given moment each individual atom of matter in the world is in one or other of these forms of motion, or in several forms of them at once. All rest, all equilibrium, is only relative, and only has meaning in relation to one or other definite form of motion. A body, for example, may be on the ground in mechanical equilibrium, may be mechanically at rest; but this in no way prevents it from participating in the motion of the earth and in that of the whole solar system, just as little as it prevents its most minute physical parts from carrying out the oscillations determined by its temperature, or its atoms from passing through a chemical process. Matter without motion is just as unthinkable as motion without matter. Motion is therefore as uncreatable and indestructible as matter itself; as the older philosophy (Descartes) expressed it, the quantity of motion existing in the world is always the same. Motion therefore cannot be created; it can only be transferred. When motion is transferred from one body to another, in so far as it transfers itself, is active, it may be regarded as the cause of motion, in so far as the latter is transferred, is passive. We call this active motion *force*, and the passive, the *manifestation of force*. In this it is as clear as daylight that the force is equal to its manifestation, because in fact it is the *same* motion which takes place in both.

A motionless state of matter is therefore one of the most empty and ridiculous of ideas—a "delirious phantasy" of the purest water. In order to arrive at such an idea it is necessary to conceive the relative mechanical equilibrium, in which state a body on the earth may in fact be, as absolute rest, and then to extend this over the whole universe. This is certainly made easier if universal motion is reduced to purely mechanical force. And the restriction of motion to purely mechanical force has the further advantage that a force can be conceived as at rest, as tied up, and as therefore for the moment inactive. When in fact, as is very often the case, the transfer of a motion is a somewhat complex process containing a number of intermediate points, it is possible to postpone the actual transmission to any moment desired by omitting the last link in the chain. This is the case for instance if a man loads a gun and postpones the moment when, through the pulling of the trigger, the discharge, the transfer of the motion set free by the explosion of the powder, takes place. It is therefore possible to imagine that during its motionless, identical state, matter was loaded with force, and this, if anything at all, seems to be what Herr Dühring understands by the unity of matter and mechanical force. This concept is nonsensical, because it transfers to the universe, as if it were absolute, a state which by its nature is relative and therefore can only apply to *one part* of matter at one time. Even if we overlook this point, the difficulty still remains: first, how did the world come to be loaded, since nowadays guns do not load themselves; and second, whose finger was it then that pulled the trigger? We may turn and twist as much as we like, but under Herr Dühring's guidance we always come back again to—the finger of God.

From astronomy our philosopher of reality passes on to mechanics and physics, and complains that the mechanical theory of heat has not, in the generation since its discovery, been materially advanced beyond the point to which Robert Mayer had himself gradually developed it. Apart from this, he says that the whole business is still very obscure; we must "always remember that in the states of motion of matter, static relations are also present and that these latter are not measured by the mechanical work ... if previously we described Nature as a great workwoman, and if we now take this expression literally, we must nevertheless add that the identical state and static relations do not represent mechanical work. So once again we miss the bridge from the static to the dynamic, and if so-called latent heat has up to now remained a stumbling-block for the theory, we must recognise a defect in this too, which can least be denied in its cosmic application."

This whole oracular discourse is once again nothing but the out-pouring of a bad conscience, which is very well aware that with its creation of motion out of absolute immobility it is irretrievably lost, but is nevertheless ashamed to appeal to the only possible saviour, namely, the creator of heaven and earth. If even in mechanics, including the mechanics of heat, the bridge from the static to the dynamic, from equilibrium to motion, cannot be found, how can Herr Dühring be compelled to find the bridge from his motionless state to motion? And that would then relieve him of the difficulty.

In ordinary mechanics the bridge from the static to the dynamic is—the external stimulus. If a stone weighing a hundredweight is raised from the ground ten yards into the air and is freely suspended in such a way that it remains hanging there in an identical state and in a relation of rest, it would be necessary to have an audience of sucklings to be able to maintain that the present state of this body does not represent any mechanical work, or that its distance from its previous position is not measured by mechanical work. Every passer-by will easily explain to Herr Dühring that the stone did not rise of itself to the rope, and any textbook of mechanics will tell him that if he lets the stone fall again it exerts in falling just as much mechanical work as was necessary to raise it the ten yards in the air. Even the simple fact that the stone is hanging up there represents mechanical work, for if it remains hanging long enough the rope breaks, as soon as chemical decomposition makes it no longer strong enough to bear the weight of the stone. But it is to such simple basic forms, to use Herr Dühring's language, that all mechanical processes can be reduced, and the engineer is still to be born who cannot find the bridge from the static to the dynamic, so long as he has at his disposal a sufficient external impulse.

To be sure, it is a hard nut and a bitter pill for our metaphysician that motion should find its measure in its opposite, in rest. That is indeed a crying contradiction, and every contradiction, according to

Herr Dühring, is nonsensical. It is none the less a fact that the suspended stone, just like the loaded gun, represents a definite quantity of mechanical motion, that this definite quantity is measurable exactly by its weight and its distance from the ground, and that the mechanical motion may be used in various ways at will, for example, by its direct fall, by sliding down an inclined plane, or by turning a shaft. From the dialectical standpoint, the possibility of expressing motion in its opposite, in rest, presents absolutely no difficulty. To dialectical philosophy the whole contradiction, as we have seen, is only relative; there is no such thing as absolute rest, unconditional equilibrium. Each separate movement strives toward equilibrium, and the motion as a whole puts an end to the equilibrium. When therefore rest and equilibrium occur they are the result of arrested motion, and it is self-evident that this motion is measurable in its result, can be expressed in it, and can be restored out of it again in one form or another. But Herr Dühring cannot allow himself to be satisfied with such a simple presentation of the matter. As a good metaphysician he first tears open a yawning gulf, which does not exist in reality, between motion and equilibrium, and is then surprised that he cannot find any bridge across this self-fabricated gulf. He might just as well mount his metaphysical Rosinante and chase the Kantian "thing-in-itself"; for it is that and nothing else which in the last analysis is hiding behind this undiscoverable bridge.

But what about the mechanical theory of heat and the latent heat which "has remained a stumbling-block" for this theory?

If, under normal atmospheric pressure, a pound of ice is transformed by heat from a temperature of freezing point into a pound of water of the same temperature, a quantity of heat is lost which would be sufficient to warm the same pound of water from $0°$ to $79.4°$ of the centigrade thermometer, or to warm 79.4 pounds of water by one degree. If this pound of water is heated up to boiling point, that is, to $100°$, and is then transformed into steam of $100°$ the amount of heat that disappears, by the time the last of the water has changed into steam, is almost seven times greater, sufficient to raise the temperature of 537.2 pounds of water by one degree. This heat that disappears is called *latent*. If, by re-cooling, the steam is again transformed into water, and the water, in its turn, to ice, the same quantity of heat as was previously latent is now again set *free*, *i.e.*, can be felt and measured as heat. This liberation of heat by the condensation of steam and the freezing of water is the reason why steam, when cooled to 100°, is only gradually transformed into water, and why a mass of water at the temperature of freezing point is only very gradually transformed into ice. These are the facts. The question is, what happens to the heat when it is latent?

The mechanical theory of heat, according to which the heat of a body consists in a greater or less vibration, depending on the temperature and state of aggregation, of its smallest physical active parts (molecules), a vibration which under certain conditions can change into any other form of motion—this theory explains the facts on the basis that the heat that disappears has done active work, has been transformed into work. When ice melts, the close and firm connection between the various molecules is broken, and transformed into a loose juxtaposition; when water at boiling point becomes steam a state is reached in which the individual molecules no longer have any noticeable influence on each other, and under the influence of heat even fly apart in all directions. It is clear that the single molecules of a body are endowed with far greater energy in the gaseous state than they are in the fluid state, and in the fluid state again more than in the solid state. The latent heat therefore has not disappeared; it has merely been transformed, and has assumed the form of molecular tension. As soon as the conditions cease to exist under which the separate molecules are able to maintain their absolute or relative freedom in regard to one another—that is, as soon as the temperature falls below the minimum of 100° or 0° as the case may be, this tension is relaxed, the molecules again press towards each other with the same force with which they had previously flown apart; and this force disappears, but only to reappear as precisely the same quantity of heat as had previously been latent. This explanation is of course a hypothesis, as is the whole mechanical theory of heat, inasmuch as no one has up to now ever seen a molecule, not to mention one in vibration. Just for this reason it is certain to be as full of defects as all other theories which are still very new, but it can at least explain what happens without in any way coming into conflict with the principle that motion can neither be destroyed nor created, and it is even able to indicate to us the whereabouts of heat during its transformations. Latent heat is therefore in no way a stumbling-block for the mechanical theory of heat. On the contrary, this theory provides the first rational explanation of what takes place, and it involves no stumbling-block except in so far as physicists continue to describe heat which has been transformed into another form of molecular energy by means of the term "latent," which has become out of date and unsuitable.

The identical states and resting conditions in the solid, in the liquid and in the gaseous state of aggregation represent therefore in all cases mechanical work, in so far as the mechanical work is the measure of heat. Both the solid crust of the earth and the water of the ocean, in their present physical condition, represent a definite quantity of heat set free, which of course corresponds to an equally definite quantity of mechanical force. In the transition of the gaseous ball, from which the earth has developed, into the liquid and subsequently into the largely solid state, a definite quantity of molecular energy was radiated as heat into space. The difficulty which Herr Dühring whispers of in this mysterious manner therefore does not exist, and though it is true that even in applying the theory cosmically we may come up against defects and gaps—which must be attributed to our inadequate means of knowledge—we never come up against theoretically insuperable difficulties. The bridge from the static to the dynamic is here too the external impulse—the cooling or heating brought about by other bodies acting on the body which is in a state of equilibrium. The further we explore this natural philosophy of Dühring's, the more impossible appear all attempts to explain motion out of immobility or to find the bridge over which purely static equilibrium can *by itself* pass over into a dynamic condition, motion.

With this we have fortunately rid ourselves for a time of the original identical state. Herr Dühring passes on to chemistry, and takes the opportunity to reveal to us three natural laws of permanence which have already been discovered by his philosophy of reality, as follows:

(1) The quantity of matter in the universe, (2) the quantity of

the simple (chemical) elements, and (3) the quantity of mechanical force are constant.

Thus: the law that matter, and also its indivisible particles in so far as it is made up of these, can neither be created nor destroyed, and that this is true also of motion—these old, familiar facts, expressed most inadequately—these are the only positive things which Herr Dühring can provide us with as a result of this natural philosophy of the inorganic world. We knew all this long ago. But what we did not know was that they were "laws of permanence" and as such "schematic properties of the system of things." We are being treated as Kant was above: Herr Dühring picks up some old familiar quip, sticks a Dühring label on it, and calls the result: "absolutely original conclusions and views...system-creating ideas...deep-rooted science."

But we need not by any means despair on this account. Whatever defects even the most deeply-rooted science and the best-ordered society may have, Herr Dühring can at any rate assert one thing with confidence: "the amount of gold present in the universe must at all times have been the same, and it can have been increased or diminished in quantity just as little as can matter in general." Unfortunately Herr Dühring does not tell us what we can buy with this gold "present in the universe."

VII. NATURAL PHILOSOPHY. THE ORGANIC WORLD

"A single and uniform ladder of intermediate steps leads from the mechanics of pressure and impact to the linking together of sensations and ideas." With this assurance Herr Dühring saves himself the trouble of saying anything further about the origin of life, although it might reasonably have been expected that a thinker who had traced the evolution of the world back to its identical state, and is so much at home on other celestial bodies, would have had exact information also on this point. For the rest, however, the assurance he gives us is only half true, unless it is completed by the Hegelian nodal line of measure-relations which has already been mentioned. In spite of all intermediate steps, the transition from one form of motion to another always remains a leap, a decisive change. This is true of the transition from the mechanics of celestial bodies to that of smaller masses on a particular celestial body; it is equally true of the transition from the mechanics of masses to the mechanics of molecules—including the forms of motion investigated in physics proper: heat, light, electricity, magnetism. In the same way, the transition from the physics of molecules to the physics of atoms— chemistry—in turn involves a definite leap; and this is even more clearly the case in the transition from ordinary chemical action to the chemistry of albumen which we call life. Then within the sphere of life the leaps become ever more infrequent and imperceptible.—Once again, therefore, it is Hegel who has to correct Herr Dühring.

The idea of purpose provides Herr Dühring with his conceptual transition to the organic world. Once again, this is borrowed from Hegel, who in his *Logic—the Science of the Idea*—makes the transition from chemistry to life by means of teleology or the science of purpose. Wherever we look in Herr Dühring we stumble up against a Hegelian "crudity," which he quite unblushingly hands on to us as his own deep-rooted science. It would take us too far to examine here to what extent it is legitimate and appropriate to apply the ideas of end and means to the organic world. In any case the utilisation of the Hegelian "inner purpose"—*i.e.*, a purpose which is not imported into Nature by some third party acting purposively, such as the wisdom of providence, but lies in the necessity of the thing itself—constantly leads, with people who are not well versed in philosophy, to the unthinking interpolation of conscious and purposive activity. That same Herr Dühring who is filled with boundless moral indignation at the slightest "spiritistic" tendency in other people assures us "with certainty that the instincts were primarily created for the sake of the sense of pleasure which is associated with their activity." He tells us that poor Nature "is obliged incessantly to maintain order in the objective world," and moreover in doing so she has to solve more than one problem "which requires on the part of Nature more subtlety than is usually credited to her." But Nature not only *knows* why she does one thing and another; she has not only to perform the duties of a housemaid, she not only possesses subtlety, in itself a very pretty accomplishment in subjective conscious thought; she has also a will. For what the instincts do in addition, fulfilling real natural functions such as nutrition, propagation, etc., "we should not regard as directly, but only indirectly, *willed*." So we have arrived at a consciously thinking and acting Nature, and are thus already standing on the "bridge"—not indeed from the static to the dynamic, but from pantheism to deism. Or is Herr Dühring perhaps just for once indulging in a little "natural-philosophical semi-poetry"?

It is impossible. All that our philosopher of reality can tell us of organic Nature is restricted to the fight against this natural-philosophical semi-poetry, against "charlatanism with its frivolous superficialities and pseudo-scientific mystifications," against the "poetising features" of *Darwinism*.

The main reproach levelled against Darwin is that he transferred the Malthusian population theory from economics into natural science, that he never got beyond the ideas of an animal breeder, and that in his theory of the struggle for existence he pursued unscientific semi-poetry, and that the whole of Darwinism, after deducting what has been borrowed from Lamarck, is a piece of brutality directed against humanity.

Darwin brought back from his scientific travels the view that plant and animal species are not constant but subject to variation. In order to follow up these ideas after his return home there was no better field available than that of the breeding of animals and plants. It is precisely in this field that England is the classical country; the achievements of other countries, for example Germany, fall far short of what England has achieved in this connection. Moreover, most of these successes have been won during the last hundred years, so that there is very little difficulty in establishing the facts. Darwin found that this breeding has produced artificially, among animals and plants of the same species, differences greater than those found in what are generally recognised as different species. Thus was established on the one hand the variability of species up to a certain point, and on the other, the possibility of a common ancestry for organisms with different specific characteristics. Darwin then investigated whether there were not possibly causes to be found in Nature which—without conscious purpose on the part of the breeder—would nevertheless in the long run produce in living organisms changes similar to those produced by artificial breeding. He discovered these causes in the disproportion between the immense number of germs created by Nature and the insignificant number of organisms which actually attain maturity. But as each germ strives to develop, there necessarily arises a struggle for existence which manifests itself not merely as direct bodily combat or devouring, but also as a struggle for space and light, even in the case of plants. And it is evident that in this struggle those individual organisms which have some particular characteristic, however insignificant, which gives them an advantage in the struggle for existence will have the best prospect of reaching maturity and propagating themselves. These individual characteristics have furthermore the tendency to be inherited, and when they occur among many individuals of the same species, to increase through accumulated heredity in the direction once taken; while those individual organisms which do not possess these characteristics succumb more easily in the struggle for existence and gradually disappear. In this way a species is altered through natural selection, through the survival of the fittest.

Against this Darwinian theory, however, Herr Dühring says that the origin of the idea of the struggle for existence, as, he claims, Darwin himself admitted, has to be sought in a generalisation of the views of the economic theorist of population, Malthus, and the idea is therefore marked by all the defects peculiar to the parsonical views of Malthus on the pressure of population.—Now Darwin would not dream of saying that the *origin* of the idea of the struggle for existence is to be found in Malthus. He only says that his theory of the struggle for existence is the theory of Malthus applied to the animal and plant world as a whole. However great the blunder made by Darwin in accepting so naïvely and without reflection the Malthusian theory, nevertheless anyone can see at the first glance that no Malthusian spectacles are required in order to perceive the struggle for existence in Nature—the contradiction between the countless host of germs which Nature so lavishly produces and the small number of those which ever reach maturity; a contradiction which in fact for the most part finds its solution in a struggle for existence which is often of extreme cruelty. And just as the law of wages has maintained its validity even after the Malthusian arguments on which Ricardo based it have long been exploded, so likewise the struggle for existence can take place in Nature, even without any Malthusian interpretation. For that matter, the organisms of Nature also have their laws of population, which have been left almost entirely uninvestigated, although their formulation would be of decisive importance for the theory of the evolution of species. But who was it that gave the most definite impulse to work in this direction? No other than Darwin.

Herr Dühring carefully avoids an examination of this positive side of the question. Instead, he does nothing but make repeated attacks on the struggle for existence. It is obvious, according to him, that there can be no talk of a struggle for existence among unconscious plants and good-natured plant-eaters: "In the precise and definite sense the struggle for existence is found only in the realm of brutality, in so far as animals get their nourishment by seizing prey by force and devouring it." And after he has reduced the idea of the struggle for existence to these narrow limits he can give full play of his indignation at the brutality of this idea, which he himself has restricted to brutality. But this moral indignation applies only to Herr Dühring himself, who is indeed the only author of the struggle for existence in this limited conception and is therefore also solely responsible for it. It is consequently not Darwin who "sought the laws and understanding of all Nature's actions in the kingdom of the brutes"—Darwin had in fact expressly included the whole of organic nature in the struggle—but an imaginary bugbear dressed up by Herr Dühring himself. The *name:* the struggle for existence, can for the matter be willingly handed over to Herr Dühring's exceedingly moral indignation. That the *fact* exists also among plants can be demonstrated to him by every meadow, every cornfield, every wood; and the question at issue is not what it is to be called, whether "struggle for existence" or "lack of conditions for existence and mechanical effects," but how this fact influences the fixity or variation of species. On this point Herr Dühring maintains an obstinate and "identical" silence. Therefore for the time being in regard to natural selection it will certainly continue to be applied.

But Darwinism "produces its transformation and differences out of nothing." It is true that Darwin, when considering natural selection, leaves out of account the *causes* which have produced the variations in separate individuals, and deals in the first place with the way in which such individual variations gradually become the characteristics of a race, variety or species. To Darwin it was of less immediate importance to discover these causes—which up to the present are in part absolutely unknown, and in part can only be stated in quite general terms—than to establish a rational form according to which their effects are preserved and acquire permanent significance. It is true that in doing this Darwin attributed to his discovery too wide a field of action, made it the sole agent in the alteration of species and neglected the causes of the repeated individual variations, concentrating rather on the form in which these variations become general; but this is a mistake which he shares in common with most other people who make any real advance. Moreover, if Darwin produces his individual variations out of nothing, and in so doing applies exclusively "the wisdom of the breeder," the

breeder also must produce *out of nothing* his changes in animal and
plant forms which are not merely imaginary but occur in reality. But
once again, the man who gave the impetus to science to investigate
how exactly these variations and differences arise is no other than
Darwin.

Recently—by Haeckel, to be precise—the idea of natural selection
has been extended, and the variation of species conceived as the
result of the mutual interaction of adaptation and heredity, in which
conception adaptation is taken as the factor which produces variations, and heredity as the conserving factor in the process. This is
also not regarded as satisfactory by Herr Dühring. "Real adaptation
to conditions of life which are offered or withheld by Nature presupposes impulses and actions, determined by ideas. Otherwise the
adaptation is only apparent, and the causality displayed here does
not rise above the low grades of causality in physics, chemistry and
the physiology of plants." Once again it is the name which makes
Herr Dühring angry. But whatever name he may give to the process,
the question here is whether through such processes variations in
the species of organisms are produced or not. And again Herr
Dühring gives no answer.

"If, in growing, a plant takes the direction in which it will receive
most light, this effect of the stimulus is nothing but a combination
of physical forces and chemical agents, and any attempt to describe
it—not metaphorically, but precisely—as adaptation must introduce a *spiritistic* confusion into the idea." Such is the severity
meted out to others by the very man who knows exactly by whose
will Nature does one thing or another, who speaks of Nature's
subtlety and even of her *will!* Spiritistic confusion, yes—but where,
in Haeckel or in Herr Dühring?

And not only spiritistic, but also logical confusion. We saw that
Herr Dühring insists with all his might on establishing the validity
in Nature of the idea of purpose: "The relation of means to end does
not in the least presuppose a conscious purpose." What then is the
adaptation without conscious purpose, without the mediation of
ideas, which he so zealously opposes, but such an unconscious
purposive activity?

If therefore tree-frogs and leaf-eating insects are green, desert animals are sandy yellow, and animals of the polar regions are mainly snow-white in colour, they have certainly not adopted these colours on purpose or in conformity with any ideas; on the contrary, the colours can only be explained on the basis of physical forces and chemical agencies. And yet it cannot be denied that these animals, because of those colours, are fittingly *adapted* to the environment in which they live, in such a way that they are far less visible to their enemies. In just the same way the organs with which certain plants seize and devour insects alighting on them are adapted to this action, and even purposively adapted. But if Herr Dühring insists that this adaptation must be affected through ideas, he only says in other words that the purposive activity must also be brought about through ideas, must be conscious and intentional. And this brings us, as is usually the case in his philosophy of reality, to a purposive creator, to God. "An expedient of this kind used to be called deism, and was not thought much of"—Herr Dühring tells us—"but in this connection also *we* now seem to have developed backwards."

From adaptation we come to heredity. Here too, according to Herr Dühring, Darwinism is completely on the wrong track. The whole organic world, Darwin is said to have asserted, is derived from one original creature, is so to speak the progeny of one single being. Dühring states that, in Darwin's view, there is no such thing as the independent co-ordination of similar products of nature except in so far as these have common descent; and therefore that Darwin in his restrospectively directed views had perforce to come to an end at the point where the thread of begetting, or other form of propagation, breaks.

The statement that Darwin traced all existing organisms back to one original creature is, to put it politely, a product of Herr Dühring's "own free creation and imagination." Darwin expressly says on the last page but one of his *Origin of Species*, sixth edition, that he regards "all beings, not as special creations, but as the lineal descendants *of some few beings*." And Haeckel even goes considerably further, assuming "a quite independent stock for the vegetable kingdom, and a second for the animal kingdom," and between the two "a number of independent stocks of Protista, each of which has developed out of one special archegon of the Moneron type" (*The*

History of Creation p. 397). This original being was only invented
by Dühring in order to bring it into as great disrepute as possible
by drawing a parallel with the original Jew Adam; and in this he
—that is to say, Herr Dühring—suffers from the misfortune of not
having the faintest idea that his original Jew had been shown by
Smith's Assyrian discoveries to have been an original Semite, and
that the whole history of creation and the flood turns out to be a
part of the old heathen religious myths which the Jews have in
common with the Babylonians, Chaldeans and Assyrians.

It is certainly a bitter reproach against Darwin, and one for which
he has no defence, that he comes to an end at the point where the
thread of descent breaks off. Unfortunately it is a reproach which
can be levelled at the whole of our natural science. Where the thread
of descent breaks off for it, it "ends." It has not yet succeeded in
producing organic beings without descent from others; indeed, it
has not yet succeeded even in producing simple protoplasm or
other albuminous bodies out of their chemical elements. With regard
to the origin of life, therefore, up to the present, science is only
able to say with certainty that it must have arisen as a result of
chemical action. However, perhaps, the philosophy of reality is in
a position to give some help on this point, as it has at its disposal
independently co-ordinated products of Nature which are without
common descent. How can these have come into existence? By
spontaneous generation? But up to now even the most presumptuous
advocates of spontaneous generation have not claimed that this
produced anything but bacteria, fungi and other very primitive
organisms—no insects, fishes, fowls or mammals. But if these similar
products of Nature—organic, of course, as here we are only dealing
with these—are not connected by descent, they or each of their
ancestors must, at the point "where the thread of descent breaks off,"
have been put into the world by a separate act of creation. So we
arrive once again at a creator and at what is called deism.

Herr Dühring further declares that it was very superficial on
Darwin's part "to make the mere act of the sexual combination of
characteristics into the fundamental principle of how these characteristics arose." This is another free creation and imagination of our
deeply-rooted philosopher. Darwin definitely states the opposite:

the expression natural selection only implies the *preservation* of variations, not their origin (p. 63). This new allegation of things which Darwin never said nevertheless serves to help us forward to the following depth of Dühringian mentality: "If some principle of independent variation had been sought in the inner schematism of generation, this idea would have been quite rational; for it is a natural conception to combine the principle of the genesis of everything with that of sexual propagation into a unity, and to regard the so-called spontaneous generation, looked at from a higher standpoint, not as the absolute antithesis of reproduction but just as a production." And the man who can write such rubbish is not ashamed to reproach Hegel for his "jargon"!

But enough of the peevish, contradictory grumbling and nagging through which Herr Dühring expresses his anger at the colossal impetus which science owes to the driving force of the Darwinian theory. Neither Darwin nor his disciples among scientists ever think of in any way belittling the great services rendered by Lamarck; in fact, they are the very people who first put him again up on his pedestal. But we must not overlook the fact that in Lamarck's time science was as yet far from being in possession of sufficient material to enable it to answer the question as to the origin of species except in an anticipatory way, as it were prophetically. In addition to the enormous mass of material, but of specimens collected and of the results of anatomical investigation, which botany and zoology have accumulated in the intervening period, two completely new sciences have arisen since Lamarck's time, and these are of decisive importance for this question: research into the development of plant and animal germs (embryology) and research into the various organic remains preserved in the various strata of the earth's supper crust (palæontology). There is in fact a peculiar similarity between the gradual development of organic germs into mature organisms, and the succession of plants and animals following each other in the history of the earth. And it is precisely this similarity which has given the theory of evolution its most secure basis. The theory of evolution itself is however still in a very early stage, and it therefore cannot be doubted that further research will modify in very important respects our present conceptions, including strictly Darwinian ones, of the course of the evolution of species.

What has the philosophy of reality to tell us, of a positive character, concerning the evolution of organic life?

"The...variability of species" is a presupposition which can be accepted. But alongside of it there holds also "the independent co-ordination of similar products of Nature, without the mediation of heredity." From this we are apparently to infer that the dissimilar products of Nature, *i.e.*, the species which show variations, have common descent, but that this is not the case with the similar products. But this too is not altogether correct; for even with species which show variations "mediation by heredity is on the contrary quite a secondary act of Nature." So we get heredity after all, but only "second class." We must rejoice that after Herr Dühring has attributed so much to it that is obscure and evil, we nevertheless find it in the end readmitted by the back door. It is the same with natural selection, for after all his moral indignation over the struggle for existence through which natural selection operates we suddenly find: "The deeper basis of the constitution of organic beings is nevertheless to be found in the condition of life and cosmic relations, while the natural selection emphasised by Darwin can only come in as a secondary factor." So after all, natural selection, though only second class; and along with natural selection also the struggle for existence, and with that also the parsonical Malthus' pressure of population! That is all, and for the rest Herr Dühring refers us to Lamarck.

In conclusion he warns us against the misuse of the terms metamorphosis and development. Metamorphosis, he maintains, is an unclear idea, and the idea of development is permissible only in so far as laws of development can be really established. In place of both these terms we should use the term "composition," and then everything would be all right. It is the old story over again: things remain as they were, and Herr Dühring is quite satisfied as soon as we just alter the names. When we speak of the development of the chicken in the egg we are creating confusion, for we are only able to prove the laws of development in an incomplete way. But if we speak of its composition, then it all becomes clear. We shall therefore no longer say: This child is developing finely, but: It is composing itself magnificently. We can congratulate Herr Dühring on being a worthy peer of the author of the *Nibelungenring* not only in his honourable self-esteem but also in his capacity as composer of the future.

VIII. NATURAL PHILOSOPHY. THE ORGANIC WORLD
(CONCLUSION)

"The reader must try to realise... what was positive scientific knowledge was required to equip our section on Natural Philosophy with all its scientific hypotheses. Its basis is provided firstly by all the fundamental achievements of mathematics, and then the main discoveries of exact science in mechanics, physics and chemistry, as well as the general conclusions of natural science in physiology, zoology and similar branches of enquiry."

Such is the confidence and assurance with which Herr Dühring speaks of the mathematical and scientific erudition of Herr Dühring. It is impossible to detect from the meagre section concerned, and still less from its paltry conclusions, what deep-rooted positive knowledge lies behind them. In any case, in order to create the Dühring oracle on physics and chemistry, it is not necessary to know any more of physics than the equation which expresses the mechanical equivalent of heat, or any more of chemistry than that all bodies can be divided into elements and combinations of elements. Moreover, a person who can talk of "gravitating atoms," as Herr Dühring does, only proves that he is completely "in the dark" as to the difference between atoms and molecules. As is well known, atoms do not exist in relation to gravitation or other mechanical or physical forms of motion, but only in relation to chemical action. And if anyone reads the chapter on organic Nature, with its vacuous, self-contradictory and, at the decisive point, oracularly senseless meandering verbiage, and its absolutely futile final conclusion, from the very start he will not be able to avoid forming the opinion that Herr Dühring is here speaking of things of which he knows remarkably little. This opinion, however, becomes absolute certainty when the reader reaches his suggestion that in the science of organic beings (biology) the term composition should henceforth be used instead of development. The person who can put forward such a suggestion shows that he has not the faintest suspicion of the constitution of organic bodies.

All organic bodies, except the very lowest, consist of cells, small particles of albumen which are only visible when considerably magnified, with a nucleus inside them. As a rule the cells also develop an outer membrane and the contents are then more or less fluid. The lowest cellular bodies consist of a single cell; the immense majority of organic beings are multicellular, interdependent complexes of many cells which in lower organisms remain of a homogeneous type, but in higher organisms develop more and more varied forms, groupings and activities. In the human body, for example, bones, muscles, nerves, tendons, ligaments, cartilages, skin, in a word all tissues, are either composed of cells or originated from them. But in all organic cellular structures, from the amœba, which is a simple and usually skinless protoplasmic particle with a nucleus inside it, up to man, and from the tiniest unicellular Desmidiacæ up to the most highly developed plant, the manner in which the cells multiply is the same; by division. The nucleus first becomes constricted in the middle, the constriction separating the two ends of the nucleus gets more and more pronounced, and at last they separate from each other and form two nuclei. The same process takes place in the cell itself; each of the two nuclei becomes the centre of an accumulation of protoplasm, linked to the other by a strip which is steadily growing narrower, until at last the two separate from each other and continue to exist as distinct cells. Through such repeated cell division the whole complete animal is gradually developed out of the embryo of the animal egg, after it has been fertilized, and the replacement of used-up tissue is effected in the same way in the adult animal. To call such a process composition, and to say that to describe it as "development" is "pure imagination," certainly indicates a person who—however difficult this may be to believe at the present day—knows absolutely nothing of this process; in it there is just precisely and *exclusively* development and indeed in the most literal sense, and absolutely nothing that is composition!

Later on we shall have something more to say as to what Herr Dühring understands in general by life. In particular his conception of life is as follows: "The inorganic world too is a system of self-fulfilling impulses; but it is only at the point where we get real division into members, with the circulation of substances through special channels from one internal point and according to a germ-scheme transmissible to a smaller structure, that we may venture to speak of real life in the narrower and stricter sense."

This sentence is, in the narrower and stricter sense, a system of self-fulfilling impulses (whatever sort of things these may be) of nonsense, even apart from the hopeless confusion of grammar in it. If life first begins where real articulation commences, then we must declare that the whole Haeckelian kingdom of Protista and perhaps a good many others too are dead, according to the meaning we attach to the idea of articulation. If life first begins when this articulation can be transmitted through a smaller germ-scheme, then at least all organisms up to and including unicellular organisms are dead. If the circulation of substances through special channels is the characteristic of life, then, in addition to the foregoing, we must also strike out of the ranks of the living the whole of the higher class of Cœlenterata, excepting however the Medusæ, that is, all Polyps and other plant-animals. But if the circulation of substances through special channels from one internal point is the essential mark of life, then we must declare that all those animals which have no heart, and those which have more than one heart, are dead. Under this would fall, in addition to those already enumerated, all worms, starfish and rotifers (Annuloida and Annulosa, Huxley's classification), a section of the Crustacea (crabs), and finally even a vertebrate animal, the Amphioxus. And moreover all plants.

In undertaking, therefore, to define real life in the narrower and stricter sense, Herr Dühring gives us four characteristics of life which totally contradict each other, one of which condemns to eternal death not only the whole plant kingdom but also about half the animal kingdom. Really no one can say that he misled us when he promised us "from the foundation upwards original conclusions and views"!

Another passage runs: "In Nature, too, one simple type is the basis of all organisations from the lowest to the highest," and this type is "fully and completely present in its general form even in the most subordinate impulse of the most undeveloped plant." This statement is again "full and complete" nonsense. The most simple type found in the whole of organic Nature is the cell; and it certainly is the basis of the highest organisations. On the other hand, among the lowest organisms there are many which are far below the cell—the Protamœba, a simple protoplasmic particle without any differentiation whatever, and a whole series of other Monera and all bladder seaweeds (Siphoneæ). All of these are linked with the higher organisms only by the fact that their essential component is protoplasm and that they consequently function as protoplasm, *i.e.*, they live and die.

Herr Dühring further tells us: "Physiologically, sensation is associated with the presence of some kind of nerve apparatus, however simple its form. It is therefore characteristic of all animal structures that they are capable of sensation, *i.e.*, subjective conscious awareness of their condition. The sharp boundary line between plants and animals lies at the point where the leap to sensation takes place. Far from being obliterated by the known intermediate structures, the dividing line first really attains logical necessity through these extremely indefinite or indefinable forms." And again: "On the other hand plants are completely and eternally devoid of the slightest trace of sensation, and even lack any apparatus for it."

In the first place Hegel says (*Natural Philosophy*, § 351, Note) that "sensation is the *differentia specifica*, the absolute distinguishing characteristic of the animal." So once again we find a Hegelian "crudity," which through the simple process of appropriation by Herr Dühring is raised to the honourable position of a final and ultimate truth.

In the second place, we hear for the first time of intermediate structures, extremely indefinite or indefinable forms (fine gibberish!) between plants and animals. That these intermediate forms exist; that there are organisms of which we simply cannot say whether they are plants or animals; that therefore we are quite unable to draw a sharp dividing line between plants and animals—precisely this fact makes it a logical necessity for Herr Dühring to establish a criterion of differentiation which in the same breath he admits will not hold water! But we have absolutely no need to go back to the doubtful territory between plants and animals; are the sensitive plants which at the slightest touch fold their leaves or close their flowers, are the insect-eating plants devoid of the slightest trace of sensation and do they even lack any apparatus for it? This cannot be maintained even by Herr Dühring without "unscientific semi-poetry."

In the third place, it is once again a free creation and imagination on Herr Dühring's part when he asserts that sensation is psychologically bound up with the presence of some kind of nerve apparatus, however simple it may be. Not only all primitive animals, but also the plant-animals, or at any rate the great majority of them, show no trace of a nerve apparatus. It is only from the worms on that such a nerve apparatus is regularly found, and Herr Dühring is the first person to make the assertion that those animals have no sensation because they have no nerves. Sensation is not necessarily associated with nerves, but probably with certain protoplasmic bodies which up to now have not been more precisely determined.

For the rest, Herr Dühring's biological knowledge is sufficiently characterised by the question which he has the impudence to put to Darwin: "Is it to be supposed that animals have developed out of plants?" Such a question could only be put by a person who has not the slightest knowledge of either animals or plants.

Of life in general Herr Dühring is only able to tell us: "The metabolism which is carried out through a plastically creating schematisation (what in the world can that be?) remains always a distinguishing characteristic of the real life process."

That is all we learn about life, while in the "plastically creating schematisation" we are left knee-deep in the meaningless gibberish of the purest Dühring jargon. If therefore we want to know what life is, we shall evidently have to look a little more closely at it ourselves.

That organic exchange of matter is the most general and most characteristic phenomenon of life has been said times without number during the last thirty years by physiological chemists and chemical physiologists, and it is here merely translated by Herr Dühring into his own elegant and clear language. But to define life as organic exchange of matter is to define life as—life; for organic exchange of matter or metabolism with plastic creative schematisation is in fact a phrase which needs explanation through life, explanation through the distinction between the organic and the inorganic, that is, the living and the non-living. This explanation therefore does not carry us any further.

Exchange of matter as such takes place even without life. There is a whole series of processes in chemistry which with an adequate supply of raw material constantly reproduce their own conditions, a definite body being the carrier of the process. This is the case in the manufacture of sulphuric acid by the burning of sulphur. In this process sulphur dioxide, SO_2, is produced, and when steam and nitric acid are added, the sulphur dioxide absorbs hydrogen and oxygen and is converted into sulphuric acid, H_2SO_4. In the process the nitric acid gives off oxygen and is reduced to nitric oxide; this nitric oxide immediately absorbs new oxygen from the air again and is transformed into the higher oxides of nitrogen, but only to transfer this oxygen again immediately to sulphur dioxide and to go through the same process again; so that theoretically an infinitely small quantity of nitric acid would suffice to change an unlimited quantity of sulphur dioxide, oxygen and water into sulphuric acid. Exchange of matter also takes place in the passage of fluids through dead organic and even through inorganic membranes, as in Traube's artificial cells. Here too it is clear that we cannot get any further by means of exchange of matter; for the special exchange of matter which is to explain life itself needs in turn to be explained through life. We must therefore try some other way.

Life is the mode of existence of albuminous substances, and this mode of existence essentially consists in the constant self-renewal of the chemical constituents of these substances.

The term albuminous substance is to be understood here in the sense used by modern chemistry, which includes under this name all substances constituted similarly to ordinary white of egg, otherwise also known as protein substances. The name is awkward, because ordinary white of egg plays the most lifeless and passive role of all the substances related to it, since, together with the yolk, it is merely food for the developing embryo. But while so little is yet known of the chemical composition of albuminous substances, this name is yet better than any other because it is more general.

Everywhere where we find life we find it associated with an albuminous body, and everywhere where we find an albuminous body not in process of dissolution, there also without exception we find the phenomena of life. Undoubtedly the presence of other chemical combinations also is necessary in a living body in order to produce particular differentiations of these phenomena of life; but they are not requisite for naked life, except in so far as they enter into it as food and are transformed into albumen. The lowest living creatures known to us are indeed nothing but simple particles of albumen, and they already exhibit all the essential phenomena of life.

But what are these universal phenomena of life which are equally present among all living organisms? They consist above all in that an albuminous body absorbs other appropriate substances from its environment and assimilates them, while other, older parts of the body are consumed and excreted. Other, non-living bodies also change and are consumed or enter into combinations in the course of natural processes; but in doing this they cease to be what they were. A rock worn away by atmospheric action is no longer a rock; metal which oxidizes turns into rust. But what with non-living bodies is the cause of destruction, with albumen is *the fundamental condition of existence*. From the moment when this uninterrupted metamorphosis of its constituents, this constant alternation of nutrition and excretion, no longer takes place in an albuminous body, from that moment the albuminous body itself comes to an end and decomposes, that is, *dies*. Life, the mode of existence of albuminous substance, therefore consists primarily in the fact that at each moment it is itself and at the same time something else; and this does not take place as the result of a process to which it is subjected from without, as is the way in which this can occur in the case of inanimate bodies. On the contrary, life, the exchange of matter which takes place through nutrition and excretion, is a self-completing process which is inherent in and native to its medium, albumen, without which it cannot exist. And hence it follows that if chemistry ever succeeds in producing albumen artificially, this albumen must show the phenomena of life, however weak these may be. It is certainly open to question whether chemistry will at the same time also discover the right food for this albumen.

From the exchange of matter which takes place through nutrition and excretion as the essential function of albumen, and from its peculiar plasticity, proceed also all the other most simple characteristics of life: response to stimuli, which is already included in the mutual interaction between the albumen and its food; contractility, which is shown even by very low forms in the consumption of food; the possibility of growth, which in the lowest forms includes propagation by fission, internal movement, without which neither the consumption nor the assimilation of food is possible.

Our definition of life is naturally very inadequate, inasmuch as, far from including *all* the phenomena of life, it has to be limited to those which are the most common and the simplest. From a scientific standpoint all definitions are of little value. In order to gain a really exhaustive knowledge of what life is, we should have to go through all the forms in which it appears, from the lowest up to the highest. But for ordinary usage, however, such definitions are very convenient and in places cannot well be dispensed with; moreover, they can do no harm, provided their inevitable deficiencies are not forgotten.

But back to Herr Dühring. When things are going somewhat badly with him in the sphere of earthly biology, he knows how to find consolation; he takes refuge in his starry heaven.

"It is not merely the special apparatus of an organ of sensation, but the whole objective world, which is adapted to the production of pleasure and pain. For this reason we take it for granted that the antithesis of pleasure and pain, and moreover *exactly* in the form with which we are familiar, is a universal antithesis, and must be represented *in the various worlds of the universe* by essentially similar feelings. . . . This general conformity, however, is of *no little* significance, for it is the key to the *universe of sensations*. . . . And moreover the subjective cosmic world is for us not much more unfamiliar than the objective. The constitution of both spheres must be conceived according to one concordant type, and in this we have the beginnings of a science of consciousness whose range is wider than merely terrestrial."

What do a few gross blunders in terrestrial natural science matter to the man who carries in his pocket the key to the universe of sensation? *Allons donc!*

IX. MORALITY AND LAW. ETERNAL TRUTHS

We refrain from giving samples of the mish-mash of platitudes and oracular sayings, in a word, of the simple *balderdash,* with which Herr Dühring regales his readers for fifty full pages as the deep-rooted science of the elements of consciousness. We will cite only this: "The person who can only think by means of language has never yet learnt what is meant by *abstract* and *pure* thought." On this basis animals are the most abstract and purest thinkers, because their thought is never obscured by the officious intrusion of language. In any case one can see from the Dühringian thoughts and the language in which they are expressed how little suited these thoughts are to any language, and how little suited the German language is to these thoughts.

At last the fourth section is reached, and we are saved; apart from the liquefying pap of rhetoric, it does at least offer us, here and there, something tangible on the subject of *morality* and *law.* Right at the outset, on this occasion, we are invited to take a trip to the other celestial bodies: the elements of morality "must occur in concordant fashion among all non-human beings whose active reason has to deal with the conscious ordering of life impulses in the form of instincts. . . . And yet our interest in such deductions will remain small. . . . Nevertheless it always remains an idea which *beneficently extends* our range of vision, when we think that on other celestial bodies the life of the individuals and of the community must be based on a scheme which . . . is unable to abrogate or escape from the general fundamental constitution of a rationally acting being."

In this case, by way of exception, the validity of the Dühringian truths also for all other possible worlds is put at the beginning instead of the end of the chapter concerned; and for a very good reason. If the validity of the Dühringian conceptions of morals and justice is first established for all *worlds,* it is all the more easy to beneficently extend their validity to all *times.* But once again what

is involved is nothing less than final and ultimate truth. The moral
world "just as much as the world of knowledge in general," has "its
permanent principles and simple elements." The moral principles
stand "above history and above the present difference in national
characteristics. . . . The special truth out of which, in the course
of evolution, the more complete moral consciousness and, so to speak,
conscience are built up, in so far as their ultimate basis is understood, may claim a validity and range similar to the concepts
and applications of mathematics. *Pure truths are absolutely immutable* . . . so that it is altogether a stupidity to think that the validity
of knowledge is something that can be affected by time and changes
in reality." Hence the certitude of exact knowledge and the adequacy
of more common cognition leave no room, when we reflect, for
doubting the absolute validity of the principles of knowledge. "Even
persistent doubt is itself a diseased condition of weakness and only
the expression of *sterile confusion*, which sometimes seeks to maintain the appearance of something stable in the systematic consciousness of its *nothingness*. In the sphere of morals, the denial
of general principles clutches at the geographical and historical
variety of customs and principles, and if one concedes the inevitable
necessity of moral wickedness and evil, it believes that it has then all
the more got beyond the recognition of the real validity and actual
efficacy of concordant moral instincts. This *mordant scepticism*,
which is not only directed against particular false doctrines but
against mankind's capacity to develop conscious morality, resolves
itself ultimately into a real Nothing, in fact into something that is
worse than mere nihilism. . . . It flatters itself that it can easily
dominate within its *confused chaos* of dissolved moral ideas and
open the gates to unprincipled caprice. But it makes a gross error in
this: for mere reference even to the inevitable fate of the mind when
it is concerned with error and truth suffices to show by this analogy
alone that the natural law of fallibility does not necessarily exclude
the attainment of accuracy."

Up to now we have calmly put up with all these pompous phrases
of Herr Dühring's about final and ultimate truths, the sovereignty
of thought, absolute certainty of knowledge, and so forth, because
it is only at the point which we have now reached that the matter can

be brought to a head. Up to this point it has been enough to enquire how far the separate assertions of the philosophy of reality had "sovereign validity" and "unconditional claim to truth"; now we come to the question whether any, and if so which, products of human knowledge ever can have sovereign validity, and an unconditional claim to truth. When I say "of *human* knowledge" I do not use the phrase with the intention of insulting the inhabitants of other celestial bodies, whom I have not had the pleasure of knowing, but only for the reason that animals also have knowledge, though it is in no way sovereign. To a dog his master is divine, though this master may be the biggest scoundrel on earth.

Is human thought sovereign? Before we can answer yes or no we must first enquire: what is human thought? Is it the thought of the individual human being? No. But it exists only as the individual thought of many billions of past, present and future men. If then, I say that the total thought of all these human beings, including future ones, which is embraced in my idea, is *sovereign*, able to know the world as it exists, if only mankind lasts long enough and in so far as no limits are imposed on its knowledge by its perceptive organs or the objects to be known, then I am saying something which is pretty banal and, in addition, pretty barren. For the most valuable result from it would be that it should make us extremely distrustful of our present knowledge, inasmuch as in all probability we are but little beyond the beginning of human history, and the generations which will put *us* right are likely to be far more numerous than those whose knowledge we—often enough with a considerable degree of contempt—are in a position to correct.

Herr Dühring himself declares that consciousness, and therefore also thought and knowledge, of necessity can only become manifest in a number of individual beings. We can only ascribe sovereignty to the thought of each of these individuals in so far as we are not aware of any power which would be able to impose any idea forcibly on him, when he is of sound mind and wide awake. But as for the sovereign validity of the knowledge in each individual's mind, we all know that there can be no talk of such a thing, and that all previous experience shows that without exception such knowledge always contains much more that is capable of being improved upon than that which cannot be improved upon or is correct.

In other words, the sovereignty of thought is realised in a number of extremely unsovereignly-thinking human beings; the knowledge which has an unconditional claim to truth is realised in a number of relative errors; neither the one nor the other can be fully realised except through an endless eternity of human existence.

Here once again we find the same contradiction as we found above, between the character of human thought, necessarily conceived as absolute, and its reality in individual human beings with their extremely limited thought. This is a contradiction which can only be solved in the infinite progression, or what is for us, at least from a practical standpoint, the endless succession, of generations of mankind. In this sense human thought is just as much sovereign as not sovereign, and its capacity for knowledge just as much unlimited as limited. It is sovereign and unlimited in its disposition, its vocation, its possibilities and its historical goal; it is not sovereign and it is limited in its individual expression and in its realisation at each particular moment.

It is just the same with eternal truths. If mankind ever reached the stage at which it could only work with eternal truths, with conclusions of thought which possess sovereign validity and an unconditional claim to truth, it would then have reached the point where the infinity of the intellectual world, both in its actuality and in its potentiality had been exhausted, and this would mean that the famous miracle of the infinite series which has been counted would have been performed.

But in spite of all this, are there any truths which are so securely based that any doubt of them seems to us to amount to insanity? That twice two makes four, that the three angles of a triangle are equal to two right angles, that Paris is in France, that a man who gets no food dies of hunger, and so forth? Are there then nevertheless *eternal* truths, final and ultimate truths?

Certainly there are. We can divide the whole realm of knowledge in the traditional way into three great departments. The first includes all sciences which are concerned with inanimate Nature and are to a greater or less degree susceptible of mathematical treatment:

mathematics, astronomy, mechanics, physics, chemistry. If it gives anyone any pleasure to use mighty words for very simple things, it can be asserted that *certain* results obtained by these sciences are eternal truths, final and ultimate truths; for which reason these sciences are also known as the *exact* sciences. But very far from all their results have this validity. With the introduction of variable magnitudes and the extension of their variability to the infinitely small and infinitely large, mathematics, in other respects so strictly moral, fell from grace; it ate of the tree of knowledge, which opened up to it a career of most colossal achievements, but at the same time a path of error. The virgin state of absolute validity and irrefutable certainty of everything mathematical was gone forever; mathematics entered the realm of controversy, and we have reached the point where most people differentiate and integrate not because they understand what they are doing but from pure faith, because up to now it has always come out right. Things are even worse with astronomy and mechanics, and in physics and chemistry we are surrounded by hypotheses as by a swarm of bees. And it must of necessity be so. In physics we are dealing with the motion of molecules, in chemistry with the formation of molecules out of atoms, and if the interference of light waves is not a myth, we have absolutely no prospect of ever seeing these interesting objects with our own eyes. As time goes on, final and ultimate truths become remarkably rare in this field.

We are even worse off for them in geology, which by its nature is concerned chiefly with events which took place not only in our absence but in the absence of any human being whatever. The winning of final and absolute truths in this field is therefore a very troublesome business, and the crop is extremely meagre.

The second department of science is the one which covers the investigation of living organisms. In this field there is such a multitude of reciprocal relations and causalities that not only does the solution of each question give rise to a host of other questions, but each separate problem can usually only be solved piecemeal, through a series of investigations which often requires centuries to complete; and even then the need for a systematic presentation of the interrelations makes it necessary again and again to surround the final and ultimate truths with a luxuriant growth of hypotheses. What a long series of intermediaries from Galen to Malpighi was necessary for correctly establishing such a simple matter as the circulation of the blood in mammals, how slight is our knowledge of the origin of blood corpuscles, and how numerous are the missing links even today, for example, in our attempts to bring the symptoms of a disease into some rational relationship with its causes! And often enough discoveries, such as that of the cell, are made which compel us to revise completely all formerly established final and ultimate truths in the realm of biology, and to put whole piles of them on the scrap heap once and for all. Anyone who wants to establish really pure and immutable truths in this science will therefore have to be content with such platitudes as: all men are mortal, all female mammals have lacteal glands, and the like; he will not even be able to assert that the higher mammals digest with their stomach and intestines and not with their heads, for the nervous activity which is centralised in the head is indispensable to digestion.

But eternal truths are in an even worse plight in the third, the historical group of sciences. The subjects investigated by these in their historical sequence and in their present forms are the conditions of human life, social relationships, forms of law and the state, with their ideal superstructure of philosophy, religion, art, etc. In organic nature we are at least dealing with a succession of phenomena which, so far as our immediate observation is concerned, recur with fair regularity between very wide limits. Organic species have on the whole remained unchanged since the time of Aristotle. In social history, however, the repetition of conditions is the exception and not the rule, once we pass beyond the primitive stage of man, the so-called Stone Age; and when such repetitions occur, they never arise under exactly similar conditions—as for example the existence of an original common ownership of the land among all civilised peoples, and the way in which this came to an end. In the realm of human history our knowledge is therefore even more backward than in the realm of biology. Furthermore, when by way of exception the inner connection between the social and political forms of existence in an epoch come to be recognized, this as a rule only occurs when these forms are already out of date and are nearing extinction. Therefore, knowledge is here essentially relative, inasmuch as it is limited to the perception of relationships and consequences of certain social and state forms which exist only at a particular epoch and among particular people and are of their very nature transitory. Anyone therefore who sets out on this field to hunt down final and ultimate truths, truths which are pure and absolutely immutable, will bring home but little, apart from platitudes and commonplaces of the sorriest kind—for example, that generally speaking man cannot live except by labour; that up to the present mankind for the most part has been divided into rulers and ruled; that Napoleon died on May 5, 1821, and so on.

Now it is a remarkable thing that it is precisely in this sphere that we most frequently encounter truths which claim to be eternal, final and ultimate and all the rest of it. That twice two make four, that birds have beaks, and similar statements, are proclaimed as eternal truths only by those who aim at deducing, from the existence of eternal truths in general, the conclusion that there are also eternal truths in the sphere of human history—eternal morality, eternal justice, and so on—which claim a validity and scope equal to those of the truths and deductions of mathematics. And then we can confidently rely on this same friend of humanity taking the first opportunity to assure us that all previous fabricators of eternal truths have been to a greater or lesser degree asses and charlatans, that they have all fallen into error and made mistakes; but that *their* error and *their* fallibility has been in accordance with natural law, and prove the existence of truth and accuracy *in his case;* and that he, the prophet who has now arisen, has in his bag, all ready made, final and ultimate truth, eternal morality and eternal justice. This has all happened so many hundreds and thousands of times that we can only feel astonished that there should still be people credulous enough to believe this, not of others, but of themselves. Nevertheless we have here before us at least another such prophet, who also, quite in the accustomed way, flies into highly moral indignation when other people deny that any individual whatsoever is in a position to hand out to us the final and ultimate truth. Such a denial, or indeed mere doubt of it, is weakness, sterile confusion, nothingness, mordant critcism, worse than nihilism, incoherent chaos and other such pleasantries. As with all prophets, instead of critical and scientific examination and judgment we get moral condemnation out of hand.

We might have made mention above of the sciences which investigate the laws of human thought, *i.e.*, logic and dialectics. In these, however, we do not fare any better as regards eternal truths. Herr Dühring declares that dialectics proper is pure nonsense, and the many books which have been and in the future will be written on logic provide abundant proof that also in this science final and ultimate truths are much more sparsely sown than is commonly believed.

For that matter, there is absolutely no need to be alarmed at the fact that the stage of knowledge which we have now reached is as little final as all that have preceded it. It already embraces a vast mass of facts and requires very great specialisation of study on the part of anyone who wants to become an expert in any particular science. But a man who applies the measure of pure, immutable, final and ultimate truth to knowledge which, by the very nature of its object, must either remain relative for long successions of generations and be completed only step by step, or which, as in cosmogony, geology and the history of man, must always remain defective and incomplete because of the faultiness of the historical material— such a man only proves thereby his own ignorance and perversity, even if the real background to his pretensions is not, as it is in this case, his claim to personal infallibility. Truth and error, like all concepts which are expressed in polar opposites, have absolute validity only in an extremely limited field, as we have just seen, and as even Herr Dühring would realise if he had any acquaintance with the first elements of dialectics, which deal precisely with the inadequacy of all polar opposites. As soon as we apply the antithesis between truth and error outside of that narrow field which has been referred to above it becomes relative and therefore unserviceable for exact scientific modes of expression; and if we attempt to apply it as absolutely valid outside that field we then really find ourselves beaten: both poles of the antithesis become transformed into their opposites, truth becomes error and error truth. Let us take as an example the well-known Boyle's law, by which, if the temperature remains constant, the volume of gases varies inversely with the pressure to which they are subjected. Regnault found that this law did not hold good in certain cases. Had he been a philosopher of reality he would have had to say: Boyle's law is mutable, and is therefore not a pure truth, therefore it is not a truth at all, therefore it is an error. But had he done this he would have committed an error far greater than the one that was contained in Boyle's law; his grain of truth would have been lost sight of in a sandhill of error; he would have distorted his originally correct conclusion into an error compared with which Boyle's law, along with the little particle of error that clings to it, would have seemed like truth. But Regnault, being a man of science, did not indulge in such childishness, but continued his investigations and discovered that Boyle's law is in general only approximately correct, and in particular loses its validity in the case of gases which can be liquefied by pressure, as soon as the pressure approaches the point at which liquefaction begins. Boyle's law therefore was proved to be correct only within definite limits. But is it absolutely and finally true even within those limits? No physicist would assert that this was so. He would say that it holds good within certain limits of pressure and temperature and for certain gases; and even within these more restricted limits he would not exclude the possibility of a still narrower limitation or altered formulation as the result of future investigations.* This is how things stand with final and ultimate truths in physics for example. Really scientific works therefore as a rule avoid such dogmatic and moral expressions as error and truth, while these expres-

* Since I wrote the above it would seem already to have been confirmed. According to the latest researches carried out with more exact apparatus by Mendeleyev and Bogusky, all true gases show a variable relation between pressure and volume; the coefficient of expansion for hydrogen, at all the pressures so far applied, has been positive, that is, the diminution of volume was slower than the increase of pressure; in the case of atmospheric air and the other gases examined, there is for each a zero point of pressure, such that with pressure below this point their coefficients are positive, and with pressure above this point their coefficients are negative. So Boyle's law, which has always hitherto been usable for practical purposes, will need completion by a whole series of special laws. We also know now—1885—that there are no "true" gases at all. They have all been reduced to a liquid form. [Note by F. Engels.]

sions meet us everywhere in works such as the philosophy of reality, in which empty phrase-mongering attempts to impose on us as the sovereign result of sovereign thought.

But, a naïve reader may ask, where has Herr Dühring expressly stated that the content of his philosophy of reality is final and even ultimate truth? Where? Well, for example, in the dithyramb on his system (page 13), a part of which we cited in Chapter II. Or when he says, in the passage quoted above: Moral truths, in so far as their ultimate basis is understood, claim the same validity as mathematical truths. And does not Herr Dühring assert that, from his really critical standpoint and by means of those researches of his which go to the roots of things, he has forced his way through to these ultimate foundations, to the basic schemata, and has thus bestowed final and ultimate validity on moral truths? Or, if Herr Dühring does not advance this claim either for himself or for his age, if he only meant to say that some day in the dark and nebulous future it will be possible to establish final and ultimate truths, if therefore he meant to say much the same, only in a more confused way, as those he charges with "mordant scepticism" and "barren confusion"—then, in that case, what is all the noise about, and what is Herr Dühring driving at?

If we have not made much progress with truth and error, we can make even less with good and bad. This antithesis belongs exclusively to the domain of morals, that is, a domain belonging to the history of mankind, and it is precisely in this field that final and ultimate truths are most sparsely sown. The conceptions of good and bad have varied so much from nation to nation and from age to age that they have often been in direct contradiction to each other. But all the same, someone may object, good is not bad and bad is not good; if good is confused with bad there is an end to all morality, and everyone can do and leave undone whatever he cares. This is also, stripped of all oracular phrases, Herr Dühring's opinion. But the matter cannot be so simply disposed of. If it was such an easy business there would certainly be no dispute at all over good and bad; everyone would know what was good and what was bad. But how do things stand today? What morality is preached to us today? There is first Christian-feudal morality, inherited from past periods of faith; and this again has two main subdivisions, Catholic and Protestant moralities, each of which in turn has no lack of further subdivisions from the Jesuit-Catholic and Orthodox-Protestant to loose "advanced" moralities. Alongside of these we find the modern bourgeois morality and with it too the proletarian morality of the future, so that in the most advanced European countries alone the past, present and future provide three great groups of moral theories which are in force simultaneously and alongside of one another. Which is then the true one? Not one of them, in the sense of having absolute validity; but certainly that morality which contains the maximum of durable elements is the one which, in the present, represents the overthrow of the present, represents the future: that is, the proletarian.

But when we see that the three classes of modern society, the feudal aristocracy, the bourgeoisie and the proletariat, each have their special morality, we can only draw the conclusion, that men, consciously or unconsciously, derive their moral ideas in the last resort from the practical relations on which their class position is based—from the economic relations in which they carry on production and exchange.

But nevertheless there is much that is common to the three moral theories mentioned above—is this not at least a portion of a morality which is externally fixed? These moral theories represent three different stages of the same historical development, and have therefore a common historical background, and for that reason alone they necessarily have much in common. Even more. In similar or approximately similar stages of economic development moral theories must of necessity be more or less in agreement. From the moment when private property in movable objects developed, in all societies in which this private property existed there must be this moral law in common: Thou shalt not steal. Does this law thereby become an eternal moral law? By no means. In a society in which the motive for stealing has been done away with, in which therefore at the very most only lunatics would ever steal, how the teacher of morals would be laughed at who tried solemnly to proclaim the eternal truth: Thou shalt not steal!

We therefore reject every attempt to impose on us any moral

dogma whatsoever as an eternal, ultimate and forever immutable moral law on the pretext that the moral world too has its permanent principles which transcend history and the differences between nations. We maintain on the contrary that all former moral theories are the product, in the last analysis, of the economic stage which society had reached at that particular epoch. And as society has hitherto moved in class antagonisms, morality was always a class morality; it has either justified the domination and the interests of the ruling class, or, as soon as the oppressed class has become powerful enough, it has represented the revolt against this domination and the future interests of the oppressed. That in this process there has on the whole been progress in morality, as in all other branches of human knowledge, cannot be doubted. But we have not yet passed beyond class morality. A really human morality which transcends class antagonisms and their legacies in thought becomes possible only at a stage of society which has not only overcome class contradictions but has even forgotten them in practical life. And now it is possible to appreciate the presumption shown by Herr Dühring in advancing his claim, from the midst of the old class society and on the eve of a social revolution, to impose on the future classless society an eternal morality which is independent of time and changes in reality. Even assuming—what we do not know up to now—that he understands the structure of the society of the future at least in its main outlines.

Finally, one more revelation which is "absolutely original" but for that reason no less "going to the roots of things." With regard to the origin of evil, we have "the fact that the *type of the cat* with the guile associated with it is found in animal form, and the similar fact that a similar type of character is found also in human beings. ... There is therefore nothing mysterious about evil, unless someone wants to scent out something mysterious in the existence of that *cat* or of any animal of prey." Evil is—the cat. The devil therefore has no horns or cloven hoof, but claws and green eyes. And Goethe committed an unpardonable error in presenting Mephistopheles as a black dog instead of the said cat. Evil is the cat! That is morality, not only for all worlds, but also—of no use to anyone!

X. MORALITY AND LAW. EQUALITY

We have already had more than one occasion to make ourselves acquainted with Herr Dühring's method. It consists in analysing each group of objects of knowledge into what is claimed to be their simplest elements, applying to these elements similarly simple and what are claimed to be self-evident axioms, and then continuing to operate with the aid of the results so obtained. Even a problem in the sphere of social life "must be decided axiomatically, in accordance with particular simple basic forms, just as if we were dealing with the simple...basic forms of mathematics." And thus the application of the mathematical method to history, morals and law is to give also in these fields mathematical certainty of the truth of the results obtained, to give them the character of pure, immutable truths.

This is only another form of the old favourite ideological method, also known as the *a priori* method, which consists in arriving at the properties of an object deductively, from the concept of the object, instead of learning them from the object itself. First the concept of the object is formed from the object; then the spit is turned round, and the object is measured by its image, the concept of it. The object is then made to conform to the concept, not the concept to the object. With Herr Dühring the simplest elements, the most ultimate abstractions which he can reach, do service for the concept, which does not alter the case, for these simplest elements are at best of a purely conceptual nature. The philosophy of reality is revealed here again, therefore, as pure ideology, the deduction of reality not from itself but from its mental image.

And when such an ideologist proceeds to construct morality and law from the concept or the so-called simplest elements of "society" instead of from the real social relations of the people round him, what material is then available for this construction? The material is clearly of two kinds: first, the meagre residue of real content which may possibly survive in those abstractions from which he starts and, secondly, the content which our ideologist once more introduces into it from his own consciousness. And what does he find in his consciousness? For the most part, moral and juridical notions which are a more or less accurate expression (positive or negative, approving or attacking) of the social and political relations amid which he lives; perhaps also ideas drawn from the literature on the subject; and finally, it may be, some additional idiosyncrasies. Our ideologist may turn and twist as he likes, but the historical reality which he cast out at the door comes in again at the window, and while he thinks he is framing a doctrine of morals and law for all times and for all worlds, he is in fact only making an image of the conservative or revolutionary tendencies of his time—an image which is distorted because it has been torn from its real basis and, like a reflection in a concave mirror, is standing on its head.

Herr Dühring thus analyses society into its simplest elements, and accordingly discovers that the simplest society consists of at least *two* people. With these two people he then proceeds to operate axiomatically. And so the basic moral axiom spontaneously presents itself: "Two human wills are as such *entirely equal* to each other, and in the first place the one can demand positively nothing of the other." And with this "the basic form of moral justice is characterised," and also that of juridical equity, for "we need only the completely simple and elementary relation of *two persons* for the development of the fundamental concepts of law."

That two people or two human wills are as such *entirely* equal in relation to each other is not only not an axiom but is even a great exaggeration. In the first place, two people, even as such, may be unequal in sex, and this simple fact leads us on at once to the fact that the simplest elements of society—if we enter into this childishness for a moment—are not two people, but a man and a woman, who found a *family*, the simplest and first form of association for the purpose of production. But this cannot in any way suit Herr Dühring. For on the one hand the two founders of society must be made as equal as possible; and secondly even Herr Dühring could not succeed in deducing from the primitive family the moral and juridical equality of man and woman. Of two alternatives, one:

either the Dühringian social molecule, by the multiplication of which the whole of society is to be built up, is from the first doomed to disaster, because the two men can never by themselves bring a child into the world; or we must conceive them as two heads of families. And in this case the whole simple basic scheme is turned into its opposite: instead of the equality of men it proves at most the equality of heads of families, and as the wives are not considered, it further proves that they are subordinate.

We have now to make an unpleasant announcement to the reader: that from this point on for some considerable time he will not get rid of these famous two men. In the sphere of social relations they play a similar role to that hitherto played by the inhabitants of other celestial bodies, with whom it is to be hoped we have now finished. Whenever there is a question of economics, politics, etc., to be solved, the two men instantly march up and settle the matter in the twinkling of an eye, "axiomatically." An excellent creative and system-producing discovery on the part of our philosopher of reality. But unfortunately, if we want to pay regard to truth, the two men are not his discovery. They are the common property of the whole eighteenth century. They are already to be found in Rousseau's *Discours sur l'origine de l'inégalité parmi les hommes* [*Discourse on the Origin of Inequality among Men*] (1754)—where, by the way, they prove axiomatically the opposite of Herr Dühring's contentions. They play a leading part among the economists from Adam Smith to Ricardo; but with these they are at least unequal in that each of the two carries on a different trade—as a rule one is a hunter and the other a fisherman—and they mutually exchange their products. Through the whole eighteenth century, too, they serve in the main as purely illustrative examples, and Herr Dühring's originality consists only in that he elevates this method of illustration into a basic method for all social science and a measure of all historical forms. Certainly it would be impossible to simplify further the "strictly scientific conception of things and men."

In order to establish the fundamental axiom that two people and their wills are absolutely equal to each other and that neither lords it over the other, we cannot use any couple of people at random. They must be two persons who are so thoroughly detached from all reality, from all national, economic, political and religious relations which are found in the world, from all sex and personal differences, that nothing is left of either person beyond the mere idea: person— and then of course they are "entirely equal." They are therefore two complete phantoms conjured up by that very Herr Dühring who everywhere scents out and denounces "spiritistic" tendencies. These two phantoms, of course, are obliged to do everything which the man who conjured them into existence wants them to do, and for that very reason all their masterpieces have no interest whatever for the rest of the world.

But let us pursue Herr Dühring's axiomatics a little further. The two wills can demand nothing positive of each other. If nevertheless one of them does so, and carries through his demand by force, this gives rise to a condition of injustice; and by this fundamental scheme Herr Dühring explains injustice, oppression, servitude, in short, the whole reprehensible history of the past. Now Rousseau, in the treatise referred to above, made use of these same two men to prove, equally axiomatically, the very opposite: that is, given two men, A cannot enslave B by force, but only by putting B into a position in which the latter cannot do without A; a conception which, however, is much too materialistic for Herr Dühring. Let us put the same thing in a slightly different way. Two shipwrecked persons are alone on an island, and form a society. Their wills are, formally, entirely equal, and this is acknowledged by both. But from a material standpoint there is great inequality. A has determination and energy, B is irresolute, inert and slack. A is quick-witted, B stupid. How long will it be before A regularly imposes his will on B, first by persuasion, subsequently by virtue of habit, but always in a voluntary form? Servitude remains servitude, whether the voluntary form is retained or is trampled underfoot. Voluntary entry into servitude was known throughout the Middle Ages, in Germany until after the Thirty Years' War. When serfdom was abolished in Prussia after the defeats of 1806 and 1807, and with it the obligation of the lords to provide for their retainers in need, illness and old age, the peasants petitioned the king asking to be left in servitude—for otherwise who would look after them when in distress? The formula of the two men is therefore just as appropriate to inequality and serfdom as to equality and mutual help; and inasmuch as we are forced, on pain of extinction, to assume that they are heads of families, hereditary serviture is also included in the idea from the start.

But let us leave all this on one side for the moment. Let us assume that Herr Dühring's axiomatics have convinced us and that we are enthusiastic supporters of the entire equality of rights as between the two wills, of "general human sovereignty," of the "sovereignty of the individual"—veritable verbal colossi, compared with whom Stirner's "ego" with his property is a mere dwarf, although he also can claim a modest part in them. Well, then, we are now all *entirely equal* and independent. All? No, not quite all, however. There are also "dependent" relations which are permissible, but these are to be explained "on grounds which are to be found not in the activity of the two wills as such, but in a third sphere, as for example in the case of children, in the inadequacy of their self-determination."

Indeed! The ground of dependent relations is not to be found in the activity of the two wills as such! Naturally not, for the activity of one of the wills is thereby restricted! But in a third sphere! And what is this third sphere? The concrete determination of the subjected will as "inadequate"! Our philosopher of reality has so far departed from reality that, as against the abstract term "will," which is devoid of content, he regards the real content, the characteristic determination of this will, as a "third sphere." But be that as it may, we are obliged to note that the equality of rights has certain exceptions. It does not hold good for a will which is afflicted with inadequacy of self-determination. *Retreat Number One.*

To proceed. "Where the animal and the human are blended in one individual the question may be asked, on behalf of a second entirely human individual, whether his conduct should be the same as if he were dealing with persons who, so to speak, were only human ... our hypothesis of two morally unequal persons, one of whom in some sense or other has something of the real beast in his character, is therefore the typical basic form for all relations which, as a result of this difference, may come about within and between groups of people." And now let the reader see for himself the pitiful diatribe that follows these embarrassed subterfuges, in which Herr Dühring turns and twists like a Jesuit priest in order to deter· mine casuistically how far the human man can go against the bestial man, how far he is entitled to show distrust and employ stratagems and harsh, even terrorist measures of deception against him, without himself deviating in any way from the requirements of immutable morality.

So, when two persons are "morally unequal," again there is no longer equality. But then it was surely not worth while to conjure up two entirely equal people, for there are no two persons who are morally entirely equal. But the inequality is supposed to consist in one being a human person and the other having in him a touch of the beast. It is, however, inherent in the descent of man from the animal world that he can never entirely rid himself of animal characteristics, so that it is always only a question of more or less, of a difference in the degree of bestiality or of humanity. A division of mankind into two sharply differentiated groups, into human men and beast men, into good and bad, sheep and goats, is only found—apart from the philosophy of reality—in Christianity, which quite logically also has its supreme judge to make the differentiation. But who is to be the supreme judge in the philosophy of reality? Presumably the procedure here will have to be the same as in Christian practice, in which the pious lambs themselves assume the office of supreme judge in relation to their mundane goat-neighbours, and discharge this duty with notorious success. The sect of philosophers of reality, if it ever comes into being, will assuredly not be less competent in this respect than the pious of the land. This, however, is of no concern to us now; what interests us is the admission that, as a result of the moral inequality between men, once more equality has vanished. *Retreat Number Two.*

But, again, let us proceed.

"If one of the two men acts on the basis of truth and science, and the other on the basis of some superstition or prejudice, then... as a rule mutual interference must occur.... At a certain degree of incompetence, brutality or perversity of character, conflict is always inevitable.... It is not only children and madmen in relation to whom the ultimate resource is *force*. The characteristics of whole natural groups and cultural classes in mankind may make the *sub-jection* of their will, which is hostile because of its perversity, an inevitable necessity, in order to draw it back again under the influence of the common ties which unite society. Even in such cases the hostile will is respected as *having equal rights;* but the perversity of its destructive and hostile activity has provoked an *adjustment,* and if it is subjected to force, it is only reaping the reaction of its own unrighteousness."

So not only moral but also mental inequality is enough to destroy the "entire equality" of the two wills and to call into being a system of morality by which all the crimes of civilised robber states against backward peoples, down to the Russian infamies in Turkestan, can be justified. When in the summer of 1873, General Kaufmann ordered the Tartar tribe of the Yomuds to be attacked, their tents to be burnt and their wives and children butchered—"in the good Caucasian way," as the order was worded—he too declared that the subjection of the hostile, because perverted, will of the Yomuds, with the object of guiding it back to the common ties which unite society, had become an inevitable necessity; that the means employed by him were the best suited to the purpose; and that whoever willed the end must also will the means. Only he was not so cruel as also to insult the Yomuds and to say that it was just through massacring them for the purpose of adjustment that he was respecting their will as having equal right. And once again in this conflict it is the elect, those who claim to be acting on the basis of truth and science and therefore in the last resort the philosophers of reality, who have to decide what are superstition, prejudice, brutality and perversity of character and when force and subjection are necessary for adjustment. Equality, therefore, is now—adjustment by force; and the second will is recognised by the first to have equal rights through subjection. *Retreat Number Three,* here already degenerating into ignominious flight.

Incidentally, the phrase that the hostile will is recognised as having equal rights precisely through bringing about an adjustment by means of force is only the inversion of the Hegelian theory, according to which punishment is the right of the criminal: "in that punishment is regarded as containing his own right, the criminal is honoured as a reasonable being" (Philosophy of Law, § 100, Note).

With that we might break off. It would be superfluous to follow Herr Dühring further in his piecemeal destruction of the equality which he set up so axiomatically, of his general human sovereignty and so on; to observe how indeed he manages to set up society with his two men, but in order to create the state he requires a third because—to put the matter briefly—without this third person no majority decisions can be arrived at, and without these, and so also without the rule of the majority over the minority, no state can exist; and then how he gradually steers into calmer waters where he constructs his socialitarian state of the future, where one fine morning we shall have the honour to look him up. We have sufficiently observed that the entire equality of the two wills only exists so long as these two wills *will nothing*; that as soon as they cease to be human wills as such, and are transformed into real, individual wills, into the wills of two real men, equality comes to an end; that childishness, madness, so-called bestiality, what is supposed to be superstition, alleged prejudice and assumed incapacity on the one hand, and fancied humanity and knowledge of truth and science on the other hand—that therefore every difference in the quality of the two wills and in that of the intelligence associated with them—justifies an inequality of treatment which may go as far as subjection. What more can we ask, when Herr Dühring has so deep-rootedly, from the foundation up, laid his own edifice of equality in ruins?

But even though we have finished with Herr Dühring's puerile and superficial treatment of the idea of equality, this does not mean that we have yet finished with the idea itself, which especially thanks to Rousseau played a theoretical, and during and since the Great Revolution a practical political role, and even today still plays an important agitational role in the socialist movement of almost every country. The establishment of its scientific content will also determine its value for proletarian agitation.

The idea that all men, as men, have something in common, and that they are therefore equal so far as these common characteristics go, is of course primeval. But the modern demand for equality is something entirely different from that; this consists rather in deducing from those common characteristics of humanity, from that equality of men as men, a claim to equal political or social status for all human beings, or at least for all citizens of a state or all members of a society. Before the original conception of relative equality could lead to the conclusion that men should have equal rights in the state and in society, before this conclusion could appear to be something even natural and self-evident, however, thousands of years had to pass and did pass. In the oldest primitive communities equality of rights existed at most for members of the community; women, slaves and strangers were excluded from this equality as a matter of course. Among the Greeks and Romans the inequalities of men were of greater importance than any form of equality. It would necessarily have seemed idiotic to the ancients that Greeks and barbarians, freemen and slaves, citizens and dependents, Roman citizens and Roman subjects (to use a comprehensive term) should have a claim to equal political status. Under the Roman Empire all these distinctions gradually disappeared, except the distinction between freemen and slaves, and in this way there arose, for the freemen at least, that equality as between private individuals on the basis of which Roman law developed—the complete elaboration of law based on private property which we know. But so long as the distinction between freemen and slaves existed, there could be no talk of drawing legal conclusions from the fact of general equality *as men;* and we saw this again quite recently, in the slave-owning states of the North American Union.

Christianity knew only *one* point in which all men were equal: that all were equally born in original sin—which corresponded perfectly with its character as the religion of the slaves and the oppressed. Apart from this is recognised, at most, the equality of the elect, which however was only stressed at the very beginning. The traces of common ownership which are also found in the early stages of the new religion can be ascribed to the solidarity of a proscribed sect rather than to real equalitarian ideas. Within a very short time the establishment of the distinction between priests and laymen put an end even to this tendency to Christian equality. The overrunning of Western Europe by the Germans abolished for centuries all ideas of equality, through the gradual building up of a complicated social and political hierarchy such as had never before existed. But at the same time the invasion drew Western and Central Europe into the course of historical development, created for the first time a compact cultural area, and within this area also for the first time a system of predominantly national states exerting mutual influence on each other and mutually holding each other in check. Thereby it prepared the ground on which alone the question of the equal status of men, of the rights of man, could at a later period be raised.

The feudal middle ages also developed in its womb the class which was destined in the future course of its evolution to be the standard-bearer of the modern demand for equality: the bourgeoisie. Itself in its origin one of the "estates" of the feudal order, the bourgeoisie developed the predominantly handicraft industry and the exchange of products within feudal society to a relatively high level, when at the end of the fifteenth century the great maritime discoveries opened to it a new and more comprehensive career. Trade beyond the confines of Europe, which had previously been carried on only between Italy and the Levant, was now extended to America and India, and soon surpassed in importance both the mutual exchange between the various European countries and the internal trade within each separate country. American gold and silver flooded Europe and forced its way like a disintegrating element into every fissure, hole and pore of feudal society. Handicraft industry could no longer satisfy the rising demand; in the leading industries of the most advanced countries it was replaced by manufacture.

But this mighty revolution in the economic conditions of life in society was not followed immediately by any corresponding change in its political structure. The state order remained feudal, while society became more and more bourgeois. Trade on a large scale, that is to say, international and, even more, world trade, requires free owners of commodities who are unrestricted in their movements and have equal rights as traders to exchange their commodities on the basis of laws that are equal for them all, at least in each separate place. The transition from handicraft to manufacture presupposes the existence of a number of free workers—free on the one hand from the fetters of the guild and on the other from the means whereby they could themselves utilise their labour power:

workers who can contract with their employers for the hire of their labour power, and as parties to the contract have rights equal with his. And finally the equality and equal status of all human labour, because and in so far as it is *human* labour, found its unconscious but clearest expression in the law of value of modern bourgeois economics, according to which the value of a commodity is measured by the socially necessary labour embodied in it.* But where economic relations required freedom and equality of rights, the political system opposed them at every step with guild restrictions and special privileges. Local privileges, differential duties, exceptional laws of all kinds affected in trading not only foreigners or people living in the colonies, but often enough also whole categories of the nationals of each country; the privileges of the guilds everywhere and ever anew formed barriers to the path of development of manufacture. Nowhere was the path open and the chances equal for the bourgeois competitors—and yet this was the first and ever more pressing need.

The demand for liberation from feudal fetters and the establishment of equality of rights by the abolition of feudal inequalities was bound soon to assume wider dimensions from the moment when the economic advance of society first placed it on the order of the day. If it was raised in the interests of industry and trade, it was also necessary to demand the same equality of rights for the great mass of the peasantry who, in every degree of bondage from total serfdom upwards, were compelled to give the greater part of their labour time to their feudal lord without payment and in addition to render innumerable other dues to him and to the state. On the other hand, it was impossible to avoid the demand for the abolition also of feudal privileges, the freedom from taxation of the nobility, the political privileges of the various feudal estates. And as people were no longer living in a world empire such as the Roman Empire had been, but in a system of independent states dealing with each other on an equal footing and at approximately the same degree of bourgeois development, it was a matter of course that the demand for equality should assume a general character reaching out beyond the indi-

* This tracing of the origin of the modern ideas of equality to the economic conditions of bourgeois society was first developed by Marx in *Capital*. [*Note by F. Engels.*]

vidual state, that freedom and equality should be proclaimed as *human rights*. And it is significant of the specifically bourgeois character of these human rights that the American Constitution, the first to recognize the rights of man, in the same breath confirmed the slavery of the coloured races in America: class privileges were proscribed, race privileges sanctified.

As is well known, however, from the moment when, like a butterfly from the chrysalis, the bourgeoisie arose out of the burghers of the feudal period, when this "estate" of the Middle Ages developed into a class of modern society, it was always and inevitably accompanied by its shadow, the proletariat. And in the same way the bourgeois demand for equality was accompanied by the proletarian demand for equality. From the moment when the bourgeois demand for the abolition of class *privileges* was put forward, alongside of it appeared the proletarian demand for the abolition of the *classes themselves*—at first in religious form, basing itself on primitive Christianity, and later drawing support from the bourgeois equalitarian theories themselves. The proletarians took the bourgeoisie at their word: equality must not be merely apparent, must not apply merely to the sphere of the state, but must also be real, must be extended to the social and economic sphere. And especially since the time when the French bourgeoisie, from the Great Revolution on, brought bourgeois equality to the forefront, the French proletariat has answered it blow for blow with the demand for social and economic equality, and equality has become the battle-cry particularly of the French proletariat.

The demand for equality in the mouth of the proletariat has therefore a double meaning. It is either—as was especially the case at the very start, for example in the peasants' war—the spontaneous reaction against the crying social inequalities, against the contrast of rich and poor, the feudal lords and their serfs, surfeit and starvation; as such it is the simple expression of the revolutionary instinct, and finds its justification in that, and indeed only in that. Or, on the other hand, the proletarian demand for equality has arisen as the reaction against the bourgeois demand for equality, drawing more or less correct and more far-reaching demands from this bourgeois demand, and serving as an agitational means in order to rouse the workers against the capitalists on the basis of the capitalists' own assertions; and in this case it stands and falls with bourgeois equality itself. In both cases the real content of the proletarian demand for equality is the demand for the *abolition of classes*. Any demand for equality which goes beyond that, of necessity passes into absurdity. We have given examples of this, and shall find enough additional ones later when we come to Herr Dühring's phantasies of the future.

The idea of equality, therefore, both in its bourgeois and in its proletarian form, is itself a historical product, the creation of which required definite historical conditions which in turn themselves presuppose a long previous historical development. It is therefore anything but an eternal truth. And if today it is taken for granted by the general public—in one sense or another—if, as Marx says, it "already possesses the fixity of a popular prejudice," this is not the consequence of its axiomatic truth, but the result of the general diffusion and the continued appropriateness of the ideas of the eighteenth century. If therefore Herr Dühring is able without more ado to make his famous two men conduct their economic relations on the basis of equality, this is because it seems quite natural to popular prejudice. And in fact Herr Dühring calls his philosophy *natural* because it is derived from things which seem to him quite natural. But why they seem to him quite natural—is a question which he does not ask.

XI. MORALITY AND LAW. FREEDOM AND NECESSITY

"In the sphere of politics and law the principles expounded in this course are based on the *most exhaustive specialised studies*. It is therefore... necessary to realise from the start that what we have here... is the logical exposition of the *conclusions* reached in the sphere of legal and political science. My original special subject was in fact jurisprudence, and I not only devoted to it the customary three years of theoretical university preparation, but also, during a further three years of legal practice, continued to study it particularly with a view to the *deepening* of its scientific content.... And *certainly* the critique of private law and of the legal shortcomings in this field could not have been put forward with *such confidence* but for the consciousness of *knowing* all the weaknesses of the subject as well as its stronger sides."

A man who is justified in saying this of himself must from the outset inspire confidence, especially in contrast to the "early, admittedly scamped legal studies of Herr Marx." And for that reason it must surprise us to find that the critique of private law which steps on to the stage with such confidence is restricted to telling us that "the scientific character of jurisprudence... has not developed far," that positive civil justice is injustice in that it sanctions property based on force, and that the "natural basis" of criminal law is *revenge*—an assertion which in any case is only new in its mystical wrapping of "natural basis." The results in political science are limited to the transactions of the famous three men, one of whom has hitherto held down the others by force; in dealing with which Herr Dühring in all seriousness conducts an investigation into whether it was the second or the third who first introduced violence and subjection.

However, let us go a little more deeply into our confident jurist's most exhaustive specialised study and scientific content deepened by three years of legal practice.

119

Herr Dühring tells us of Lassalle that he was prosecuted for "*inciting* to an attempt to steal a cash-box" but that "no decision to convict could be reached by the court, as the so-called *provisional acquittal*, which was *then still possible*, supervened...this *half* acquittal."

The Lassalle case referred to here came up in the summer of 1848, before the assizes at Cologne, where, as in almost the whole of the Rhine province, French criminal law was in force. The Prussian *Landrecht* had been introduced by way of exception only for political offences and crimes, but already in April 1848 this exceptional application had been abrogated by Camphausen. French law has no knowledge whatever of the Prussian *Landrecht's* loose category of "inciting" to a crime, let alone inciting to an attempt at a crime. It knows only *instigation* to crime, and this is only punishable if it takes the form of "gifts, promises, threats, abuse of authority or of power, deceitful machinations or criminal artifices" (*Code pénal*, art. 60). The State Ministry, steeped in the Prussian *Landrecht*, overlooked, just as Herr Dühring does, the essential difference between the sharp and definite French code and the vague indefiniteness of the Prussian *Landrecht*, and prosecuted Lassalle for political reasons, egregiously failing in the case. Only a person who is completely ignorant of modern French law can venture to assert that French criminal procedure permits the Prussian *Landrecht* form of provisional acquittal, this *half* acquittal; criminal procedure under French law admits no intermediate form, but only conviction or acquittal.

And so we are forced to say that Herr Dühring would certainly not have been able to apply this "historical treatment in the grand style" in relation to Lassalle if he had ever had the *Code Napoléon* in his hands. We must therefore conclude that modern French law, the *only* modern bourgeois law code, which rests on the social achievements of the Great French Revolution and translates them into legal form, is *completely unknown* to Herr Dühring.

In another place, in the criticism of trial by jury with majority decision which was adopted throughout the Continent from the French model, we are taught: "Yes, it will *even* be necessary to familiarise oneself with the idea, which for that matter is not without precedent in history, that a conviction *where opinions are divided* would be one of the impossible forms of institution in a perfect community.... This *important and profoundly intelligent* conception, however, as already indicated above, must of necessity seem unsuitable for the traditional political forms, because it is *too good* for them."

Once again, Herr Dühring is ignorant of the fact that the unanimity of the jury is absolutely essential, not only for criminal convictions but also for decisions in civil suits, under English common law, *i.e.*, the unwritten law of custom which has been in force since time immemorial, certainly at least since the fourteenth century. The important and profoundly intelligent conception, which according to Herr Dühring is *too good* for the present-day world, has therefore had legal validity in England as far back as the darkest Middle Ages, and from England it was transported to Ireland, the United States of America and all the English colonies. And yet the most exhaustive specialised study failed to reveal to Herr Dühring even the faintest whisper of all this! The area in which a unanimous verdict by the jury is required is therefore not only infinitely greater than the tiny area where the Prussian *Landrecht* is in force, but is also much more extensive than all the areas taken together on which jury decisions are reached by a majority. Not only is French law, the only modern legal code, totally unknown to Herr Dühring; he is also equally ignorant of the only Germanic law which has developed independently of the influence of Roman law up to the present day and spread to all parts of the world—English law. And why does Herr Dühring know nothing of it? Because English manner of juridical thought, "would, however, not be able to stand up against German juridical studies in the pure concepts of the classical Roman jurists," says Herr Dühring; and further he says "what is the English-speaking world with its childish hodge-podge of language as compared with our natural language forms?" To which we might answer with Spinoza: *"Ignorantia non est argumentum.* Ignorance is no argument."

We can accordingly come to no other final conclusion than that Herr Dühring's most exhaustive specialised study consisted in his absorption for three years in the theoretical study of the *Corpus juris,* and for a further three years in the practical study of the noble

Prussian *Landrecht*. That is certainly quite meritorious, and should qualify him to be a really respectable district judge or advocate in Old Prussia. But when a person undertakes to compose a legal philosophy for all worlds and all ages, he should at least have some degree of acquaintance with legal systems like those of the French, English and Americans, nations which have played quite a different role in history from that played by the little corner of Germany in which the Prussian *Landrecht* flourishes. But let us follow him a little further.

"The variegated medley of local, provincial and national laws, which clash with one another in the most various directions, in very arbitrary fashion, sometimes as common law, sometimes as written law, often cloaking the most important issues in a purely statutory form—this pattern-book of confusion and contradiction, in which particular cases override general principles, and then at times general principles override particular rules—is really not calculated to enable anyone to form a clear conception of jurisprudence."—But where does this confusion exist? Once again, within the area where the Prussian *Landrecht* holds sway, where alongside, over or under this *Landrecht* there are also provincial laws and local statutes, here and there also common law and other trash, ranging through the most diverse degrees of relative authority and making all practising jurists give that scream for help which Herr Dühring here so sympathetically echoes. He need not even go outside his beloved Prussia —he need only come as far as the Rhine to convince himself that all this has been forgotten for seventy years—not to speak of other civilised countries, where these antiquated conditions have long since been abolished.

Further: "In a less crude form the glossing over of the natural responsibility of individuals occurs by means of secret and therefore anonymous collective decisions and actions on the part of *collegia* or other official institutions which mask the personal share of each separate member." And in another place: "As things are at the present time, it will be regarded as an *astonishing* and extremely far-reaching claim if one opposes the glossing over and covering up of individual responsibility through the medium of collective bodies." Perhaps Herr Dühring will regard it as an astonishing piece of

information when we tell him that in the sphere of English law
each member of the judicial collegium has to give his decision
separately in public session, stating the grounds on which it is based;
that administrative collective bodies which are not elected, and do
not transact business and vote publicly, are essentially a *Prussian*
institution and are unknown in most other countries, and that therefore his claim can only be regarded as astonishing and extremely
far-reaching—in *Prussia*.

In the same way his complaints about the compulsory introduction of religious practices in birth, marriage, death and burial, apply
to Prussia alone of all the greater civilised nations, and since the
introduction of civil registration they no longer apply even to Prussia. What Herr Dühring only accomplishes by means of a future
"socialitarian" state of things, even Bismarck has meanwhile managed by a simple law. It is just the same with his complaint in
connection with "the inadequate preparation of jurists for their
profession," a complaint which could also be extended to cover the
"administrative officials"—it is a specifically Prussian jeremiad;
and even his hatred of Jews, exaggerated to the verge of absurdity,
which he exhibits on every possible occasion, is a feature which if
not specifically Prussian is yet specific to the region east of the Elbe.
That same philosopher of reality who has a sovereign contempt for
all prejudices and superstitions is himself so deeply imbued with
personal crotchets that he calls the popular prejudice against the
Jews, inherited from the bigotry of the Middle Ages, a "natural
judgment" based on "natural grounds," and he rises to the pyramidal
heights of the assertion that "socialism is the only power which can
oppose population conditions with a strong Jewish admixture."
(Conditions with a Jewish admixture! What "natural" German
language!)

Enough of this. The grandiloquent boasts of judicial erudition
have as their basis—at best—only the most commonplace specialised
knowledge of quite an ordinary jurist of Old Prussia. The sphere
of legal and political science whose results Herr Dühring logically
expounds "is identical" with the area where the Prussian *Landrecht*
holds sway. Apart from the Roman law with which every jurist is
fairly familiar, now even in England, his juridical knowledge is

limited simply and solely to the Prussian *Landrecht*—that legal
code of an enlightened patriarchal despotism which is written in a
German such as Herr Dühring appears to have been trained in, and
which, with its moral glosses, its juristic vagueness and inconsequen-
tiality, its flogging as a means of torture and punishment, still belongs entirely to the pre-revolutionary epoch. Whatever exists beyond
this Prussian law Herr Dühring regards as evil—both modern
bourgeois French law, and English law with its quite exceptional
developments and its safeguarding of personal liberty to an extent
unknown anywhere on the Continent. The philosophy which "cannot
allow the validity of any merely *apparent* horizon, but in its mighty
revolutionising sweep involves all earths and heavens of external
and inward nature"—has as its *real* horizon: the boundaries of the
six eastern provinces of old Prussia, and in addition in any case only
the few other patches of land where the noble *Landrecht* still holds
sway; and beyond this horizon it involves neither earths nor heavens,
whether of external or of internal nature, but only the crassest ignorance of what is happening in the rest of the world.

It is difficult to deal with morality and law without coming up
against the question of so-called free will, of human responsibility,
of the relation between freedom and necessity. And the philosophy
of reality also has not only one but even two solutions of this
problem.

"All false theories of freedom must be replaced by what we know
from experience is the nature of the relation between rational judgment on the one hand and instinctive impulse on the other, a relation
which *so to speak* unites them into a single mean force. The fundamental facts of this form of dynamics must be drawn from observation, and for the calculation in advance of events which have not
yet occurred must also be estimated *as closely as possible*, in general
both as to their nature and magnitude. In this way the foolish delu-
sions of inner freedom, which have been a source of worry and
anxiety for thousands of years, are not only thoroughly cleared away,
but are also replaced by something positive, which can be made
use of for the practical regulation of life."—On this basis freedom
consists in rational judgment pulling a man to the right while irrational impulses pull him to the left, and in this parallelogram of

forces the actual movement follows the direction of the diagonal. Freedom is therefore the mean between judgment and impulse, reason and unreason, and its degree in each individual case can be determined on the basis of experience by a "personal equation," to use an astronomical expression. But a few pages later on we find: "We base moral responsibility on freedom, which however in our view means nothing more than susceptibility to conscious motives in accordance with our natural and acquired intelligence. All such motives operate with the inevitable force of natural law, notwithstanding our awareness of the possible contradiction in the actions; but it is precisely on this inevitable compulsion that we rely when we bring in the moral lever."

This second definition of freedom, which quite unceremoniously gives a knock-out blow to the other, is again nothing but an extremely superficial rendering of the Hegelian conception of the matter. Hegel was the first to state correctly the relation between freedom and necessity. To him, freedom is the appreciation of necessity. "Necessity is *blind* only *in so far as it is not understood*." Freedom does not consist in the dream of independence of natural laws, but in the knowledge of these laws, and in the possibility this gives of systematically making them work towards definite ends. This holds good in relation both to the laws of external nature and to those which govern the bodily and mental existence of men themselves— two classes of laws which we can separate from each other at most only in thought but not in reality. Freedom of the will therefore means nothing but the capacity to make decisions with real knowledge of the subject. Therefore the *freer* a man's judgment is in relation to a definite question, with so much the greater *necessity* is the content of this judgment determined; while the uncertainty, founded on ignorance, which seems to make an arbitrary choice among many different and conflicting possible decisions, shows by this precisely that it is not free, that it is controlled by the very object it should itself control. Freedom therefore consists in the control over ourselves and over external nature which is founded on knowledge of natural necessity; it is therefore necessarily a product of historical development. The first men who separated themselves from the animal kingdom were in all essentials as unfree as the animals themselves, but each step forward in civilisation was a step towards freedom. On the threshold of human history stands the discovery that mechanical motion can be transformed into heat: the production of fire by friction; at the close of the development so far gone through stands the discovery that heat can be transformed into mechanical motion: the steam engine. And, in spite of the gigantic and liberating revolution in the social world which the steam engine is carrying through—and which is not yet half completed—it is beyond question that the generation of fire by friction was of even greater effectiveness for the liberation of mankind. For the generation of fire by friction gave man for the first time control over one of the forces of Nature, and thereby separated him for ever from the animal kingdom. The steam engine will never bring about such a mighty leap forward in human development, however important it may seem in our eyes as representing all those powerful productive forces dependent on it—forces which alone make possible a state of society in which there are no longer class distinctions or anxiety over the means of subsistence for the individual, and in which for the first time there can be talk of real human freedom and of an existence in harmony with the established laws of Nature. But how young the whole of human history still is, and how ridiculous it would be to attempt to ascribe any absolute validity to our present views, is evident from the simple fact that all past history can be characterised as the history of the epoch from the practical discovery of the transformation of mechanical motion into heat up to that of the transformation of heat into mechanical motion.

It is true that Herr Dühring's treatment of history is different from this. In general, as the record of error, ignorance and barbarity, violence and subjugation, it is a repulsive object to the philosophy of reality; but considered in detail it is divided into two great periods, namely (1) from the identical state of matter up to the French revolution; (2) from the French revolution up to Herr Dühring; at the same time, the nineteenth century remains "still in essence reactionary, indeed from the intellectual standpoint even more so than the eighteenth." Nevertheless, it bears socialism in its womb, and therewith "the germ of a mightier regeneration than was concocted (!) by the forerunners and the heroes of the French revolution." The philosophy of reality's contempt for all past history is justified as follows: "The few thousand years, the historical memory of which has been transmitted in original documents, with the development of human nature so far, are *of little significance* when one thinks of the succession of thousands of years which are still to come. ... The human race as a whole is still very young, and when scientific memory will look back on tens of thousands instead of thousands of years, the intellectual immaturity and childishness of our institutions will not be contested and will be a self-evident axiom in relation to our epoch, which will then be considered as primeval antiquity."

Without dwelling on the really "natural language form" of the last sentence, we must note two points. First, that this "primeval antiquity" will in any case still remain a historical epoch of the greatest interest for all future generations, because it is the basis for all subsequent higher development, having for its starting point the emergence of man from the animal kingdom, and for its content the overcoming of obstacles such as will never again face the associated human race of the future. And secondly, that the close of this "primeval antiquity" (in contrast with which future periods of history, which will no longer be held back by these difficulties and obstacles, hold the promise of quite other scientific, technical and social achievements) is in any case a very strange moment to choose to lay down prescriptions for these thousands of years that are to come, in the form of final and ultimate truths, immutable truths and deep-rooted conceptions which have been discovered on the basis of the intellectually immature childishness of our so extremely "backward" and "retrogressive" century. Only the Richard Wagner of philosophy—but without Wagner's talents—could fail to see that all the depreciatory terms slung at historical development up to the present day remain sticking also on what is claimed to be its final outcome—the so-called philosophy of reality.

One of the most significant morsels of the new deep-rooted science is the section on the "individualisation" and the "increasing value" of life. In this section oracular commonplaces bubble up and gush forth in an irresistible torrent for three full chapters. Unfortunately we must limit ourselves to a few short samples.

"The deeper nature of all sensation and therefore of all forms of subjective life rests on the *difference* of one state from another.... But it can also be shown quite easily (!) that, for a *full* (!) life, it is not the continuation of a particular state but the transition from one state of life to another through which the appreciation of life is heightened and the decisive stimuli are developed.... The state which approximates to the identical which is *so to speak* in permanent inertia and *so to say* continues in the same position of equilibrium, whatever its nature may be, has but little significance for the appreciation of life.... Habituation and *so to speak* familiarisation with one's life makes it something of absolute indifference and unconcern to us, something which is not very distinct from death. The torment of boredom at most also enters into it as a kind of negative life-impulse.... A life of stagnation extinguishes all passion and all interest in existence, both for individuals and for peoples. *But it is our law of difference through which all these phenomena become explicable.*"

The rapidity with which Herr Dühring establishes his "fundamentally original conclusions"—passes all belief. The commonplace that the continued stimulation of the same nerves or the continuation of the same stimulus fatigues each nerve or each nervous system, and that therefore in a normal condition nerve stimuli must be interrupted and varied—which for many years has been in every textbook of physiology, and is known to every philistine from his own experience—is first translated into the language of the philosophy of reality. And this platitude, which is as old as the hills, has hardly been translated into the mysterious formula that the deeper nature of all sensation rests on the difference of one state from another, when it is immediately further transformed into "*Our* law of difference." And this law of difference makes "absolutely explicable" a whole series of phenomena which in turn are nothing more than illustrations and examples of the pleasantness of variety which requires no explanation even for the most common philistine understanding and gains not the breadth of an atom in clarity by reference to this alleged law of difference.

But the deep-rootedness of "*our* law of difference" is far from being exhausted by what has been given above: "The sequence of ages in life, and the emergence of different conditions of life bound up with them, furnish a very obvious example which demonstrates *our* principle of difference. Child, boy, youth and man experience the intensity of their feeling of life at each stage not so much when the state in which they find themselves has already become set, as in the periods of transition from one to the other." Even this is not enough. "*Our* law of difference can be given an even more extended application if we take into consideration the fact that the repetition of what we have already tried or done has no attraction for us." And now the reader can imagine for himself the oracular twaddle for which sentences of the depth and deep-rootedness of those cited form the starting point. Herr Dühring may well shout triumphantly at the end of his book: "The law of difference is both in theory and in practice decisive for the appraisement and heightening of the value of life!" This is certainly true of Herr Dühring's appraisement of the intellectual value of his public: he must believe that it is composed exclusively of sheer asses or philistines.

We are further given the following extremely practical rules of life: "The method whereby total interest in life can be kept active" (a fitting task for philistines and those who want to become philistines!) "consists in allowing the particular and *so to speak* elementary interests, of which the total interest is composed, to develop and succeed each other in accordance with natural periods. For the same state we may resort to the replacement of the lower and more easily satisfied stimuli by the higher and more permanently effective excitations in order to avoid the occurrence of any gaps which are entirely devoid of interest. But it will also be necessary to ensure that the natural excitations or those arising in the normal course of social existence are not arbitrarily multiplied or forced or—the contrary form of perversion—satisfied by the lightest stimulus, and thus prevented from developing a want which is capable of gratification. In this as in other cases the maintenance of the natural rhythm is the pre-condition of all harmonious and agreeable movement. Nor should anyone set before himself the impossible task of trying to prolong the stimuli of any situation beyond the period allotted them by nature or by the circumstances of the case"—and so on. The worthy fellow who takes as his rule of life these solemn oracles of philistine pedantry subtilising over the shallowest platitudes will certainly not have to complain of "gaps which are entirely devoid of interest." It will take him all his time to prepare his pleasures and get them in the right order, so that he will not have a moment left to enjoy them.

We should try out life, full life. There are only two things which Herr Dühring prohibits: firstly "the uncleanliness of using tobacco," and secondly drink and food which "have properties which rouse disgust or are in general repugnant to the finer feelings." In his *Course of Political Economy*, however, Herr Dühring writes such a dithyramb on distilling that it is impossible that he should include spirits in this category; we are therefore forced to conclude that his prohibition covers only wine and beer. He has only also to prohibit meat, and then he will have raised the philosophy of reality to the same height as that on which the late Gustav Struve moved with such great success—the height of pure childishness.

For the rest, Herr Dühring might be slightly more liberal in regard to spirituous liquors. A man who, by his own admission, still cannot find the bridge from the static to the dynamic has surely every reason to be indulgent in judging some poor devil who has for once dipped too deep in his glass and as a result also cannot find the bridge from the dynamic to the static.

XII. DIALECTICS. QUANTITY AND QUALITY

"The first and most important principle of the basic logical characteristics of being is the *exclusion of contradiction*. Contradiction
is a category which can only appertain to a combination of thoughts,
but not to reality. There are no contradictions in things, or, to put it
another way, contradiction applied to reality is itself the apex of
absurdity.... The antagonism of contrary forces measured against
each other is in fact the basic form of all actions in the life of the
world and of the creatures on it. But this opposition of forces, which
is found both in the elements and in individuals, is not even in the
most distant way identical with the absurd idea of contradictions.
... We can be content here with having cleared the fogs which generally rise from the supposed mysteries of logic by presenting a clear
picture of the actual absurdity of contradictions in reality, and with
having shown the uselessness of the incense which is burnt in some
quarters in honour of the dialectics of contradiction—the very clum-
sily carved wooden doll which is substituted for the antagonistic
world schematism."—This is practically all we are told about dialectics in the *Course of Philosophy*. In his *Critical History*, on the
other hand, the dialectics of contradiction, and with it Hegel, is
treated quite differently. "Contradiction, indeed, according to the
Hegelian logic (or rather Logos doctrine), is not present in thought,
which by its nature can only be conceived as subjective and conscious, but is objectively present themselves in things and processes
and so to speak appears in corporeal form, so that absurdity does
not remain an impossible combination of thoughts but becomes an
actual force. The reality of the absurd is the first article of faith
in the Hegelian unity of the logical and the illogical.... The more
contradictory a thing the truer it is, or in other words the more
absurd the more credible it is. This maxim, which is not even newly
invented but is borrowed from the theology of the Revelation and

131

from mysticism, is the undisguised expression of the so-called dialectical principle."

The thought-content of the two passages cited is contained in the statement that contradiction = absurdity, and therefore cannot be found in the real world. People who in other respects show a fair degree of common sense may regard this statement as having the same self-evident validity as the statement that a straight line cannot be a curve and a curve cannot be straight. But, regardless of all protests made by common sense, the differential calculus assumes that under certain circumstances straight lines and curves are nevertheless identical, and with this assumption reaches results which common sense, insisting on the absurdity of straight lines being identical with curves, can never attain. And in view of the important role which the so-called dialectics of contradiction has played in philosophy from the time of the earliest Greeks up to the present, even a stronger opponent than Herr Dühring should have felt obliged to attack it with other arguments besides one assertion and a good many abusive epithets.

So long as we consider things as static and lifeless, each one by itself, alongside of and after each other, it is true that we do not run up against any contradictions in them. We find certain qualities which are partly common to, partly diverse from, and even contradictory to each other, but which in this case are distributed among different objects and therefore contain no contradiction. Within the limits of this sphere of thought we can get along on the basis of the usual metaphysical mode of thought. But the position is quite different as soon as we consider things in their motion, their change, their life, their reciprocal influence on one another. Then we immediately become involved in contradictions. Motion itself is a contradiction: even simple mechanical change of place can only come about through a body at one and the same moment of time being both in one place and in another place, being in one and the same place and also not in it. And the continuous assertion and simultaneous solution of this contradiction is precisely what motion is.

Here, therefore, we have a contradiction which "is objectively present in things and processes themselves and so to speak appears in corporeal form." And what has Herr Dühring to say about it? He asserts that up to the present there is absolutely "no bridge, in rational mechanics, from the strictly static to the dynamic." The reader can now at last see what is hiding behind this favourite phrase of Herr Dühring's—it is nothing but this: the mind which thinks metaphysically is absolutely unable to pass from the idea of rest to the idea of motion, because the contradiction pointed out above blocks its path. To it, motion is simply incomprehensible because it is a contradiction. And in asserting the incomprehensibility of motion, it thereby against its will admits the existence of this contradiction, and in so doing admits the objective presence of a contradiction in things and processes themselves, a contradiction which is moreover an actual force.

And if simple mechanical change of place contains a contradiction, this is even more true of the higher forms of motion of matter, and especially of organic life and its development. We saw above that life consists just precisely in this—that a living thing is at each moment itself and yet something else. Life is therefore also a contradiction which is present in things and processes themselves, and which constantly asserts and solves itself; and as soon as the contradiction ceases, life too comes to an end, and death steps in. We likewise saw that in the sphere of thought also we could not avoid contradictions, and that for example the contradiction between man's inherently unlimited faculty of knowledge and its actual realisation in men who are limited by their external conditions and limited also in their intellectual faculties finds its solution in what is, for us at least, and from a practical standpoint, an endless succession of generations, in infinite progress.

We have already noted that one of the basic principles of higher mathematics is the contradiction that in certain circumstances straight lines and curves are identical. It establishes also this other contradiction: that lines which intersect each other before our eyes nevertheless, only five or six centimetres from their point of intersection, can be shown to be parallel, that is, that they will never meet even if extended to infinity. And yet, working with these and with even far greater contradictions, it can attain results which are not only correct but are also quite unattainable for lower mathematics.

But even lower mathematics teems with contradictions. It is for example a contradiction that a root of a should be a power of a, and yet $a^{1/2} = \sqrt{a}$. It is a contradiction that a negative magnitude should be the square of anything, for every negative magnitude multiplied by itself gives a positive square. The square root of minus one is therefore not only a contradiction, but even an absurd contradiction, a real absurdity. And yet $\sqrt{-1}$ is in many cases a necessary result of correct mathematical operations; in fact, we might go further and ask: where would mathematics—either lower or higher—be, if it were prohibited from operating with $\sqrt{-1}$?

In its operations with variable magnitudes mathematics itself enters the field of dialectics, and it is significant that it was a dialectical philosopher, Descartes, who first introduced this advance in mathematics. The relation between the mathematics of variable and the mathematics of constant magnitudes is in general the same as the relation of dialectical to metaphysical thought. But this does not prevent the great mass of mathematicians from recognising dialectics only in the sphere of mathematics, and a good many of them from continuing to work in the old, limited metaphysical way with methods that have been obtained dialectically.

It would only be possible to go more closely into Herr Dühring's antagonism of forces and his antagonistic world schematism if he had given us something more on this theme than the mere *phrase*. After giving us the phrase, this antagonism is not even once shown to us at work, either in his *World Schematism* or in his *Philosophy of Nature*—the most adequate admission that Herr Dühring can produce absolutely nothing of a positive character with his "basic form of all actions in the life of the world and of the creatures on it." When someone has in fact reduced Hegel's *Theory of Essence* to the platitude of forces moving in opposite directions but not in contradictions, certainly the best thing he can do is to avoid any application of this commonplace.

Marx's *Capital* furnishes Herr Dühring with another occasion for venting his anti-dialectical spleen. "The absence of natural and intelligible logic which characterises these dialectical frills and mazes and these arabesques of ideas... even to the part that has already appeared we must apply the principle that in a certain respect and also in general (!), according to a well-known philosophical assumption, all is in each and each in all, and that therefore, according to these mixed and misconceived ideas, everything is all one in the end." This insight into the well-known philosophical assumption also enables Herr Dühring to prophesy with assurance what will be the "end" of Marx's economic philosophising, that is, what the following volumes of *Capital* will contain, and this he does exactly seven lines after he has declared that "speaking frankly and plainly it is really impossible to divine what is still to come in the two (final) volumes."

This, however, is not the first time that Herr Dühring's writings are revealed to us as belonging to the category of "things" in which "contradiction is objectively present and so to speak appears in corporeal form." But this does not prevent him from going on victoriously with the following: "Yet sound logic, it can be predicted, will triumph over its caricature.... This pretence of superiority and this mystifying dialectical rubbish will tempt no one who has even a remnant of sound judgment left to have anything to do with these deformities of thought and style. With the death of the last relics of these dialectical follies this method of duping ... will lose its treacherous influence, and no one will any longer believe that he has to torture himself in order to get behind some profound piece of wisdom, the kernel of which, when cleared of its frills, reveals at best the features of everyday theories if not of absolute common-places.... It is quite impossible to reproduce the (Marxian) mazes in accordance with the Logos doctrine without prostituting sound logic." Marx's method, according to Herr Dühring, consists in "performing dialectical miracles for his faithful followers," and so on.

We are not in any way concerned here with the correctness or incorrectness of the economic results of Marx's researches, but only with the dialectical method applied by Marx. But this much is certain: most readers of *Capital* will have learnt for the first time from Herr Dühring what it is in fact that they have read. And among them will also be Herr Dühring himself, who in the year 1867 (*Ergänzungsblätter* III, No. 3) was still able to make what, for a thinker of his calibre, was a relatively rational analysis of the book; and he did this without first being obliged, as he now declares is absolutely necessary, to translate the Marxian argument into Dühringian language. And though even then he committed the blunder of identifying Marxian dialectics with the Hegelian, he had not quite lost capacity to distinguish between the method and the results obtained by using it, and to understand that the latter are not refuted in detail by the general undermining of the former.

The most astonishing piece of information given by Herr Dühring is, however, that from the Marxian standpoint "everything is all one in the end," that therefore to Marx, for example, capitalists and wage-earners, feudal, capitalist and socialist systems of productions are also "all one"—no doubt in the end even Marx and Herr Dühring are "all one." Such arrant nonsense can only be explained if we suppose that the mere word dialectics throws Herr Dühring into such a state of mental incompetence that, as a result of certain mixed and misconceived ideas, what he says and does is "all one" in the end.

We have here a sample of what Herr Dühring calls "*my* historical treatment in the grand style," or "the summary treatment which takes genus and type into account, and does not sink so low as to honour what a Hume called the learned mob by an exposition in micrological detail; this treatment in a higher and nobler style is the only one that is compatible with the interests of complete truth and with one's duty to the public which is outside the exclusive professional circle." Historiography in the grand style and the summary treatment of genus and type is indeed very convenient for Herr Dühring, inasmuch as this method enables him to omit all known facts as micrological and equate them to zero, so that instead of proving anything he need only use general phrases, make assertions and thunder his denunciations. The method has the further advantage that it offers no real foothold to an opponent, who is consequently left with almost no other possibility of reply except by making similar summary assertions in the grand style, by resorting to general phrases and finally thundering back denunciations at Herr Dühring —in a word, as the saying is, by a slanging match, which is not to everyone's taste. We must therefore be grateful to Herr Dühring for occasionally, by way of exception, dropping the higher and nobler style, and giving us at least two examples of the detestable Marxian Logos doctrine.

"What a comical effect is produced by the reference to the confused and foggy Hegelian conception that quantity changes into quality, and that therefore an advance, when it reaches a certain size, becomes capital by this mere quantitative increase!"

In this "purged" presentation by Herr Dühring it certainly looks curious enough. But let us see how it looks in the original, in Marx. On page 336,* Marx, on the basis of the previous examination of constant and variable capital and surplus value, draws the conclusion that "not every sum of money, or of value, is at pleasure transformable into capital. To effect this transformation, in fact, a certain minimum of money or of exchange-value must be presupposed in the hands of the individual possessor of money or commodities."

He then takes as an example the case of a labourer in any branch of industry, who works eight hours for himself—that is, in producing the value of his wages—and the following four hours for the capitalist, in producing surplus value, which immediately flows into the pocket of the capitalist. In this case a capitalist would have to dispose of a sum of value sufficient to enable him to provide two labourers with raw materials, instruments of labour, and wages, in order to appropriate enough surplus value every day to enable him to live on it even as well as one of his labourers. And as the aim of capitalist production is not mere subsistence but the increase of wealth, our man with his two labourers would still not be a capitalist. Now in order that he may live twice as well as an ordinary labourer, and besides turn half of the surplus value produced again into capital, he would have to be able to employ eight labourers, that is, he would have to dispose of four times the sum of value assumed above. And it is only after this, and in the course of still further explanations elucidating and establishing the fact that not every petty sum of value is enough to be transformable into capital, but that the minimum sum required varies with each period of development and each branch of industry, it is only then that Marx observes: "Here, as in natural science, is *verified* the correctness of the law discovered by Hegel (in his *Logic*) that merely quantitative changes beyond a certain point are transformed into qualitative differences."

And now let the reader admire the higher and nobler style, by

* *Capital*, Vol. I (Kerr edition).

virtue of which Herr Dühring attributes to Marx the opposite of what he really said. Marx says: The fact that a sum of value can only be transformed into capital when it has reached a certain size, varying according to the circumstances, but in each case with a definite minimum—this fact is a *proof of the correctness* of the Hegelian law. Herr Dühring makes him say: *Because,* according to the Hegelian law, quantity changes into quality, *"therefore"* "an advance, when it reaches a certain size, becomes capital." That is to say, the very opposite.

In connection with Herr Dühring's putting Darwin on trial we have already got to know his habit, "in the interests of complete truth" and because of his "duty to the public which is outside the exclusive professional circle," of citing passages incorrectly. It becomes more and more evident that this habit is an inner necessity of the philosophy of reality, and it is certainly a very "summary treatment." Not to mention the fact that Herr Dühring further makes Marx speak of any kind of "advance" whatsoever, whereas Marx only refers to an advance made in the form of raw materials, instruments of labour, and wages; and that in doing this Herr Dühring succeeds in making Marx speak pure nonsense. And then he has the cheek to describe as *comic* the nonsense which he has himself fabricated. Just as he built up a fantastic image of Darwin in order to try out his strength against it, so here he builds up a fantastic image of Marx. It is indeed a "historical treatment in the grand style"!

We have already seen earlier, in regard to world schematism, that in connection with this Hegelian nodal line of measure-relations—in which quantitative change suddenly produces, at certain points, a qualitative difference—Herr Dühring had a little accident: in a weak moment he himself recognised and made use of this principle. We gave there one of the best-known examples—that of the change of the state of water, which under normal atmospheric pressure changes at O° C. from the liquid into the solid state, and at 100° C. from the liquid into the gaseous state, so that at both these turning-points the merely quantitative change of temperature brings about a qualitative change in the condition of the water.

In proof of this law we might have cited hundreds of other similar facts from Nature as well as from human society. Thus, for example, the whole of Part IV of Marx's *Capital—Production of Relative Surplus Value—Co-operation, Division of Labour and Manufacture, Machinery and Large Scale Industry*—deals with innumerable cases in which quantitative change alters the quality, and also qualitative change alters the quantity, of the things under consideration; in which therefore, to use the expression which is so hated by Herr Dühring, quantity is transformed into quality and *vice versa*. As for example the fact that the co-operation of a number of people, the fusion of many forces into one single force, to use Marx's phrase, creates a "new power," which is essentially different from the sum of its individual powers.

Over and above this, in the passage which, in the interests of complete truth, Herr Dühring perverted into its opposite, Marx added a footnote: "The molecular theory of modern chemistry first scientifically worked out by Laurent and Gerhardt rests on no other law." But what does that matter to Herr Dühring? He knew that: "the eminently modern elements of education provided by the scientific mode of thought are lacking precisely among those who, like Marx and his rival Lassalle, make half-science and a little philosophistics the meagre equipment on which their learning rests"—while with Herr Dühring "the main achievements of exact knowledge in mechanics, physics and chemistry" and so forth are his basis—we have seen how. However, in order to enable third persons also to reach a decision in the matter, we shall look a little more closely into the example cited in Marx's footnote.

What is referred to here is the homologous series of carbon compounds, of which a great many are already known and each of which has its own algebraic formula of composition. If for example, as is done in chemistry, we denote an atom of carbon by C, an atom of hydrogen by H, an atom of oxygen by O, and the number of atoms of carbon contained in each compound by n, the molecular formulæ for some of these series can be expressed as follows:

C_nH_{2n+2} — the series of normal paraffins.
$C_nH_{2n+2}O$ — the series of primary alcohols.
$C_nH_{2n}O_2$ — the series of the normal fatty acids.

Let us take as an example the last of these series, and let us assume successively that $n = 1$, $n = 2$, $n = 3$, etc. We then obtain the following results (omitting the isomers):

CH_2O_2	— formic acid	boiling point 100°; melting point 1°
$C_2H_4O_2$	— acetic acid	boiling point 118°; melting point 17°
$C_3H_6O_2$	— propionic acid	boiling point 140°; melting point —
$C_4H_8O_2$	— butyric acid	boiling point 162°; melting point —
$C_5H_{10}O_2$	— valerianic acid	boiling point 175°; melting point —

and so on to $C_{30}H_{60}O_2$, melissic acid, which melts only at 80° and has no boiling point, because it does not evaporate at all without decomposing.

Here therefore we have a whole series of qualitatively different bodies, formed by the simple quantitative addition of elements, and in fact always in the same proportion. This is most clearly evident in cases where the quantity of all the elements of the compound changes in the same proportion; thus in the normal paraffins $C_nH_{2n}{+}2$ the lowest is methane, CH_4, a gas; the highest known, hexadecane, $C_{16}H_{34}$, is a body forming hard, colourless crystals which melts at 21° and does not boil below 278°. Each new member of both series comes into existence through the addition of CH_2, one atom of carbon and two atoms of hydrogen, to the molecular formula of the preceding member, this quantitative change in molecular composition produces at each step a qualitatively different body.

These series, however, are only one particularly obvious example; throughout practically the whole of chemistry, even in the various nitrogen oxides and oxygen acids of phosphorus or sulphur, there are instances of "quantity being transformed into quality," and this alleged confused nebulous Hegelian conception is to be found so to speak in corporeal form in things and processes—although no one but Herr Dühring is confused and befogged by it. And if Marx was the first to call attention to it, and if Herr Dühring read the reference without even understanding what it meant (otherwise he would certainly not have allowed this unparalleled outrage to pass unchallenged), this is enough—even without looking back at Herr Dühring's famous *Philosophy of Nature*—to make it clear which of the two, Marx or Herr Dühring, is lacking in "the eminently modern elements of education provided by the scientific mode of thought" and in acquaintance with the "main achievements of ... chemistry."

In conclusion we shall call one more witness for the transformation of quantity into quality, namely—Napoleon. He makes the following reference to the fights between the French cavalry, who were bad riders but disciplined, and the Mamelukes, who were undoubtedly the best horsemen of their time for single combat, but lacked discipline: "Two Mamelukes were undoubtedly more than a match for three Frenchmen: 100 Mamelukes were equal to 100 Frenchmen; 300 Frenchmen could generally beat 300 Mamelukes, and 1,000 Frenchmen invariably defeated 1,500 Mamelukes." Just as with Marx a definite, though varying, minimum sum of exchange value was necessary to make possible its transformation into capital, so with Napoleon a detachment of cavalry had to be of a definite minimum number in order to make it possible for the force of discipline, embodied in closed order and planned application, to manifest itself and rise superior even to greater numbers of irregular cavalry, in spite of the latter being better mounted, more skilful horsemen and fighters, and at least as brave as the former. But what does this prove as against Herr Dühring? Was not Napoleon miserably vanquished in his conflict with Europe? Did he not suffer defeat after defeat? And why? Simply as a result of his having introduced confused nebulous Hegelian conceptions into his cavalry tactics!

XIII. DIALECTICS. NEGATION OF THE NEGATION

"This historical sketch (of the genesis of the so-called primitive accumulation of capital in England) is relatively the best part of Marx's book, and would be even better if it had not relied on dialectical crutches to help out its scholarly basis. The Hegelian negation of the negation, in default of anything better and clearer, has in fact to serve here as the midwife to deliver the future from the womb of the past. The abolition of individual property, which since the sixteenth century has been effected in the way indicated, is the first negation. It will be followed by a second, which bears the character of a negation of the negation, hence the restoration of 'individual property,' but in a higher form, based on common ownership of the land and of the instruments of labour. Herr Marx also calls this new 'individual property'—'social property,' and in this we have the Hegelian higher unity, in which the contradiction is resolved, that is to say, in the Hegelian verbal jugglery, it is both overcome and preserved.... According to this, the expropriation of the expropriators is as it were the automatic result of historical reality in its material external relations.... It would be difficult to convince a sensible man of the necessity of the common ownership of land and capital on the basis of Hegelian word-juggling such as the negation of the negation.... The nebulous hybrids of Marx's conceptions will however surprise no one who realises what phantasies can be built up with the Hegelian dialectics as the scientific basis, or rather what absurdities necessarily spring from it. For the benefit of the reader who is not familiar with these artifices, it must be expressly pointed out that Hegel's first negation is the idea of the fall from grace, which is taken from catechism, and his second is the idea of a higher unity leading to redemption. The logic of facts can hardly be based on his nonsensical analogy borrowed from the religious sphere.... Herr Marx remains cheerfully in the nebulous world of his property which is at the same time both individual and social and leaves it to his adepts to solve for themselves this profound dialectical enigma." Thus far Herr Dühring.

So Marx has no other way of proving the necessity of the social revolution and the establishment of a social system based on the common ownership of land and of the means of production produced by labour, except by appealing to the Hegelian negation of the negation; and because he bases his socialist theory on these nonsensical analogies borrowed from religion, he arrives at the result that in the society of the future there will be property which is at the same time both individual and social, as the Hegelian higher unity of the sublated contradiction.

Let us for the moment leave the negation of the negation to look after itself, and let us have a look at the "property which is at the same time both individual and social." Herr Dühring characterises this as a "nebulous world," and curiously enough he is really right on this point. Unfortunately, however, it is not Marx but on the contrary Herr Dühring himself who is in this nebulous world. Just as his proficiency in the Hegelian method of "delirious raving" enabled him without any difficulty to determine what the still unfinished volumes of *Capital* are sure to contain, so here too without any great effort he can put Marx right *à la* Hegel, by foisting on him the higher unity of a property, of which there is not a word in Marx. Marx says: *

It is the negation of negation. This does not re-establish private property for the producer, but gives him individual property based on the acquisitions of the capitalist era; *i.e.*, on co-operation of free labourers and the possession in common of the land and of the means of production.

The transformation of scattered private property, arising from individual labour, into capitalist private property is, naturally, a process incomparably more protracted, violent, and difficult, than the transformation of capitalistic private property, already practically resting on socialised production, into socialised property.

That is all. The state of things brought about through the expropriation of the expropriator is therefore characterised as the reestablishment of individual property, but *on the basis* of the social ownership of the land and of the means of production produced by

* *Capital*, Vol. I, p. 837 (Kerr edition).

labour itself. To anyone who understands English this means that social ownership extends to the land and the other means of production, and private ownership to the products, that is, the articles of consumption. And in order to make the matter comprehensible even to children of six, Marx assumes on page 90 * "a community of free individuals, carrying on their work with the means of production in common, in which the labour power of all the different individuals is consciously applied as the combined labour power of the community" that is, a society organised on a socialist basis; and he says: "The total product of our community is a social product. One portion serves as fresh means of production and *remains social*. But another portion is consumed by the members as means of subsistence. *A distribution of this portion among them is consequently necessary.*" And surely that is clear enough even for Herr Dühring, in spite of his having Hegel on the brain.

The property which is at the same time both private and social, this confused hybrid, this absurdity which necessarily springs from Hegelian dialectics, this nebulous world, this profound dialectical enigma, which Marx leaves his adepts to solve for themselves—is yet another free creation and imagination on the part of Herr Dühring. He thinks that Marx, as an alleged Hegelian, must produce a real higher unity as the outcome of the negation of the negation, and as Marx does not do this to Herr Dühring's taste, the latter has to fall into his higher and nobler style, and in the interests of complete truth foist on Marx things which are the products of Herr Dühring's own manufacture. A man who is so totally incapable of quoting correctly, even by way of exception, may well lapse into moral indignation at the "Chinese erudition" of other people, who without exception quote correctly, but precisely by doing this "inadequately conceal their lack of insight into the system of ideas of the various writers from whom they quote." Herr Dühring is right. Long live the historical treatment found in the grand style!

Up to this point we have proceeded from the assumption that Herr Dühring's persistent habit of quoting falsely does at least happen in good faith, and arises either from his total incapacity to understand things or from a habit of quoting from memory—a habit

* *Capital*, Vol. I (Kerr edition)

which seems to be peculiar to the historical treatment in the grand style, and outside of this would probably be described as slovenly. But we seem to have reached the point at which, even with Herr Dühring, quantity is transformed into quality. For we must take into consideration, first, that the passage in Marx is in itself perfectly clear and is moreover supplemented by a further passage in the same book, a passage which leaves no room whatever for misunderstanding; secondly, that Herr Dühring had not discovered the monstrosity of "property which is at the same time both individual and social" when he wrote either the critique of *Capital* in the *Ergänzungsblätter* which was referred to above, or even the critique contained in the first edition of his *Critical History,* but that it first appeared in the second edition—that is, when he had read Marx for the *third* time and, further, that in this second edition, which was rewritten in a socialist sense, it was necessary for Herr Dühring to make Marx say the utmost possible nonsense about the future organisation of society, in order to enable him, in contrast to this, to bring forward all the more triumphantly—as he in fact does—his "economic commune as sketched in economic and juridical outline in my *Course.*"—When we call attention to all this, we are forced to the conclusion which Herr Dühring almost compels us to accept: that the "beneficent extension" of Marx's ideas—beneficent for Herr Dühring—was here carried out of set purpose by Herr Dühring.

But what role does the negation of the negation play in Marx? On page 834 * and the following pages he sets out the conclusions which he draws from the preceding fifty pages of economic and historical investigation into the so-called primitive accumulation of capital. Before the capitalist era, at least in England, petty industry existed on the basis of the private property of the labourer in his means of production. The so-called primitive accumulation of capital consisted in this case in the expropriation of these immediate producers, that is, in the dissolution of private property based on the labour of its owner. This was possible because the petty industry referred to above is compatible only with a system of production, and a society, moving within narrow and primitive bounds, and at a certain stage of its development it brings forth the material agencies

* *Capital,* Vol. I (Kerr edition)

for its own annihilation. This annihilation, the transformation of the individual and scattered means of production into socially concentrated ones, forms the pre-history of capital. As soon as the labourers are turned into proletarians, their means of labour into capital, as soon as the capitalist mode of production stands on its own feet, the further socialisation of labour and further transformation of the land and other means of production, and therefore the further expropriation of private proprietors, takes a new form.

"That which is now to be expropriated is no longer the labourer working for himself, but the capitalist exploiting many labourers. This expropriation is accomplished by the action of the immanent laws of capitalist production itself, by the centralisation of capital. One capitalist always kills many. Hand in hand with this centralisation, or this expropriation of many capitalists by few, develop, on an ever extending scale, the co-operative form of the labour process, the conscious technical application of science, the methodical cultivation of the soil, the transformation of the instruments of labour into instruments of labour only usable in common, the economising of all means of production by their use as the means of production of combined, socialised labour. . . . Along with the constantly diminishing number of the magnates of capital, who usurp and monopolise all advantages of this process of transformation, grows the mass of misery, oppression, slavery, degradation, exploitation; but with this too grows the revolt of the working class, a class always increasing in number, and disciplined, united, organised by the very mechanism of the process of capitalist production itself. The monopoly of capital becomes a fetter upon the mode of production, which has sprung up and flourished along with, and under it. Centralisation of the means of production and socialisation of labour at last reach a point where they become incompatible with their capitalist integument. This integument is burst asunder. The knell of capitalist private property sounds. The expropriators are expropriated." *

And now I ask the reader: where are the dialectical frills and mazes and intellectual arabesques; where the mixed and misconceived ideas as a result of which everything is all one in the end;

---

* *Capital*, Vol. I, pp. 836-37 (Kerr edition).

where the dialectical miracles for his faithful followers; where the mysterious dialectical rubbish and the contortions based on the Hegelian Logos doctrine, without which Marx, according to Herr Dühring, is quite unable to accomplish his development? Marx merely shows from history, and in this passage states in a summarised form, that just as the former petty industry necessarily, through its own development, created the conditions of its annihilation, *i.e.*, of the expropriation of the small proprietors, so now the capitalist mode of production has likewise itself created the material conditions which will annihilate it. The process is a historical one, and if it is at the same time a dialectical process, this is not Marx's fault, however annoying it may be for Herr Dühring.

It is only at this point, after Marx has completed his proof on the basis of historical and economic facts, that he proceeds: "The capitalist mode of production and appropriation, and hence capitalist private property, is the first negation of individual private property founded on the labours of the proprietor. But capitalist production begets, with the inexorability of a law of Nature, its own negation. It is the negation of the negation"—and so on (as quoted above).

In characterising the process as the negation of the negation, therefore, Marx does not dream of attempting to prove by this that the process was historically necessary. On the contrary: after he has proved from history that in fact the process has partially already occurred, and partially must occur in the future, he then also characterises it as a process which develops in accordance with a definite dialectical law. That is all. It is therefore once again a pure distortion of the facts by Herr Dühring, when he declares that the negation of the negation has to serve as the midwife to deliver the future from the womb of the past, or that Marx wants anyone to allow himself to be convinced of the necessity of the common ownership of land and capital (which is itself a Dühringian corporeal contradiction) on the basis of the negation of the negation.

Herr Dühring's total lack of understanding as to the nature of dialectics is shown by the very fact that he regards it as a mere instrument through which things can be proved, as in a more limited way formal logic or elementary mathematics can be regarded. Even formal logic is primarily a method of arriving at new results, of advancing from the known to the unknown—and dialectics is the same, only in a much more important sense, because in forcing its way beyond the narrow horizon of formal logic it contains the germ of a more comprehensive view of the world. It is the same with mathematics. Elementary mathematics, the mathematics of constant magnitudes, moves within the confines of formal logic, at any rate taken as a whole; the mathematics of variable magnitudes, whose most important part is the infinitesimal calculus, is in essence nothing other than the application of dialectics to mathematical relations. In it, the simple question of proof is definitely pushed into the background, as compared with the manifold application of the method to new spheres of research. But almost all the proofs of higher mathematics, from the first—that of the differential calculus—on, are false, from the standpoint of elementary mathematics taken rigidly. And it is necessarily so, when, as happens in this case, an attempt is made to prove by formal logic results obtained in the field of dialectics. To attempt to prove anything by means of dialectics alone to a crass metaphysician like Herr Dühring would be as much a waste of time as the attempt made by Leibnitz and his pupils to prove the principles of the infinitesimal calculus to the mathematicians of his time. The differential calculus produced in them the same convulsions as Herr Dühring gets from the negation of the negation, in which, moreover, as we shall see, the differential calculus also plays a certain role. Ultimately these gentlemen—or those of them who had not died in the interval—grudgingly gave way, not because they were convinced, but because it always produced correct results. Herr Dühring, as he himself tells us, has only just entered the forties, and if he attains old age, as we hope he may, perhaps his experience will be the same.

But what then is this fearful negation of the negation, which makes life so bitter for Herr Dühring and fulfils the same role with him of the unpardonable crime as the sin against the Holy Ghost does in Christianity?—A very simple process which is taking place everywhere and every day, which any child can understand, as soon as it is stripped of the veil of mystery in which it was wrapped by the old idealist philosophy and in which it is to the advantage of helpless metaphysicians of Herr Dühring's calibre to keep it enveloped. Let us take a grain of barley. Millions of such grains of barley are milled, boiled and brewed and then consumed. But if such a grain of barley meets with conditions which for it are normal, if it falls on suitable soil, then under the influence of heat and moisture a specific change takes place, it germinates; the grain as such ceases to exist, it is negated, and in its place appears the plant which has arisen from it, the negation of the grain. But what is the normal life-process of this plant? It grows, flowers, is fertilised and finally once more produces grains of barley, and as soon as these have ripened the stalk dies, is in its turn negated. As a result of this negation of the negation we have once again the original grain of barley, but not as a single unit, but ten, twenty or thirty fold. Species of grain change extremely slowly, and so the barley of today is almost the same as it was a century ago.

But if we take an ornamental plant which can be modified in cultivation, for example a dahlia or an orchid: if we treat the seed and the plant which grows from it as a gardener does, we get as the result of this negation of the negation not only more seeds, but also qualitatively better seeds, which produce more beautiful flowers, and each fresh repetition of this process, each repeated negation of the negation increases this improvement. With most insects, this process follows the same lines as in the case of the grain of barley. Butterflies, for example, spring from the egg through a negation of the egg, they pass through certain transformations until they reach sexual maturity, they pair and are in turn negated, dying as soon as the pairing process has been completed and the female has laid its numerous eggs. We are not concerned at the moment with the fact that with other plants and animals the process does not take such a simple form, that before they die they produce seeds, eggs or offspring not once but many times; our purpose here is only to show that the negation of the negation *takes place in reality* in both divisions of the organic world. Furthermore, the whole of geology is a series of negated negations, a series arising from the successive shattering of old and the depositing of new rock formations. First the original earth-crust brought into existence by the cooling of the liquid mass was broken up by oceanic, meteorological and atmospherico-chemical action, and these distintegrated masses were deposited on the ocean floor. Local elevations of the ocean floor above the surface of the sea subject portions of these first strata once more to the action of rain, the changing temperature of the seasons and the oxygen and carbonic acid of the atmosphere. These same influences acted on the molten masses of rock which issued from the interior of the earth, broke through the strata and subsequently solidified. In this way, in the course of millions of centuries, ever new strata are formed and in turn are for the most part destroyed, ever anew serving as material for the formation of new strata. But the result of this process has been a very positive one: the creation, out of the most varied chemical elements, of a mixed and mechanically pulverised soil which makes possible the most abundant and diverse vegetation.

It is the same in mathematics. Let us take any algebraical magnitude whatever: for example, a. If this is negated, we get $-a$ (minus a). If we negate that negation, by multiplying $-a$ by $-a$, we get $+a^2$, i.e., the original positive magnitude, but at a higher degree, raised to its second power. In this case also it makes no difference that we can reach the same a^2 by multiplying the positive a by itself, thus also getting a^2. For the negated negation is so securely entrenched in a^2 that the latter always has two square roots, namely a and $-a$. And the fact that it is impossible to get rid of the negated negation, the negative root of the square, acquires very obvious significance as soon as we get as far as quadratic equations. The negation of the negation is even more strikingly obvious in the higher analyses, in those "summations of indefinitely small magnitudes" which Herr Dühring himself declares are the highest operations of mathematics, and in ordinary language are known as the differential and integral calculus. How are these forms of calculus used? In a given problem, for example, I have two variable magnitudes x and y, neither of which can vary without the other also varying in a relation determined by the conditions of the case. I differentiate x and y, i.e., I take x and y as so infinitely small that in comparison with any real magnitude, however small, they disappear, so that nothing is left of x and y but their reciprocal relation without any, so to speak, material basis, a quantitative relation in which there is no quantity. Therefore, $\frac{dy}{dx}$, the relation between the differentials of x and y, is equal to $\frac{o}{o}$, but $\frac{o}{o}$ as the expression of $\frac{y}{x}$. I only mention in passing that this relation between two magnitudes which have disappeared, caught at the moment of their disappearance, is a contradiction; it cannot disturb us any more than it has disturbed the whole of mathematics for almost two hundred years. And yet what have I done but negate x and y, though not in such a way that I need not bother about them any more, not in the way that metaphysics negates, but in the way that corresponds with the facts of the case? In place of x and y, therefore, I have their negation, dx and dy in the formulæ of equations before me. I continue then to operate with these formulæ, treating dx and dy as magnitudes which are real, though subject to certain exceptional laws, and at a certain *point I negate the negation, i.e.,* I integrate the differential formula, and in place of dx and dy again get the real magnitudes x and y, and am not then where I was at the beginning, but by using this method I have solved the problem on which ordinary geometry and algebra might perhaps have broken their teeth in vain.

It is the same, too, in history. All civilised peoples begin with the common ownership of the land. With all peoples who have passed a certain primitive stage, in the course of the development of agriculture this common ownership becomes a fetter on production. It is abolished, negated, and after a long or shorter series of intermediate stages is transformed into private property. But at a higher stage of agricultural development, brought about by private property in land itself, private property in turn becomes a fetter on production as is the case today, both with small and large landownership. The demand that it also should be negated, that it should once again be transformed into common property, necessarily arises. But this demand does not mean the restoration of the old original common ownership, but the institution of a far higher and more developed form of possession in common which, far from being a hindrance to production, on the contrary for the first time frees production from all fetters and gives it the possibility of making full use of modern chemical discoveries and mechanical inventions.

Or let us take another example: the philosophy of antiquity was primitive, natural materialism. As such, it was incapable of clearing up the relation between thought and matter. But the need to get clarity on this question led to the doctrine of a soul separable from the body, then to assertion of the immortality of this soul, and finally to monotheism. The old materialism was therefore negated by idealism. But in the course of the further development of philosophy, idealism too became untenable and was negated by modern materialism. This modern materialism, the negation of the negation, is not the mere reestablishment of the old, but adds to the permanent foundations of this old materialism the whole thought content of two thousand years of development of philosophy and natural science, as well as of the historical development of these two thousand years. It is in fact no longer a philosophy, but a simple world outlook which has to establish its validity and be applied not in a science of sciences standing apart, but within the positive sciences. In this development philosophy is therefore "sublated," that is, "both overcome and preserved"; overcome as regards its form, and preserved as regards its real content. Where Herr Dühring sees only "verbal jugglery," closer inspection therefore reveals a positive content.

Finally: even the Rousseau theory of equality—of which Dühring's is only a feeble and distorted echo—could not have seen the light but for the midwife's services rendered by the Hegelian negation of the negation—though it was over twenty years before Hegel was born. And far from being ashamed of this, in its first presentation the theory bears almost ostentatiously the imprint of its dialectical origin. In the state of nature and savagery men were equal; and as Rousseau regards even language as a perversion of the state of nature, he is fully justified in extending the equality of animals of a single species, in so far as it applies, also to the animal-men recently classified by Haeckel in the hypothetical group, Alali: speechless. But these equal animal-men had one quality which gave them an advantage over the other animals: perfectibility, the capacity to develop further: and this was the cause of inequality. Rousseau therefore regards the rise of inequality as progress. But this progress contained an antagonism: it was at the same time retrogression. "All further progress (beyond the original state) consisted likewise of steps forward apparently towards the *perfection of the individual man*, but in reality towards the *decay of the species*. The working of metals and agriculture were the two arts the discovery of which produced this great revolution" (the transformation of the primeval forest into cultivated land, but along with this the introduction of poverty and slavery through property). "For the poets it is gold and silver, for the philosophers iron and corn, which have civilised *men* and ruined the human *race*." Each new advance of civilisation is at the same time a new advance of inequality. All institutions set up by the society which has arisen with civilisation change into the opposite of their original purpose. "It is an incontestable fact, and the basic principle of all constitutional law, that the people set up their chieftains to safeguard their liberty and not to destroy it." And nevertheless the chiefs necessarily become the oppressors of the peoples, and intensify their oppression up to the point at which inequality, carried to the utmost extreme, is again transformed into its opposite, becomes the cause of equality; before the despot all are equal—equally ciphers. "Here we have the most extreme degree of inequality, *the final point which completes the circle and meets the point from which we set out*: here all private individuals are equal, just because they are ciphers, and the subjects have no other law but the will of their master." But the despot is only master so long as he has power, and therefore when "he is driven out, he cannot complain of the use of force.... Force maintains him in power, and force overthrows him; everything proceeds in its right and natural course." And so inequality is once more transformed into equality; not, however, into the former natural equality of speechless primeval man, but into the higher equality of the social contract. The oppressors are oppressed. It is the negation of the negation.

Already in Rousseau, therefore, we find not only a sequence of ideas which corresponds exactly with the sequence developed in Marx's *Capital*, but that the correspondence extends also to details, Rousseau using a whole series of the same dialectical developments as Marx used: processes which in their nature are antagonistic, contain a contradiction, are the transformation of one extreme into its opposite; and finally, as the kernel of the whole process, the negation of the negation. And though in 1754 Rousseau was not yet able to use the Hegelian jargon, he was certainly, twenty-three years before Hegel was born, deeply bitten with the Hegelian pestilence, dialectics of contradiction, Logos doctrine, theology and so forth. And when Herr Dühring, in his superficial version of Rousseau's theory of equality, begins to operate with his victorious two men, he is himself already on the inclined plane down which he must slide helplessly into the arms of the negation of the negation. The state of things in which the equality of the two men flourished, which was also described as an ideal state, is characterised on page 271 of his *Philosophy* as the "primitive state." This primitive state, however, according to page 279, was necessarily brought to an end by the "robber system"—the first negation. But now, thanks to the philosophy of reality, we have gone so far as to abolish the robber system and establish in its stead the economic commune based on equality which has been discovered by Herr Dühring—negation of the negation, equality on a higher degree. What a delightful spectacle, and how beneficently it extends our range of vision: we find Herr Dühring's eminent self committing the capital crime of the negation of the negation!

What therefore is the negation of the negation? An extremely general—and for this reason extremely comprehensive and important—law of development of Nature, history and thought; a law which, as we have seen, holds good in the animal and plant kingdoms, in geology, in mathematics, in history and in philosophy—a law which even Herr Dühring, in spite of all his struggles and resistance, has unwittingly and in his own way to follow. It is obvious that in describing any evolutionary process as the negation of the negation I do not say anything concerning the *particular* process of development, for example, of the grain of barley from germination to the death of the fruit-bearing plant. For, as the integral calculus also is a negation of the negation, if I said anything of the sort I should only be making the nonsensical statement that the life-process of a barley plant was the integral calculus or for that matter that it was socialism. That, however, is what the metaphysicians are constantly trying to impute to dialectics. When

I say that all these processes are the negation of the negation, I bring them all together under this one law of motion, and for this very reason I leave out of account the peculiarities of each separate individual process. Dialectics is nothing more than the science of the general laws of motion and development of Nature, human society and thought.

But someone may object: the negation that has taken place in this case is not a real negation: I negate a grain of barley also when I grind it down, an insect when I crush it underfoot, or the positive magnitude *a* when I cancel it, and so on. Or I negate the sentence; the rose is a rose, when I say: the rose is not a rose; and what do I get if I then negate the negation and say: but after all the rose is a rose? —These objections are in fact the chief arguments put forward by the metaphysicians against dialectics, and they are eminently worthy of the narrow-mindedness of this mode of thought. Negation in dialectics does not mean simply saying no, or declaring that something does not exist, or destroying it in any way one likes. Long ago Spinoza said: *Omnis determinatio est negatio*—every limitation or determination is at the same time a negation. And further: the kind of negation is here determined in the first place by the general, and secondly by the particular, nature of the process. I must not only negate, but also in turn sublate the negation. I must therefore so construct the first negation that the second remains or becomes possible. In what way? This depends on the particular nature of each individual case. If I grind a grain of barley, or crush an insect, it is true I have carried out the first part of the action, but I have made the second part impossible. Each class of things therefore has its appropriate form of being negated in such a way that it gives rise to a development, and it is just the same with each class of conceptions and ideas. The infinitesimal calculus involves a form of negation which is different from that used in the formation of positive powers from negative roots. This has to be learnt, like everything else. The mere knowledge that the barley plant and the infinitesimal calculus are both governed by the negation of the negation does not enable me either to grow barley successfully or to use the calculus; just as little as the mere knowledge of the laws of the determination of sound by the thickness of strings enables me to play the violin.

But it is clear that in a negation of the negations which consists of the childish pastime of alternately writing and cancelling *a,* or of alternately declaring that a rose is a rose and that it is not a rose, nothing comes out of it but the stupidity of the person who adopts such a tedious procedure. And yet the metaphysicians try to tell us that this is the right way to carry out the negation of the negation, if we ever want to do such a thing.

Once again, therefore, it is no one but Herr Dühring who is mystifying us when he asserts that the negation of the negation is a stupid analogy invented by Hegel, borrowed from the sphere of religion and based on the story of the fall of man and redemption. Men thought dialectically long before they knew what dialectics was, just as they spoke prose long before the term prose existed. The law of the negation of the negation, which is unconsciously operative in Nature and history, and until it has been recognised, also in our heads, was only clearly formulated for the first time by Hegel. And if Herr Dühring wants to use it himself on the quiet and it is only the name which he cannot stand, let him find a better name. But if his aim is to expel the process itself from thought, we must ask him to be so good as first to banish it from Nature and history and to invent a mathematical system in which $-a \times -a$ is not $+a^2$ and in which the differential and integral calculus are prohibited under severe penalties.

XIV. CONCLUSION

We have now finished with Philosophy: such other phantasies of the future as the *Course of Philosophy* contains will be dealt with when we come to Herr Dühring's revolution in socialism.

What did Herr Dühring promise us? Everything. And what promises has he kept? Not one. "The elements of a philosophy which is real and therefore directed to the reality of Nature and of life," the "strictly scientific conception of the world," the "system-creating ideas," and all Herr Dühring's other achievements, trumpeted forth to the world by Herr Dühring in high-sounding phrases—turn out, wherever we lay hold of them, to be *pure charlatanism*. The world schematism which "without in any way compromising the profundity of thought, securely established the basic forms of being" proved to be an infinitely vulgarised plagiarism of Hegel's *Logic,* and in common with the latter shares the superstition that these "basic forms" or logical categories have led a secret existence somewhere before and out of the world to which they are "to be applied." The philosophy of nature offered us a cosmogony whose starting point is an "identical state of matter"—a state which can only be conceived by means of the most hopeless confusion as to the relation between matter and motion; a state which can also only be conceived on the hypothesis of a personal God outside the universe, who alone can help this state of matter to acquire motion. In its treatment of organic Nature, the philosophy of reality first rejected the Darwinian struggle for existence and natural selection as "a piece of brutality directed against humanity," and then had to re-admit both by the back door as factors operative in Nature though of second rank. And the philosophy of reality also found occasion to exhibit, in the biological domain, ignorance such as nowadays, when no one can avoid popular lectures on science, could hardly be found even among the daughters of the "cultured" class. In the domain of morals and law, the philosophy of reality was no more successful in its

157

superficial plagiarism of Rousseau than it had been in its previous vulgarisation of Hegel; and moreover, so far as legal science is concerned, in spite of all its assurances to the contrary, it displayed ignorance such as is rarely found even among the most ordinary jurists of Old Prussia. The philosophy "which cannot allow the validity of any merely apparent horizon" is content, in juridical matters, with a real horizon which is identical with the territory in which the Prussian *Landrecht* holds sway. We are still waiting for the "earths and heavens of external and inward Nature" which this philosophy promised to reveal to us in its mighty revolutionising sweep; just as we are still waiting for the "final and ultimate truths" and the "absolute fundamental basis." The philosopher whose mode of thought "excludes any tendency to a visionary and subjectively limited conception of the world" proves to be subjectively limited not only by what has been shown to be his extremely defective knowledge, his narrow metaphysical mode of thought and his grotesque conceit, but even also by his childish personal crotchets. He cannot produce his philosophy of reality without dragging in his repugnance to tobacco, cats and Jews as a general law valid for the whole of the rest of humanity, including the Jews themselves. His "really critical standpoint" shows itself in relation to other people by insistently foisting on them things which they never said and which are Herr Dühring's very own productions. His verbose lucubrations on themes worthy of petty-bourgeois philistines, such as the value of life and the best way to enjoy life, are themselves so philistine that they explain his anger at Goethe's Faust. It was really unpardonable of Goethe to make a hero of the unmoral Faust and not of the serious philosopher of reality, Wagner.

In short, the philosophy of reality proves to be what Hegel would call "the weakest residue of the German Enlightenment"—a residue whose tenuosity and transparent commonplace character are made more substantial and opaque only by the mixing in of crumbs of oracular rhetoric. And now that we have finished the book we are just as wise as we were at the start, and we are forced to admit that the "new mode of thought," the "conclusions and views which are original from the foundation upwards" and the "system-creating ideas," though they have certainly shown us a great variety of original nonsense, have not provided us with a single line from which we might have been able to learn something. And this man who praises his talents and his wares to the noise of cymbals and trumpets as loudly as any market quack, and behind whose great words there is nothing, absolutely and completely nothing—this man has the temerity to say of people like Fichte, Schelling and Hegel, the least of whom is a giant compared with him, that they are charlatans. Undoubtedly there is a charlatan—but who is it?

PART II

POLITICAL ECONOMY

I. SUBJECT MATTER AND METHOD

Political economy, in the widest sense, is the science of the laws governing the production and exchange of the material means of subsistence in human society. Production and exchange are two different functions. Production can occur without exchange, exchange —being necessarily only exchange of products—cannot occur without production. Each of these two social functions is subject to the action of external influences which are for the most part peculiar to it and for this reason each has also, for the most part, its own special laws. But on the other hand, they always determine and influence each other to such an extent that they might be termed the abscissa and ordinate of the economic curve.

The conditions under which men produce and exchange vary from country to country, and within each country again from generation to generation. Political economy, therefore, cannot be the same for all countries and for all historical epochs. A vast distance separates the bow and arrow, the stone knife and the rare and exceptional acts of exchange among savages, from the steam engine of a thousand horse power, the mechanical loom, the railways and the Bank of England. The Patagonians have not got as far as mass production and world trade, any more than they have experience of bill-jobbing or a Stock Exchange crash. Anyone who attempted to bring Patagonia's political economy under the same laws as are operative in present-day England would obviously produce only the most banal commonplaces. Political economy is therefore essentially a *historical* science. It deals with material which is historical, that is, constantly changing; it must first investigate the special laws of each separate stage in the evolution of production and exchange, and only when it has completed this investigation will it be able to establish the few quite general laws which hold good for production and exchange as a whole. At the same time, it goes without saying that the laws which are valid for definite modes of production and

163

forms of exchange also hold good for all historical periods in which these modes of production and forms of exchange prevail. Thus, for example, the introduction of metallic money brought into play a series of laws which remain valid for all countries and historical epochs in which metallic money is the medium of exchange.

Along with the mode and method of production and exchange in a definite historical society, and the historical conditions which have given birth to this society, the mode and method of distribution of the products is also given. In the tribal or village community with common ownership of the land—with which, or with the easily recognisable survivals of which, all civilised peoples first enter history—a fairly equal distribution of products is a matter of course; where considerable inequality of distribution among the members of the community is found, this is already an indication that the community is beginning to break up. Both large and small-scale agriculture admit of very diverse forms of distribution, according to the historical conditions in which they developed. But it is obvious that large scale farming always gives rise to a distribution which is quite different from that of small-scale farming; that large-scale agriculture presupposes or creates a class antagonism—slave-owners and slaves, feudal lords and serfs, capitalists and wage-workers—while small-scale agriculture does not necessarily involve class differences between the individuals engaged in agricultural production, and that on the contrary the mere existence of a class differentiation indicates the approaching dissolution of the small-farming economy.

The introduction and wide diffusion of metallic money in a country in which hitherto a natural economy has been universal or predominant is always associated with a more or less rapid revolutionisation of the former mode of distribution, and this takes place in such a way that the inequality of distribution among the individuals and therefore the antagonism between rich and poor becomes more pronounced. The local handicraft production of the Middle Ages, based on the guild, was incompatible with big capitalists and life-long wage-workers, just as these are necessarily produced by modern large-scale industry and the credit system of the present day, together with free competition, the form of exchange which corresponds with the development of industry and credit.

But with the differences in distribution, *class differences* emerge. Society divides into classes: the privileged and the dispossessed, the exploiters and the exploited, the rulers and the ruled; and the state, which the primitive groups of communities of the same tribe had at first arrived at only for safeguarding their common interests (such as irrigation in the East) and providing protection against external enemies, from this stage onwards acquires just as much the function of maintaining by force the economic and political position of the ruling class against the subject class.

Distribution, however, is not a merely passive result of production and exchange; it has an equally important reaction on both of these. Each new mode of production or form of exchange is at first retarded not only by the old forms and the political institutions which correspond to these, but also by the old mode of distribution; it can only secure the distribution which is essential to it in the course of a long struggle. But the more mobile a given mode of production and exchange, the more capable it is of expansion and development, the more rapidly does distribution also reach the stage in which it gets beyond its mother's control and comes into conflict with the prevailing mode of production and exchange. The old primitive communities which have already been mentioned could remain in existence for thousands of years—as in India and among the Slavs up to the present day—before intercourse with the outside world gave rise to the inequalities of property as a result of which they began to break up. Modern capitalist production, on the contrary, which is hardly three hundred years old and has only become predominant since the introduction of large-scale industry, that is, only in the last hundred years, has in this short time brought about contradictions in distribution—concentration of capital in a few hands on the one side and the concentration of the propertyless masses in the big towns on the other—which must of necessity bring about its downfall.

The connection between distribution and the material conditions of existence of society at each period is so much a matter of course that it is always reflected in popular instinct. So long as a mode of production is still in the rising stage of its development, it is enthusiastically welcomed even by those who come off worst from its corresponding mode of distribution. This was the case with the English workers in the beginnings of large-scale industry. So long as this mode of production remains normal for society, there is general contentment with the distribution, and if objections to it begin to be raised, these come from within the ruling class itself (Saint-Simon, Fourier, Owen) and at first find no response among the exploited masses. Only when the mode of production in question has already a good part of its declining phase behind it, when it has half out-lived its day, when the conditions of its existence have to a large extent disappeared, and its successor is already knocking at the door —it is only at this stage that the constantly increasing inequality of distribution appears as unjust, it is only then that appeal is made from the facts which have had their day to so-called eternal justice. From a scientific standpoint, this appeal to morality and justice does not help us an inch further; to economic science, moral indig-nation, however justifiable, cannot serve as an argument, but only as a symptom. The task of economic science is rather to show the social abuses which are now developing as necessary consequences of the existing mode of production, but at the same time also as the indications of its imminent dissolution; and to reveal, within the already dissolving economic development, the elements of the future new organisation of production and exchange which will put an end to those abuses. The indignation which creates the poet is abso-lutely in place in describing these terrible conditions, and also in attacking those apostles of harmony in the service of the ruling class who either deny or palliate these abuses; but how little it can *prove* anything for the particular case is evident from the fact that in *each* epoch of all past history there has been no lack of material for such indignation.

Political economy, however, as the science of the conditions and forms under which the various human societies have produced and exchanged and on this basis have distributed their products—politi-cal economy in this wider sense has still to be brought into being. Such economic science as we have up to the present is almost exclu-sively limited to the genesis and development of the capitalist mode of production; it begins with the critique of the survivals of the feudal forms of production and exchange, shows the necessity of their replacement by capitalist forms, and then develops the laws of the capitalist mode of production and its corresponding forms of exchange in their positive aspects, that is, the aspects in which they further the general aims of society, and ends with the socialist critique of the capitalist mode of production, that is, with the statement of its laws in their negative aspects, with the demonstration that this mode of production, through its own development, drives towards the point at which it makes itself impossible. This critique proves that the capitalist forms of production and exchange become more and more an intolerable fetter on production itself, that the mode of distribution necessarily determined by these forms has produced a class position which is daily becoming more intolerable—the antagonism, sharpening from day to day, between capitalists, constantly decreasing in number but constantly growing richer, and propertyless wage workers, whose number is constantly increasing and whose conditions, taken as a whole, are steadily deteriorating; and finally, that the colossal productive forces developed within the capitalist system of production, which the latter can no longer master, are only waiting to be taken possession of by a society organised for co-operative working on a planned basis to ensure to all members of society the means of existence and the full development of their capacities, and indeed in constantly increasing measure.

In order to carry out this critique of bourgeois economy completely, an acquaintance with the capitalist form of production, exchange and distribution did not suffice. The forms which had preceded it or those which still exist alongside it in less developed countries had also, at least in their main features, to be examined and compared. Such an investigation and comparison has up to the present been made only by Marx, and we therefore owe almost exclusively to his researches all that has up to now been established on the theory of pre-bourgeois political economy.

Although it first took shape in the minds of a few men of genius towards the end of the seventeenth century, political economy in the narrow sense, in its positive formulation by the physiocrats and Adam Smith, is nevertheless essentially a child of the eighteenth century, and takes its place with the achievements of the contemporary great French philosophers of the Enlightenment, sharing with them all the merits and defects of that period. What we have said of the philosophers of the Enlightenment is also true of the contemporary economists. To them, the new science was not the expression of the conditions and requirements of their epoch, but the expression of eternal Reason; the laws of production and exchange discovered by them were not laws of a historically determined form of these activities, but eternal laws of Nature; they were deduced from the nature of man. But this man, when examined more closely, was the middle burgher of that epoch, in the state of transition to the modern bourgeois, and his nature consisted in making commodities and trading in accordance with the historically determined conditions of that period.

Now that we have acquired sufficient knowledge of our maker of "critical foundations," Herr Dühring, and his method on the philosophical field, it will not be difficult for us to foretell the way in which he will also handle political economy. In philosophy, in so far as his writings were not simply drivel (as in the philosophy of nature), his mode of outlook was a distortion of that of the eighteenth century. It was not a question of historical laws of development, but of laws of Nature, eternal truths. Social relations such as morality and law were determined, not by the actual historical conditions of the age, but by the famous two men, one of whom either oppressed the other or did not—though the latter alternative, sad to say, has never yet come to pass. We are therefore hardly likely to go astray if we conclude that Herr Dühring will base political economy also on final and ultimate truths, eternal laws of Nature, and the most empty and barren tautological axioms; that nevertheless he will smuggle in again by the back door the whole positive content of political economy, so far as this is known to him; and that he will not develop distribution, as a social phenomenon, out of production and exchange, but that he will hand it over to his famous two men for them to solve in a final form. And as all these are tricks with which we are already familiar, our treatment of this question can be all the shorter.

In fact, even on page 2, Herr Dühring tells us that his economics links up with what has been "*established*" in his philosophy, and "in certain essential points depends on *truths* of a higher order

which have already been settled in a higher field of investigation."
Everywhere the same importunate eulogy of himself; everywhere
Herr Dühring is triumphant at what Herr Dühring has established
and put out. Put out, yes, we have seen it to surfeit—but put out in
the way that people put out a sputtering candle.

Immediately afterwards we find "the most general *laws of Nature*
governing all economy"—so our forecast was right. But a correct
understanding of past history, we are told, can only be given by
these laws if they are "investigated in that more precise determination which their results have experienced through the political forms
of subjection and grouping. Institutions such as slavery and serfdom along with which is associated their twin brother, property
based on force, must be regarded as social and economic constitutional forms of a purely political nature, and in the world up to
now they have constituted the frame within which the consequences
of the economic laws of Nature could alone manifest themselves."

This sentence is the fanfare which, like a *leitmotif* in Wagner's
operas, announces the approach of the famous two men. But it is
more than this: it is the basic theme of Herr Dühring's whole book.
In the sphere of law, Herr Dühring could only give us a bad translation of Rousseau's theory of equality into the language of socialism, such as one has long been able to hear more effectively rendered in any tavern in Paris where workers foregather. Now he gives
us an equally bad socialist translation of the economist's laments
over the falsification of the eternal economic laws of Nature and of
their effects owing to the intervention of the state, of force. And in
this Herr Dühring stands, deservedly, absolutely alone among socialists. Every socialist worker, no matter of what nationality, knows
quite well that force only protects exploitation, but does not cause
it; that the relation between capital and wage labour is the basis
of his exploitation, and that this arose through purely economic
causes and not at all by means of force.

Then we are further told that in all economic questions "two
processes, that of production and that of distribution, can be distinguished." Also that J. B. Say, notorious for his superficiality,
mentioned in addition a third process, that of use, of consumption,
but that he was unable to say anything intelligible about it, any

more than his successor. That exchange or circulation is, however, only a sub-department of production, which covers all the operations required for the products to reach the final and actual consumers.—By confounding the two essentially different, though also reciprocally influencing, processes of production and circulation, and asserting quite calmly that the avoidance of this confusion can only "give rise to confusion," Herr Dühring merely shows that he either does not know or does not understand the colossal development which precisely circulation has undergone during the last fifty years—as indeed is further borne out by the rest of his book.

But this is not all. After thus lumping together production and exchange into one, as simply production, he then puts distribution *alongside* of production, as a second, quite external process, which has nothing whatever to do with the first. Now we have seen that distribution, in its decisive features, is always the necessary result of the production and exchange relations of a particular society, as well as of the historical conditions in which this society arose; so much so that when we know these relations and conditions, we can confidently infer the mode of distribution which operates in this society. But we see also that if Herr Dühring does not want to be unfaithful to the basic principles "established" by him in his theories of morality, law and history, he is compelled to deny this elementary economic fact, and in fact that he must deny it if he is to smuggle his indispensable two men into economics. And once distribution has been happily deprived of all connection with production and exchange, this great event can come to pass.

Let us first recall how Herr Dühring developed his argument in morals and law. He started originally with one man, and he said: "One man conceived as being alone, or, what is in effect the same, out of all relation with other men, can have no *obligations*; for such a man there can be no question of *duty* but only of his own will." But what is this man, conceived as being alone and without obligations, but the unfortunate "original Jew Adam" in Paradise, where he is without sin precisely because there is no possibility for him to commit any? However, even this "philosopher of reality" Adam is destined to fall into sin. Alongside of this Adam there suddenly appears—not, it is true, an Eve with rippling tresses, but a second Adam. And instantly Adam acquires obligations and—breaks them. Instead of treating his brother as having equal rights and clasping him to his breast, he subjects him to his domination, he makes a slave of him—and it is the consequences of this first sin, the original sin of the subjection of man, from which the world has suffered through the whole course of history up to the present day—and it is this, too, that makes Herr Dühring think it is not worth three farthings.

Incidentally, Herr Dühring considered that he had brought the "negation of the negation" sufficiently into contempt by characterising it as a copy of the old story of original sin and redemption—but what are we to say of *his* latest version of the same story? (for, in due time, we shall have to "come to close quarters," to use an expression of the reptile press, with redemption as well). In any case, we must surely say that we prefer the old Semitic tribal legend, according to which it was worth their while for the man and woman to abandon the state of innocence, and that Herr Dühring will be left the uncontested glory of having constructed his original sin with two men.

Let us now see how he translates this original sin into economic terms: "We can get an appropriate conceptual scheme for the idea of production from the conception of a Robinson Crusoe who is facing Nature alone with his own powers and has not to share with anyone else. . . . Equally appropriate for the representation of what is essential in the idea of distribution is the conceptual scheme of two persons, who combine their economic forces and who must evidently come to a mutual understanding in some form as to their separate shares. In fact nothing more than this simple dualism is required to enable us accurately to portray some of the most important relations of distribution and to study their laws in germ in their logical necessity. . . . Co-operative working on an equal footing is here just as conceivable as the combination of forces through the complete subjection of one party, who is then compelled to render economic service as a slave or as a mere tool and is maintained also only as a tool. . . . Between the state of equality and

that of nullity on the one part and omnipotence and one-sided active
participation on the other, there is a range of stages which the
events of world history have filled in rich variety. A universal survey of the various historical institutions of *justice* and *injustice* is
here the essential pre-supposition" ... and finally the whole question of distribution is transformed into an "economic right of distribution."

Now at last Herr Dühring has firm ground under his feet again.
Arm in arm with his two men he can issue his challenge to his age.
But behind this trinity stands another unknown man.

"Capital has not invented surplus labour. Wherever a part of
society possesses the monopoly of the means of production, the
labourer, free or not free, must add to the working time necessary
for his own maintenance an extra working time in order to produce
the means of subsistence for the owners of the means of production,
whether this proprietor be the Athenian καλὸς κἀγαθός, Etruscan
theocrat, *Civis romanus* (Roman citizen), Norman baron, American slave owner, Wallachian Boyard, modern landlord or capitalist." *

When Herr Dühring had thus learnt what is the basic form of
exploitation common to all forms of production up to the present
day—so far as these have developed in class antagonisms—all he
had to do was to apply his two men to it, and the deep-rooted foundations of the economics of reality was completed. He did not hesi-
tate for a moment to carry out this "system-creating idea." Labour
without any payment in return, beyond the labour time necessary
for the maintenance of the labourer—that is the point. The Adam,
who is here called Robinson Crusoe, makes his second Adam—
Man Friday—drudge incessantly. But why does Friday toil more
than is necessary for his maintenance? To this question also Marx
has provided a partial answer. But this answer is far too long-
winded for the two men. The matter is settled in a trice: Robinson
Crusoe "oppresses" Friday, compels him "to render economic service as a slave or a tool" and maintains him "also only as a tool."
With this latest "creative idea" of his, Herr Dühring as it were kills
two birds with one stone. First he saves himself the trouble of

* Marx, *Capital*, Vol. I, pp. 259-60 (Kerr edition).

explaining the various forms of distribution which have hitherto existed, their differences and their causes; taken in the lump, they are simply of no account—they rest on oppression, on force. We shall have to deal with this in a moment. In the second place, his treatment of the questions transfers the whole theory of distribution from the sphere of economics to that of morals and law, that is, from the sphere of established material facts to that of more or less unstable opinions and sentiments. He therefore no longer has any need to investigate or to prove things; he can simply go on declaiming, and he can advance the claim that the distribution of the products of labour should be regulated, not in accordance with its real causes, but in accordance with what seems moral and just to Herr Dühring. But what seems just to Herr Dühring is not at all immutable, and is therefore very far from being a real truth. For real truths, according to Herr Dühring himself, are "absolutely immutable." In 1868 Herr Dühring asserted—*Die Schicksale meiner sozialen Denkschrift, etc.**—that it was "an inherent tendency of all higher civilisations *to give a more and more sharply marked character to property*, and in this, not in confusion of rights and spheres of sovereignty, lies the essence and the future of modern developments." And furthermore, he was quite unable to see "*how a transformation of wage labour into another form of acquisition is ever to be reconciled with the laws of human nature and the natural and necessary structure of the body social*." Thus in 1868, private property and wage labour are a necessity of nature and therefore just; in 1876, both of these are the emanation of force and "robbery" and therefore unjust. And we cannot possibly foretell what in a few years' time may seem moral and just to such a mighty and impetuous genius, so that in any case we should do better, in considering the distribution of wealth, to stick to the real objective, economic laws and not to depend on the momentary, changeable, subjective conceptions of Herr Dühring as to what is just or unjust.

If for the imminent overthrow of the present mode of distribution of the products of labour, with its crying contrasts of want and luxury, starvation and debauchery, we had no better guarantee than the consciousness that this mode of distribution is unjust, and that

* *The Fate of My Social Memorial, etc.*—Ed.

justice must eventually triumph, we should be in a pretty bad way, and we might have a long time to wait. The mystics of the Middle Ages who dreamed of the coming millennium were already conscious of the injustice of class contradictions. On the threshold of modern history, three hundred and fifty years ago, Thomas Münzer proclaimed it loudly to the world. In the English and the French bourgeois revolutions the same call resounded—and died away. And if today the same call for the abolition of class antagonisms and class divisions, which up to 1830 had left the working and suffering masses cold, if today this call is re-echoed a millionfold, if it takes hold of one country after another in the same order and in the same degree of intensity that large-scale industry develops in each country, if in one generation it has gained a strength that enables it to defy all the forces combined against it and to be confident of victory in the near future—what is the reason for this? The reason is that modern large-scale industry has called into being on the one hand a proletariat, a class which for the first time in history can demand the abolition, not of one particular class organization or another, or of one particular class privilege or another, but of classes themselves, and which is in such a position that it must carry through this demand on pain of sinking to the level of the Chinese coolie; while this same large-scale industry has on the other hand brought into being, in the bourgeoisie, a class which has the monopoly of all the instruments of production and means of subsistence, but which in each boom period and in each crash that follows on its heels proves that it has become incapable of any longer controlling the productive forces, which have grown beyond its power; a class under whose leadership society is racing to ruin like a locomotive whose jammed safety-valve the driver is too weak to open. In other words, it is because both the productive forces created by the modern capitalist mode of production and also the system of distribution of goods established by it have come into burning contradiction with that mode of production itself, and in fact to such a degree that, if the whole of modern society is not to perish, a revolution of the mode of production and distribution must take place, a revolution which will put an end to all class divisions. On this tangible, material fact, which is impressing itself in a more or less clear form, but with invincible necessity, on the minds of the exploited proletarians—it is on this fact, and not on the conceptions of justice and injustice held by any armchair philosopher, that modern socialism's confidence of victory is founded.

II. THE FORCE THEORY

"In my system, the relation between general politics and the forms of economic law is determined in so definite and at the same time so *original* a way that it would not be superfluous, in order to facilitate study, to make special reference to this point. The formation of *political* relationships is, *historically, the fundamental fact,* and the *economic* facts dependent on this are only an *effect* or a particular case, and are consequently always *facts of the second order.* Some of the newer socialist systems take as their guiding principle, the superficial idea of a completely reverse relationship, in that they make the political phenomena subordinate, and, as it were grow out of the economic conditions. It is true that these effects of the second order do exist as such, and are most clearly perceptible at the present time; but the *primitive* phenomenon must be sought in *direct political force* and not in any indirect economic power."

This conception is also expressed in another passage, in which Herr Dühring "starts from the principle that the political conditions are the determining cause of the economic order and that the reverse relationship represents only a reaction of a secondary character ... so long as anyone treats the political grouping not for its own sake, as the starting point, but merely as a *means through which food can be secured,* then such a person, however radical a socialist and revolutionary he may seem to be, must nevertheless be harbouring a hidden portion of reaction in his mind."

That is Herr Dühring's theory. In this and in many other passages it is merely advanced, or, so to speak, decreed. Nowhere in the three fat volumes is there even the slightest attempt to prove it or to disprove the opposite point of view. And even if the arguments for it were as cheap as blackberries, Herr Dühring would give us none of them. For the whole affair has been already proved through the famous original sin, when Robinson Crusoe made Friday his slave. That was an act of force, that is, a political act. And as this enslave-

176

ment was the starting point and the basic fact underlying all past history and inoculated it with the original sin of injustice, so much so that in the later periods it was only softened down and "transformed into the more indirect forms of economic dependence"; and inasmuch as "property founded on force" which has been maintained right through up to the present day, is likewise based on this original act of enslavement—for these reasons it is clear that all economic phenomena must be explained by political causes, that is, by force. And anyone who is not satisfied with that is a reactionary in disguise.

We must first point out that no one with less regard for himself than Herr Dühring could regard this view as so very "original," which it is not in the least. The idea that outstanding political acts and state actions are the decisive facts in history is as old as written history itself, and is the main reason why so little material has been preserved in regard to the really progressive evolution of the peoples which has taken place quietly in the background behind these noisy scenes on the stage. This idea dominated all the conceptions of historians in the past, and the first blow against it was delivered by the French bourgeois historians of the Restoration period; the only "original" thing about it is that Herr Dühring once again knows nothing of all this.

Furthermore: even if we assume for the moment that Herr Dühring is right in saying that all past history can be traced back to the enslavement of man by man, we are still very far from having got to the bottom of the matter. For the question then arises: how did Robinson Crusoe come to enslave Friday? Just for the pleasure of doing it? No such thing. On the contrary, we see that Friday "is compelled to render *economic* service as a slave or as a mere tool and is maintained only as a tool." Crusoe enslaved Friday only in order that Friday should work for Crusoe's benefit. And how can Crusoe derive any benefit for himself from Friday's labour? Only through Friday producing by his labour more of the necessaries of life than Crusoe has to give him to keep him in a fit state to work. Crusoe, therefore, in violation of Herr Dühring's express prescription, takes the political grouping arising out of Friday's enslavement "not for its own sake, as the starting point, but merely *as a means through which food can be secured*"; and now let him see for himself how he gets the better of his lord and master, Dühring.

The childish example specially selected by Herr Dühring in order to prove that force is "historically the fundamental fact," in reality, therefore, proves that force is only the means, and that the aim is economic advantage. And inasmuch as the aim is "more fundamental" than the means used to secure it, so in history the economic side of the relationship is much more fundamental than the political side. The example therefore proves precisely the opposite of what it was supposed to prove. And as in the case of Robinson Crusoe and Friday, so in all cases of domination and subjection up to the present day. Subjugation has always been—to use Herr Dühring's elegant expression—a "means through which food can be secured" (taking food securing in a very wide sense), and never and nowhere a political grouping established "for its own sake." It takes a Herr Dühring to be able to imagine that state taxes are only "effects of a secondary character," or that the present-day political grouping of the ruling bourgeoisie and the ruled proletariat has come into existence "for its own sake," and not as "a means through which food can be secured" by the ruling capitalists, that is to say, for the sake of making profits and the accumulation of capital.

However, let us get back again to our two men. Crusoe, "sword in hand," makes Friday his slave. But in order to pull it off, Crusoe needs something more besides his sword. Not every one can make use of a slave. In order to make use of a slave, a man must possess two kinds of things: first, the instruments and material for his slave's labour; and secondly, the minimum means of subsistence for him. Therefore, before slavery becomes possible, a certain level of production must already have been reached and a certain inequality of distribution must already have appeared. And before slave labour could become the dominant mode of production in a whole social group, an even far higher increase in production, trade and accumulation of wealth was essential. In the ancient primitive communities with common property in the land, slavery either does not exist at all or plays only a very subordinate role. It was the same in the originally peasant city of Rome; but when Rome became a "world city" and the ownership of the land in Italy came more and more into the hands of a numerically small class of enormously rich proprietors, the peasant population was supplanted by a population of slaves. If at the time of the Persian wars the number of slaves in Corinth rose to 460,000 and in Aegina to 470,000 and there were ten slaves to every freeman; something more than "force" was involved, namely, a highly developed arts and handicraft industry and an extensive commerce. Slavery in the United States of America was based far less on force than on the English cotton industry; in those districts where no cotton was grown or which, unlike the border states, did not breed slaves for the cotton-growing states, it died out of itself without any force being used, simply because it did not pay.

In calling property as it exists today property founded on force, and in characterising it as "that form of domination *at the root of which lies* not merely the exclusion of a fellow man from the use of the natural means of subsistence, but also, what is far more important, the subjugation of the man for menial work"—in doing this, Herr Dühring is therefore making the whole relationship stand on its head. The subjugation of a man for menial work, in all its forms, presupposes that the subjugator has at his disposal the instruments of labour with the help of which alone he is able to employ the oppressed person and in the case of slavery, in addition, the means of subsistence which enable him to keep his slave alive. In all cases, therefore, it presupposes the possession of a certain amount of property, in excess of the average. How did this come about? In any case it is clear that it may in fact have been robbed, and that therefore it may be based on *force*, but that this is by no means necessary. It may have been got by labour, it may have been stolen or it may have been obtained by trade or by fraud. In fact, it must have been obtained by labour before there is any possibility of its being robbed.

Historically, private property by no means makes its appearance as the result of robbery or violence. On the contrary. It already existed, even though it was limited to certain objects, in the ancient primitive communes of all civilised peoples. It developed even within these communes, at first through barter with strangers, till it reached the form of commodities. The more the products of the commune assumed the commodity form, that is, the less they were produced for their producers' own use and the more for the purpose of exchange, the more the original primitive division of labour was

replaced by exchange also within the commune, the more did inequality develop in the property of the individual members of
the commune, the more deeply was the ancient common ownership
of the land undermined, and the more rapidly did the commune
move towards its dissolution and transformation into a village of
small peasants. For thousands of years Oriental depotism and the
changing rule of conquering nomad peoples were unable to change
this old form of commune; it saw the gradual destruction of their
original home industry by the competition of products of large-
scale industry which brought them nearer and nearer to dissolution.
Force was as little involved in this process as in the dividing up,
still now taking place, of the cultivated land held in common in the
Gehöferschaften on the Moselle and in the Hochwald; the peasants
find it actually to their advantage that private ownership of cultivated land should take the place of common ownership. Even the
formation of a primitive aristocracy, as in the case of the Celts, the
Germans and the Indian Punjab, took place on the basis of common
ownership of the land, and at first was not based in any way on force,
but on voluntary goodwill and custom. Everywhere where private
property developed, this took place as the result of altered relations
of production and exchange, in the interests of increased production
and in furtherance of intercourse—that is to say, as a result of economic causes. Force plays no part in this at all. Indeed, it is clear
that the institution of private property must be already in existence
before the robber can *appropriate* another person's property, and
that therefore force may be able to change the possessor but cannot
create private property as such.

Nor can we use either force or property founded on force to explain the "subjugation of man for menial work" in its most modern
form—wage labour. We have already mentioned the role played
in the dissolution of the primitive communes, that is, in the direct or
indirect generalisation of private property, by the transformation
of the products of labour into commodities, their production not for
consumption of their own producers, but for exchange. In *Capital*,
Marx proved with absolute clarity—and Herr Dühring avoids even
the slightest reference to this—that at a certain stage of development the production of commodities becomes transformed into capi-

talist production, and that at this stage "the laws of appropriation or of private property, laws that are based on the production and circulation of commodities, become, by their own inner and inexorable dialectic, changed into their very opposite. The exchange of equivalents, the original operation with which we started, has now become turned round in such a way that there is only an apparent exchange. This is owing to the fact, first, that the capital which is exchanged for labour power is itself but a portion of the product of others' labour appropriated without an equivalent; and secondly, that this capital must not only be replaced by its producer, but replaced together with an added surplus.... At first the rights of property seemed to us to be based on a man's own labour.... Now, however [at the end of the Marxian development], property turns out to be the right, on the part of the capitalist, to appropriate the unpaid labour of others or its product, and, on the part of the labourer, the impossibility of appropriating his own product. The separation of property from labour has become the necessary consequence of a law that apparently originated in their identity."

In other words, even if we exclude all possibility of robbery, violence and fraud, even if we assume that all private property was originally based on the owner's individual labour, and that throughout the whole subsequent process there was only exchange of equal values for equal values, the progressive evolution of production and exchange nevertheless brings us with necessity to the present capitalist mode of production, to the monopolisation of the means of production and the means of subsistence in the hands of a numerically small class, to the degradation of the other class, constituting the immense majority, into propertyless proletarians, to the periodic succession of production booms and commercial crises and to the whole of the present anarchy of production. The whole process is explained by purely economic causes; robbery, force, the state or political interference of any kind are unnecessary at any point whatever. "Property founded on force" proves here also to be nothing but the phrase of a braggart intended to cover up his lack of understanding of the real course of things.

This course of things, expressed historically, is the history of the evolution of the bourgeoisie. If "political conditions are the decisive cause of the economic order," then the modern bourgeoisie cannot have developed in struggle with feudalism, but must be the latter's voluntarily begotten pet child. Everyone knows that what took place was the opposite. Originally an oppressed estate liable to pay dues to the ruling feudal nobility, recruited from serfs and villeins of every type, the burghers conquered one position after another in continuous struggle with the nobility, and finally, in the most highly developed countries, took power in its stead: in France, by directly overthrowing the nobility; in England, by making it more and more bourgeois, and incorporating it as the ornamental head of the bourgeoisie itself. And how did it accomplish this? Simply through a change in the "economic order," which sooner or later, voluntarily or as the outcome of struggle, was followed by a change in the political conditions. The struggle of the bourgeoisie against the feudal nobility is the struggle of the town against the country, of industry against landed property, of money economy against barter economy; and the decisive weapon of the burghers in this struggle was their *economic* power, constantly increasing through the development first of handicraft industry, at a later stage progressing to manufacturing industry, and through the extension of commerce. During the whole of this struggle political force was on the side of the nobility, except for a period when the Crown used the burghers against the nobility, in order that the two "estates" might keep each other in check; but from the moment when the burghers, still politically powerless, began to grow dangerous owing to their increasing economic power, the Crown resumed its alliance with the nobility, and by so doing called forth the bourgeois revolution, first in England and then in France. The "political conditions" in France had remained unaltered, while the "economic order" had outgrown them. In political rank the nobleman was everything, the burgher nothing; but from the social standpoint the burgher was now the most important class in the state, while the nobleman had lost all his social functions and was now only drawing in, in the revenues that came to him, payment for these functions which had disappeared. Nor was that all. In all their production the burghers had remained hemmed in by the feudal political forms of the Middle Ages, which this production—not only manufacture, but even handicraft industry—had long outgrown; they had remained hemmed in by all the thousandfold guild privileges and local and provincial customs barriers which had become mere irritants and fetters on production. The bourgeois revolution put an end to this. Not, however, by adjusting the economic order to suit the political conditions, in accordance with Herr Dühring's principle—this was precisely what the nobles and the king had been vainly trying to do for years—but by doing the opposite, by casting aside the old mouldering political rubbish and creating political conditions in which the new "economic order" could exist and develop. And in this political and legal atmosphere which was suited to its needs it developed brilliantly, so brilliantly that the bourgeoisie already almost occupies the position filled by the nobility in 1789: it is becoming more and more not only socially superfluous, but a social hindrance; it is more and more becoming separated from productive activity, and becoming more and more, like the nobility in the past, a class merely drawing in revenues; and it has accomplished this revolution in its own position and the creation of a new class, the proletariat, without any hocus-pocus of force whatever, and in a purely economic way. Even more: it did not in any way will this result of its own actions and activities—on the contrary this developed of itself with irresistible force, against the will and contrary to the intentions of the bourgeoisie; its own productive powers have grown beyond its control, and, as with the force of a law of Nature, are driving the whole of bourgeois society forward to ruin or revolution. And when the bourgeoisie now make their appeal to force in order to save the collapsing "economic order" from the final crash, by so doing they only show that they are caught in the same illusion as Herr Dühring: the illusion that "political conditions are the decisive cause of the economic order"; they show that they imagine, just as Herr Dühring does, that by making use of the "primitive phenomenon," "direct political force," they can remodel those "facts of the second order," the economic order and its inevitable development; and that therefore the economic consequences of the steam engine and the modern machinery driven by it, of world trade and the banking and credit developments of the present day, can be blown out of existence with Krupp guns and Mauser rifles.

III. THE FORCE THEORY (CONTINUATION)

But let us look a little more closely at this omnipotent "force" of Herr Dühring's. Crusoe enslaved Friday "sword in hand." Where did he get the sword from? Even on the imaginary islands of Crusoe stories, swords have not, up to now, grown on trees, and Herr Dühring gives us no answer whatever to this question. Just as Crusoe could procure a sword for himself, we are equally entitled to assume that one fine morning Friday might appear with a loaded revolver in his hand, and then the whole "force" relationship is inverted. Friday commands, and it is Crusoe who has to drudge. We must apologise to the readers for returning with such insistence to the Crusoe and Friday story, which properly belongs to the nursery and not to science—but how can we help it? We are compelled to apply Herr Dühring's axiomatic method conscientiously, and it is not our fault if in doing so we have to keep all the time within the field of pure childishness. So, then, the revolver triumphs over the sword; and this will probably make even the most childish axiomatician comprehend that force is no mere act of the will, but requires very real preliminary conditions before it can come into operation, that is to say, *instruments*, the more perfect of which vanquish the less perfect; moreover, that these instruments have to be produced, which also implies that the producer of more perfect instruments of force, *vulgo* arms, vanquishes the producer of the less perfect instrument, and that, in a word, the triumph of force is based on the production of arms, and this in turn on production in general —therefore, on "economic power," on the "economic order," on the *material* means which force has at its disposal.

Force, nowadays, is the army and navy, and both, as we all know to our cost, are "devilishly expensive." Force, however, cannot make any money; at most it can only take away money that has already been made—and even this does not help very much—as we have seen, also to our cost, in the case of the French milliards. In the last analysis, therefore, money must be provided through the medium of economic production; and so once again force is conditioned by the economic order, which furnishes the resources for the equipment and maintenance of the instruments of force. But even that is not all. Nothing is more dependent on economic pre-conditions than precisely the army and navy. Their armaments, composition, organisation, tactics and strategy depend above all on the stage reached at the time in production and communications. It is not the "free creations of the mind" of generals of genius which have revolutionised war, but the invention of better weapons and changes in the human material, the soldiers; at the very most, the part played by generals of genius is limited to adapting methods of fighting to the new weapons and combatants.

At the beginning of the fourteenth century, gunpowder came from the Arabs to Western Europe, and, as every school child knows, completely revolutionised methods of warfare. The introduction of gunpowder and firearms, however, was not at all an act of force, but a step forward in industry, that is, an economic advance. Industry remains industry, whether it is applied to the production or the destruction of things. And the introduction of firearms had a revolutionising effect not only on the waging of war itself, but also on the political relationships of domination and subjection. The provision of powder and firearms required industry and money, and both of these were in the hands of the burghers of the towns. From the outset, therefore, firearms were the weapons of the towns, and of the rising monarchy drawing its support from the towns, against the feudal nobility. The stone walls of the nobleman's castles, hitherto unapproachable, fell before the cannon of the burghers, and the bullets of the burghers' arquebuses pierced the armour of the knights. With the armour-clad cavalry of the feudal lords, the feudal lords' supremacy was also broken; with the development of the bourgeoisie, infantry and guns became more and more the decisive types of weapons; compelled by the development of artillery, the military profession had to add to its organisation a new and entirely industrial sub-section, the corps of engineers.

The improvement of firearms was a very slow process. Artillery remained clumsy and the musket, in spite of a number of inventions affecting details, was still a crude weapon. It took over three hundred years before a weapon was constructed which was suitable for the equipment of the whole body of infantry. It was not until the early part of the eighteenth century that the flint-lock musket with a bayonet finally displaced the pike in the equipment of the infantry. The foot soldiers of that period were the mercenaries of princes; they consisted of the most demoralized elements of society, rigorously disciplined, but quite unreliable and only held together by the whip; they were often enemy prisoners of war who had been pressed into service. The only type of fighting in which these soldiers could apply the new weapons was the tactics of the line, which reached its highest perfection under Frederick II. The whole infantry of an army was drawn up in triple ranks in the form of a very long, hollow square, and moved in battle order only as a whole; at very most, one or other of the two wings might move forward or withdraw a little. This cumbrous mass could only move in formation on absolutely level ground, and even then only at a very slow rate (seventy-five paces a minute); a change of formation during a battle was impossible, and once the infantry was engaged, victory or defeat was decided rapidly and at a single blow.

In the American War of Independence, these cumbrous lines came up against bands of insurgents, which although not drilled were all the better able to shoot from their rifled carbines; these rebels were fighting for their own special interests, and therefore did not desert like the mercenaries; nor did they do the English the kindness of advancing against them also in line and across the open plain, but in scattered and rapidly moving troops of sharpshooters under cover of the woods. In such circumstances the line was powerless and was defeated by its invisible and intangible opponents. Fighting in skirmishing order was re-invented—a new method of warfare which was the result of a change in the human material of war.

In the military sphere also, the French Revolution completed what the American Revolution had begun. Like the American, the French Revolution could oppose to the trained mercenary armies of the coalition only poorly trained but great masses of soldiers, the levy of the whole nation. But these masses had to protect Paris, that is, to hold a definite area, and for this purpose victory in open battle on a mass scale was essential. Mere skirmishes did not suffice; a form had to be invented for use by large bodies of troops, and this form was found in the *column*. Column formation made it possible for even poorly trained troops to move with a fair degree of order, and moreover with greater speed (a hundred paces and more in a minute); it made it possible to break through the rigid forms of the old line formation; to fight on any ground, and therefore even on ground which was extremely disadvantageous to the line formation; to group the troops in any appropriate way; and, in conjunction with attacks by scattered bands of sharpshooters, to hold up the enemy's lines, keeping them occupied and wearing them out until the moment came for masses held in reserve to break through them at the decisive point in the position. This new method of warfare, based on the combined action of skirmishes and columns and on the partitioning of the army into independent divisions or army corps, composed of all types of arms—a method brought to full perfection by Napoleon in both its tactical and strategical aspects —had become necessary primarily because of the changed material: the soldiery of the French Revolution. But it also had two other very important preliminary technical conditions: first, the lighter carriages for field guns constructed by Gribeauval, which alone made possible the more rapid movement now required of them; and secondly, the slanting of the butt, which had hitherto been quite straight, continuing the line of the barrel; introduced in France in 1777, it was copied from hunting weapons and it made it possible to shoot at an individual man without necessarily missing him. But for this improvement it would have been impossible to adopt skirmishing tactics, for which the old weapons were useless.

The revolutionary system of arming the whole people was soon restricted to compulsory conscription (with substitution for the rich, by payment of money) and in this form it was adopted by most of the large states on the Continent. Only Prussia attempted, through its *Landwehr* system, to draw to a still greater extent on the defensive power of the people. After the rifled muzzle-loader, which had been improved between 1830 and 1860 and made suitable for use in war, had played a brief role, Prussia was also the first state to equip its whole infantry with the most up-to-date weapons, the rifled breech-loader. Its successes in 1866 were due to these two factors.

The Franco-Prussian War was the first in which two armies faced each other both equipped with breech-loading rifles, and moreover both fundamentally in the same tactical formations as in the time of the old smooth-bore flint-locks. The only difference was that the Prussians had introduced the company column formation in an attempt to find a form of fighting which was better adapted to the new type of arms. But when, at St. Privat on August 18, the Prussian Guard tried to apply the company column formation seriously, the five regiments which were chiefly engaged lost in less than two hours more than a third of their strength (176 officers and 5,114 men). From that time the company column formation too was condemned, no less than the battalion column and the line; all idea of exposing troops in any kind of closed formation to enemy gunfire was abandoned, and on the German side all subsequent fighting was conducted only in those compact bodies of skirmishers into which the columns had so far regularly dissolved of themselves under a deadly hail of bullets, although this had been opposed by the higher officers on the ground that it was contrary to good discipline; and in the same way the only form of movement when under fire from enemy rifles became the *double*. Once again the soldier had been shrewder than the officer; it was he who instinctively found the only way of fighting which has proved of service up to now under the fire of breech-loading rifles, and in spite of opposition from his officers he carried it through successfully.

The Franco-Prussian War marked a turning-point which was of entirely new significance. In the first place the weapons used have reached such a stage of perfection that further progress which would have any revolutionising influence is no longer possible. Once armies have guns which can hit a battalion at any range at which it can be distinguished, and rifles which are equally effective for hitting individual men, whole loading them takes less time than aiming, then all further improvements are more or less unimportant for field warfare. The era of evolution is therefore, in essentials, closed in this direction. And secondly, this war compelled all continental Powers to introduce in a stricter form the Prussian *Landwehr* system, and with it a military burden which must bring them to ruin within a few years. The army has become the main purpose of the state, and an end in itself; the peoples are only there in addition in order to provide and feed the soldiers. Militarism dominates and is swallowing Europe. But this militarism also carries in itself the seed of its own destruction. Competition of the individual states with each other forces them, on the one hand, to spend more money each year on the army and navy, artillery, etc., thus more and more hastening financial catastrophe; and on the other hand, to take universal compulsory military service more and more seriously, thus in the long run making the whole people familiar with the use of arms; and therefore making the people more and more able at a given moment to make its will prevail in opposition to the commanding military lords. And this moment comes as soon as the mass of the people—town and country workers and peasants—*has* a will. At this point the armies of princes become transformed into armies of the people; the machine refuses to work, and militarism collapses by the dialectic of its own evolution. What the bourgeois democracy of 1848 could not accomplish, just because it was *bourgeois* and not proletarian, namely, to give the labouring masses a will whose content was in accord with their class position—socialism will infallibly secure. And this will mean the bursting asunder of militarism *from within*, and with it of all standing armies.

That is the first moral of our history of modern infantry. The second moral, which brings us back again to Herr Dühring, is that the whole organisation and method of fighting of armies, and along with these victory or defeat, proves to be dependent on material, that is, economic conditions; on the human material, and the armaments material, and therefore on the quality and quantity of the population and on technical development. Only a hunting people like the Americans could re-discover skirmishing tactics—and they were hunters as a result of purely economic causes, just as now, as a result of purely economic causes, these same Yankees of the old States have been transformed into farmers, industrialists, seamen and merchants who no longer skirmish in the primeval forests, but instead skirmish all the more effectively on the field of speculation, where they have made considerable progress with it also in its mass application. Only a revolution such as the French, which brought about the economic emancipation of the burghers and especially of the peasantry, could find the method of the mass army and at the same time the free form of movement which shattered the old rigid lines—the military counterparts of the absolutism against which they were fighting. And we have seen in case after case how advances in technique, as soon as they became usable in the military sphere and in fact were so used, immediately and almost violently produced changes in the methods of warfare and indeed revolutionised them, often even against the will of the army command. And nowadays any zealous subaltern could explain to Herr Dühring how greatly the conduct of a war depends on the productivity and means of communication of the army's own hinterland as well as of the arena of war. In short, always and everywhere it is the economic conditions and instruments of force which help "force" to victory, and without these, force ceases to be force. And anyone who tried to reform methods of warfare from the opposite standpoint, on the basis of Dühringian principles, would certainly reap nothing but a beating.*

If we pass now from land to sea, even in the last twenty years we find a complete revolution of quite a different order. The warship of the Crimean war was the wooden two and three-decker of 60 to 100 guns; these were still mainly sailing ships, with only a low-powered auxiliary steam engine. The guns on these warships were for the most part 32-pounders, weighing approximately 2½ tons, with a few 68-pounders weighing approximately 4¾ tons. Towards the end of the war, iron-clad floating batteries made their appearance; they were clumsy and almost immobile, but to the guns of that period they were invulnerable monsters. Soon the iron armour plating was applied also to warships; at first the plates were still very thin, a ship with plates four inches thick being regarded as extremely heavily armoured. But soon the progress made with artillery outstripped the armour-plating; each successive increase in the strength of the armour used was countered by a new and heavier gun which easily

* This is already perfectly well known to the Prussian General Staff. "The *basis* of warfare is primarily the general *economic* life of the peoples." This was said in a scientific lecture by Herr Max Jähns, a captain of the General Staff. (*Kölnische Zeitung*, April 20, 1876, p. 3.) [*Note by F. Engels.*]

pierced the plates. In this way we have already reached armour-plating ten, twelve, fourteen and twenty-four inches in thickness (Italy proposes to build a ship with plates three feet thick) on the one hand, and on the other, rifled guns of 25, 35, 80 and even 100 tons in weight, which can hurl projectiles, weighing 300, 400, 1,700 and up to 2,000 pounds to distances which were never dreamed of before. The warship of the present day is a gigantic armoured screw-driven vessel of 8,000 to 9,000 tons and 6,000 to 8,000 horse power, with revolving turrets and four or at most six heavy guns and with a bow extended under water into a ram for running down enemy vessels; it is a single colossal machine, in which steam not only drives the ship at a high speed, but also works the steering-gear, raises the anchor, swings the turrets, changes the elevation of the guns and loads them, pumps out water, hoists and lowers the boats— some of which are themselves also steam-driven—and so forth. And the rivalry between armour-plating and the efficacy of guns is so far from being at an end that nowadays a ship is almost always not up to requirements, already out of date, before it is launched. The modern warship is not only a product, but at the same time a speci-men of modern large-scale industry, a floating factory—producing mainly, to be sure, a lavish waste of money. The country in which large-scale industry is most highly developed has almost a monop-oly in the construction of these ships. All Turkish, almost all Rus-sian and most German armoured vessels are built in England; serviceable armour-plates are hardly made outside of Sheffield; of the three steel works in Europe which alone are able to make the heaviest guns, two (Woolwich and Elswick) are in England, and the third (Krupp) in Germany. In this sphere it is most palpably evident that the "direct political force" which, according to Herr Dühring, is the "determining cause of the economic order," is on the contrary completely subordinated to the economic order; that not only the construction but also the manipulation of the marine instrument of force, the warship, has itself become a branch of modern large-scale industry. And that this is so distresses no one more than force itself, that is, the state, which has now to pay for one ship as much as a whole fleet used to cost; which has to resign itself to seeing these ex-pensive vessels becoming already out of date, and therefore worth-

less, before they get into the water; and which must certainly be just
as disgusted as Herr Dühring that the man of the "economic order,"
the engineer, is now of far greater importance on board than the
man of "direct force," the captain. We, on the contrary, have absolutely no cause for annoyance when we see that, in this competitive
struggle between armour-plating and guns, the warship is being
developed to a pitch of perfection which is making it both outra-
geously costly and unusable in war,* and that this struggle makes
manifest also in the sphere of naval warfare those immanent dialectical laws of motion on the basis of which militarism, like all other
historical phenomena, is being brought to destruction as a result of
its own development.

Here too, therefore, we see absolutely clearly that it is not in any
way true "the primitive phenomenon must be sought in direct political force and not in any indirect economic power." On the contrary. For what in fact does "the primitive" in force itself prove to
be? Economic power, control over the means of force in large-scale
industry. Political naval power, which is dependent on modern warships, proves to be not at all "direct" but on the contrary *conditioned*
by economic power, the high development of metallurgy, and the
command of skilled technicians and productive coal mines.

And yet what is the use of it all? If we put Herr Dühring in supreme command in the next naval war, he will utterly destroy all
fleets of armoured ships, which are the slaves of the economic order,
without torpedoes or any other artifices, by sole virtue of his
"direct force."

* The perfecting of the latest production of large-scale industry for use in
naval warfare, the self-propelling torpedo, seems likely to bring this to pass;
it would mean that the smallest torpedo-boat would be superior to the most
powerful armoured battle-ship. (It should be borne in mind that the above
was written in 1878.) [*Note by F. Engels.*]

IV. THE FORCE THEORY (CONCLUSION)

"It is a circumstance of great importance that in fact the domination over *Nature*, generally speaking (!) only proceeded (a domination proceeded) through the domination of *man*. The exploitation of landed property in tracts of considerable size never took place anywhere without the antecedent subjection of man in some form of slavery or serfdom. The establishment of an economic domination over things has presupposed the political, social and economic domination of man over man. How could a large landed proprietor even be conceived without including in this idea also his domination over slaves, serfs, or others indirectly enslaved? What could the efforts of an individual, at most supplemented by those of his family, have signified and ever signify in large-scale agriculture? The exploitation of the land, or the extension of economic control over it on a scale exceeding the natural capacities of the individual, was only made possible in previous history by the establishment, either before or simultaneously with the introduction of dominion over land, of the enslavement of man which this involves. In the later periods of development this servitude was mitigated... its present form in the more highly civilised states is wage labour, to a greater or less degree carried on under police control. Thus wage labour provides the practical possibility of that form of contemporary wealth which is represented by control over wide areas of land and (!) large-scale landed property. It goes without saying that all other types of distributed wealth must be explained historically in an analogous way, and the indirect dependence of man on man, which is now the basic feature of conditions which are most fully developed economically, cannot be understood and explained from their own nature, but only as a somewhat transformed heritage of an earlier direct subjugation and expropriation." Thus Herr Dühring.

Thesis: The domination of Nature (by man) presupposes the domination of man (by man).

Proof: The exploitation of landed *property* in *tracts of consider-able size* never took place anywhere except by the use of serfs.

Proof of the proof: How can there be large landowners without serfs, for the large landowner, even with his family, could cultivate only a tiny part of his property without the help of serfs.

Therefore, so as to prove that man, in order to bring Nature under his control, must first subjugate man, Herr Dühring trans-forms "Nature" without more ado into "landed property in tracts of considerable size," and then this landed property—ownership un-specified—is immediately further transformed into the property of a large landed proprietor, who naturally cannot work his land without serfs.

In the first place "domination over Nature" and the "exploita-tion of landed property" are by no means the same thing. In indus-try, domination over Nature is exercised on quite another and much greater scale than in agriculture, which is still subject to weather conditions instead of controlling them.

Secondly, if we confine ourselves to the exploitation of landed property in tracts of considerable size, the question arises: whose landed property is it? And then we find in the early history of all civilised peoples, not the "great landlords" whom Herr Dühring interpolates here with one of his customary tricks of legerdemain, which he calls "natural dialectics," but tribal and village communi-ties with common ownership of the land. From India to Ireland the exploitation of landed property in tracts of considerable size was originally carried out by such tribal and village communities; sometimes the arable land was cultivated jointly for account of the community, and sometimes in detached parcels of land temporarily allocated to families by the community, while woodland and pas-ture-land continued to be used in common. It is once again charac-teristic of "the most exhaustive specialised studies" made by Herr Dühring "in the domain of politics and law" that he knows nothing of all this; that all his works breathe total ignorance of Maurer's epoch-making writings on the primitive constitution of the Ger-man Mark, the basis of all German law, and of the ever-increasing mass of literature, chiefly stimulated by Maurer, which is devoted to proving the primitive common ownership of the land among all civilized peoples of Europe and Asia, and showing the various forms of its existence and dissolution. Just as in the domain of French and English law Herr Dühring "himself acquired all his ignorance," great as it was, so it is with his even much greater ignorance in the domain of German law. In this domain, the man who flies into such a violent rage over the limited horizon of university professors is himself today, at the very most, where the professors were twenty years ago.

It is a pure "free creation and imagination" on Herr Dühring's part when he asserts that landed proprietors and serfs were required for the exploitation of landed property in tracts of considerable size. In the whole of the East, where the commune or the state owns the land, the very term landed proprietor is not to be found in the various languages, a point on which Herr Dühring can consult the English jurists, whose efforts in India to solve the question: who owns the land?—were as vain as those of the late Prince Heinrich LXXII of Reuss-Greiz-Schleitz-Lobenstein-Eberswalde in his attempts to solve the question of who was the nightwatchman. The Turks first introduced a form of feudal ownership of land in the countries conquered by them in the East. Greece made its entry into history, as far back as the heroic epoch, with a class structure which itself was evidently the product of a long but unknown previous history; even there, however, the land was mainly cultivated by independent peasants; the larger estates of the nobles and tribal chiefs were the exception, and moreover they disappeared soon after this period. Italy was brought under cultivation chiefly by peasants; when, in the final period of the Roman Republic, the great estates, the *latifundia*, displaced the small peasants and replaced them with slaves, they also replaced tillage with stock-raising, and, as Pliny realised, brought Italy to ruin (*latifundia Italiam perdidere*). During the Middle Ages, peasant cultivation was predominant throughout the whole of Europe (especially in bringing virgin land into cultivation); and in relation to the question we are now considering it is of no significance whether these peasants had to pay dues, and if so what dues, to any feudal lords. The colonists from Friesland, Lower Saxony, Flanders and the Lower Rhine, who brought under cultivation the land east of the Elbe which had been

wrested from the Slavs, did this as free peasants under very favourable conditions of tenure, and not at all under "some form of serfdom."—In North America, by far the largest portion of the land
was opened for cultivation by the labour of free farmers, while the
big landlords of the South, with their slaves and their improvident
robbery of the land, exhausted the soil until it could only grow
firs, so that the cultivation of cotton was forced farther and farther
west. In Australia and New Zealand, all the attempts made by the
British government to establish artificially a landed aristocracy
came to nothing. In short, if we except the tropical and sub-tropical
countries, where the climate makes agricultural labour impossible
for Europeans, the large landlord who subjugates Nature by means
of his slaves or serfs and brings the land under cultivation proves
to be a pure figment of the imagination. The very reverse is the
case. Where the large landlord makes his appearance in antiquity,
as in Italy, he does not bring waste land into cultivation, but transforms arable land brought under cultivation by peasants into stock
pastures, depopulating and bringing ruin on whole countries. Only
in a more recent period, when the increasing density of population
had raised the value of the land, and particularly since the development of agricultural science has made even poorer land more
cultivable—it is only from this period that large landowners began
to participate to any considerable extent in bringing waste land
and grassland under cultivation—and this mainly through the robbery of common land from the peasants, both in England and in
Germany. But there was another side even to this. For every acre
of common land which the large landowners brought into cultivation in England, in Scotland they transformed at least three acres
of arable land into sheep-runs and eventually even into mere tracts
for deer hunting.

We are concerned here only with Herr Dühring's assertion that
the bringing into cultivation of tracts of land of considerable size
and therefore of practically the whole area now cultivated, "never
anywhere" took place except through the agency of large landowners
and serfs—an assertion which, as we have seen, "presupposes" a
really unprecedented ignorance of history. It is not necessary,
therefore, for us to examine here either to what extent, at dif-

ferent periods, areas which were already made entirely or mainly cultivable were cultivated by slaves (as in the flourishing period of Greece) or serfs (such as in the manors of the Middle Ages); or what was the social function of the large landowners at various periods.

And after Herr Dühring has shown us this masterpiece of the imagination—in which we do not know whether the conjuring trick of deduction or the falsification of history is most to be admired —he shouts triumphantly: "It goes without saying that all other types of distributed wealth *must be explained historically in an analogous way!*" Which of course saves him the trouble of wasting even a single word more on the origin, for example, of capital.

If, with his domination of man by man as a preliminary condition for the domination of Nature by man, Herr Dühring only wanted to state in a general way that the whole of our present economic order, the stage of evolution now attained by agriculture and industry, is the result of a social history which developed in class antagonisms and relationships of domination and subjection, he is saying something which long ago, since *The Communist Manifesto*, became a commonplace. But the question at issue is how we are to explain the origin of classes and relations based on domination, and if Herr Dühring's only answer is the one word "force," this leaves us exactly where we were at the start. The mere fact that the ruled and exploited class has at all times been far more numerous than the rulers and exploiters, and that therefore it is the former who have had the real force in their hands, is enough to demonstrate the absurdity of the whole force theory. The relationships based on domination and subjection have therefore still to be explained.

They arose in two ways.

As men first emerged from the animal world—in the narrower sense of the term—so they made their entry into history; still half animal, brutal, still helpless in face of the forces of Nature, still ignorant of their own: and consequently as poor as the animals and hardly more productive than these. There prevailed a certain equality in the conditions of existence, and for the heads of families also a kind of equality of social position—at least an absence of social classes—which continued among the natural agricultural communities of the civilised peoples of a later period. In each such community there were from the beginning certain common interests the safeguarding of which had to be handed over to individuals, even though under the control of the community as a whole: such were the adjudication of disputes; repression of encroachments by individuals on the rights of others; control of water supplies, especially in hot countries; and finally, when conditions were still absolutely primitive, religious functions. Such offices are found in primitive communities of every period—in the oldest German Mark communities and even today in India. They are naturally endowed with a certain measure of authority and the beginnings of state power. The productive forces gradually increase; the increasing density of the population creates at one point a community of interests, at another, conflicting interests, between the separate communes, whose grouping into larger units brings about in turn a new division of labour, the setting up of organs to safeguard common interests and to guard against conflicting interests. These organs which, for the reason that they represent the common interests of the whole group, have a special position in relation to each individual community—in certain circumstances even one of opposition—soon make themselves even more independent, partly through heredity of functions, which comes about almost as a matter of course in a world where everything happens in a natural way, and partly because they become more and more indispensable owing to the increasing number of conflicts with the other groups. It is not necessary for us to examine here how this independence of social functions in relation to society increased with time until it developed into domination over society; how what was originally the servant developed gradually, where conditions were favourable, into the lord; how this lord, on the basis of different conditions, emerged as an Oriental despot or satrap, the dynast of a Greek tribe, chieftain of a Celtic clan, and so on; and to what extent ultimately used force in this transformation; and how finally the separate individual rulers united into a ruling class. Here we are only concerned with establishing the fact that the exercise of a social function was everywhere the basis of political supremacy; and further that political supremacy has existed for any length of time only when it fulfilled its social functions. However great the number of despotic governments which rose and fell in India and Persia, each was fully aware that its first duty was the general maintenance of irrigation throughout the valleys, without which no agriculture was possible. It was reserved for the enlightened English to lose sight of this in India; they let the irrigation canals and sluices fall into decay, and are now at last discovering, through the regularly recurrent famines, that they have neglected the one activity which might have made their rule in India at least as legitimate as that of their predecessors.

But alongside of this development of classes another was also taking place. The natural division of labour within the family cultivating the soil made possible, at a certain level of well-being, the introduction of one or more strangers as additional labour forces. This was especially the case in countries where the old common ownership of the land had already disappeared or at least the former joint cultivation had given place to the separate cultivation of parcels of land by the respective families. Production had so far developed that the labour power of a man could now produce more than was necessary for its mere maintenance; the means of maintaining additional labour forces existed; likewise the means of employing them; labour power acquired a *value*. But within the community and the association to which it belonged there were no superfluous labour forces available. On the other hand, such forces were provided by war, and war was as old as the simultaneous existence alongside each other of several groups of communities. Up to that time they had not known what to do with prisoners of war, and had therefore simply killed them; at an even earlier period, eaten them. But at the stage of the "economic order" which had now been attained the prisoners acquired a value; their captors therefore let them live and made use of their labour. Thus force, instead of controlling the economic order, was on the contrary pressed into the service of the economic order. *Slavery* was invented. It soon became the predominant form of production among all peoples who were developing beyond the primitive community, but in the end was also one of the chief causes of the decay of that system. It was slavery that first made possible the division of labour between agriculture and industry on a considerable scale, and along with this, the flower of the ancient world, Hellenism. Without slavery, no Greek state, no Greek art, and science; without slavery, no Roman Empire. But without Hellenism and the Roman Empire as a basis, also no modern Europe. We should never forget that our whole economic, political and intellectual development has as its presupposition a state of things in which slavery was as necessary as it was universally recognised. In this sense we are entitled to say: Without the slavery of antiquity, no modern socialism.

It is very easy to inveigh against slavery and similar things in general terms, and to give vent to high moral indignation at such infamies. Unfortunately all that this conveys is only what everyone knows, namely that these institutions of antiquity are no longer in accord with our present-day conditions and our sentiments, which these conditions determine. But it does not tell us one word as to how these institutions arose, why they existed, and what role they have played in history. And when we examine these questions, we are compelled to say—however contradictory and heretical it may sound—that the introduction of slavery under the conditions of that time was a great step forward. For it is a fact that man sprang from the beasts, and had consequently to use barbaric and almost bestial means to extricate himself from barbarism. The ancient communes, where they continued to exist, have for thousands of years formed the basis of the most barbarous form of state, oriental despotism, from India to Russia. It was only where these communities dissolved that the peoples made progress of themselves, and their first economic advance consisted in the increase and development of production by means of slave labour. It is clear that so long as human labour was still so little productive that it provided but a small surplus over and above the necessary means of subsistence, any increase of the productive forces, extension of trade, development of the state and of law, or beginning of art and science, was only possible by means of a greater division of labour. And the necessary basis for this was the great division of labour between the masses discharging simple manual labour and the few privileged persons directing labour, conducting trade and public affairs, and, at a later stage, occupying themselves with art and science. The simplest and most natural form of this division of labour was in fact slavery. In the historical conditions of the ancient world, and particularly of Greece, the advance to a society based on class antagonisms could only be accomplished in the form of slavery. This was an advance even for the slaves; the prisoners of war, from whom the mass of the slaves was recruited, now at least kept their lives, instead of being killed as they had been before, or even roasted, as at a still earlier period.

We may add at this point that all historical antagonisms between exploiting and exploited, ruling and oppressed classes to this very day find their explanation in this same relatively undeveloped productivity of human labour. So long as the really working population was so much occupied in their necessary labour that they had no time left for looking after the common affairs of society—the direction of labour, affairs of the state, legal matters, art, science, etc.—so long was it always necessary that there should exist a special class, freed from actual labour, to manage these affairs; and this special class never failed to impose a greater and greater burden of labour, for its own advantage, on the working masses. Only the immense increase of the productive forces attained through large-scale industry made it possible to distribute labour among all members of society without exception, and thereby to limit the labour time of each individual member to such an extent that all have enough free time left to take part in the general—both theoretical and practical—affairs of society. It is only now, therefore, that any ruling and exploiting class has become superfluous and indeed a hindrance to social development, and it is only now, too, that it will be inexorably abolished, however much it may be in possession of the "direct force."

When, therefore, Herr Dühring turns up his nose at Hellenism because it was founded on slavery, he might with equal justice reproach the Greeks with having no steam engines and electric telegraphs. And when he asserts that our modern wage-serfdom can only be explained as a somewhat transformed and mitigated heritage of slavery, and not from its own nature (that is, from the economic laws of modern society), either this only means that both wage labour and slavery are forms of subjection and class domination, which every child knows, or it is false. For with equal justice we might say that wage labour is only to be explained as a mitigated form of cannibalism, which is now established as having been the universal primitive form of disposal of vanquished enemies.

The role played in history by force as contrasted with economic development is now clear. In the first place, all political power is originally based on an economic, social function, and increases in proportion as the members of society, through the dissolution of the primitive community, become transformed into private producers, and thus become more and more separated from the administrators of the general functions of society. Secondly, after the political force has made itself independent in relation to society, and has transformed itself from society's servant into its master, it can work in two different directions. Either it works in the sense and in the direction of the regular economic development, in which case no conflict arises between them, the economic development being accelerated. Or, force works against economic development; in this case, as a rule, with but few exceptions, force succumbs to it. These few exceptions are isolated cases of conquest, in which barbarian conquerors have exterminated or driven out the population of a country and have laid waste or allowed to go to ruin productive forces which they did not know how to use. This was what the Christians in Moorish Spain did with the major part of the irrigation works on which the highly-developed agriculture and horticulture of the Moors depended. Every conquest by a more barbarian people naturally disturbs the economic development and destroys numerous productive forces. But in the immense majority of cases where the conquest is permanent, the more barbarian conqueror has to adapt himself to the higher "economic order" as it emerges from the conquest; he is assimilated by the vanquished and in most cases he has even to adopt their language. But where—apart from cases of conquest—the internal public force of a country stands in opposition to its economic development, as at a certain stage has occurred with almost every political power in the past, the contest has always ended with the downfall of the political power. Inexorably and without exception the economic evolution has forced its way through—we have already mentioned the latest and most striking example of this: the Great French Revolution. If, in accordance with Herr Dühring's theory, the economic order and with it the economic constitution of a given country were dependent simply on political force, it is absolutely impossible to understand why after 1848 Friedrich Wilhelm IV could not succeed, in spite of his "magnificent army," in grafting the mediæval guilds and other romantic whims on to the railways, the steam engines and the large-scale industry which was just then developing in his country; or why the tsar of Russia, who is certainly even much more powerful, is not only unable to pay his debts, but cannot even maintain his "force" without continuous loans from the "economic order" of Western Europe.

For Herr Dühring force is the absolute evil; the first act of force is for him the original sin; his whole exposition is a jeremiad on the contamination, which this brought about, of all subsequent history by this original sin; a jeremiad on the shameful perversion of all natural and social laws by this diabolical power, force. That force, however, plays another role in history, a revolutionary role; that, in the words of Marx, it is the midwife of every old society which is pregnant with the new, that it is the instrument by the aid of which social development forces its way through and shatters the dead, fossilised, political forms—of this there is not a word in Herr Dühring. It is only with sighs and groans that he admits the possibility that force will perhaps be necessary for the overthrow of the economic system of exploitation—unfortunately, because all use of force, forsooth, demoralises the person who uses it. And this in spite of the immense moral and spiritual impetus which has resulted from every victorious revolution! And this in Germany, where a violent collision—which indeed may be forced on the people—would at least have the advantage of wiping out the servility which has permeated the national consciousness as a result of the humiliation of the Thirty Years' War. And this parsons' mode of thought—lifeless, insipid and impotent—claims to impose itself on the most revolutionary party that history has known.

V. THEORY OF VALUE

It is now about a hundred years since the publication in Leipzig of a book which by the beginning of the nineteenth century had run through over thirty editions; it was circulated and distributed in town and country by the authorities, by preachers and philanthropists of all kinds, and was generally prescribed as a reader for use in the elementary schools. This book was Rochow's *Kinderfreund* [*Children's Friend*]. Its purpose was to teach the youthful offspring of the peasants and artisans their vocation in life and their duties to their superiors in society and in the state, and likewise to inspire in them a beneficent contentment with their lot on earth, with black bread and potatoes, corvée labour, low wages, paternal thrashings and other agreeable things of this kind, and all by means of the system of education which was then in vogue. With this aim in view the youth of the towns and of the countryside was shown how wisely Nature had ordained that man must win his livelihood and his pleasures by labour, and how happy therefore the peasant and the artisan should feel that it was granted to him to season his meal with bitter labour, instead of, like the debauched rich, suffering the pangs of indigestion or constipation, and having to gulp down the choicest titbits with repugnance. These same platitudes, which old Rochow thought good enough for the young Saxon peasants of his time, are served up to us by Herr Dühring on page 14 and the following pages of his *Course*, as the "absolutely fundamental basis" of the most up-to-date political economy.

"Human needs as such have their natural laws, and their expansion is confined within limits which can only be transgressed by unnatural acts for a time, until these acts bring their consequences in nausea, boredom with life, decrepitude, social mutilation and finally salutary annihilation. . . . Amusement consisting purely of pleasures without any further serious aim soon makes one blasé, or, what amounts to the same thing, exhausts all capacity to feel. Real

204

labour, in some form or other, is therefore the natural social law of healthy beings.... If instincts and needs were not provided with something to balance them, they could bring us hardly even a childish existence, let alone a historical evolution towards a richer life. If they could find satisfaction without limit and without trouble they would soon exhaust themselves, leaving an empty existence in the form of boring intervals lasting until they were felt again.... From every point of view, therefore, the fact that the satisfaction of the instincts and passions depends on the surmounting of economic obstacles is a salutary basic law of both external Nature and the inner nature of Man"—and so on, and so forth. It can be seen that the commonest commonplaces of the worthy Rochow are celebrating their centenary in Herr Dühring, and moreover as "the deeper foundation" of the one and only really critical and scientific "socialitarian system."

With the foundations thus laid, Herr Dühring can proceed to build. Applying the mathematical method, he first gives us, following the ancient Euclid's example, a series of definitions. This is all the more convenient because it enables him from the start to contrive his definitions in such a way that what is to be proved with their help is already partially contained in them. And so we learn at the outset that the governing concept in all past economics is wealth and that wealth, as it has been understood and as it has developed its sway in the actual past history of the world, is "economic power over men and things." This is doubly false. In the first place the wealth of the old tribal and village communities of antiquity was in no sense a domination over men. And secondly, even in societies moving in class antagonisms, in so far as wealth includes domination over men, it is mainly and almost exclusively a domination over men *by virtue of,* and *through the intermediary of,* the domination over things. From the very early period when the capture of slaves and the exploitation of slaves became separate branches of business, the exploiters of slave labour had to buy the slaves, acquiring control over men only through their prior control of things, of the purchase price of the slave and his means of subsistence and instruments of labour. Throughout the Middle Ages large landed property was the preliminary condition by means of which the feudal nobility came to have dues-paying peasants and bondsmen. And nowadays even a six-year-old child sees that wealth dominates men exclusively by means of the things which it has at its disposal.

But what is it that makes Herr Dühring concoct this false definition of wealth, and why has he to sever the real relationship which has existed in all former class societies? In order to drag wealth from the domain of economics over into that of morals. Domination over things is quite all right, but domination over men is an evil thing; and as Herr Dühring has precluded himself from explaining the domination over men by the domination over things, he can once again do an audacious trick and in a trice explain domination over men by his beloved force. Wealth, as domination over men, is "robbery"—and with this we are back again at a corrupted version of Proudhon's ancient formula: "Property is theft."

And so we have now happily brought wealth under the two essential aspects of production and distribution; wealth as domination over things—production wealth, the good side; wealth as domination over men—distribution wealth up to the present day, the bad side, away with it! Applied to the conditions of today, this runs: The capitalist mode of production is quite good and can remain, but the capitalist mode of distribution is no good and must be abolished. Such is the nonsense which comes of writing on economics without even having grasped the connection between production and distribution.

After wealth, value is defined as follows: "Value is the worth which economic things and services have in commerce." This worth corresponds to "the price or any other equivalent name, for example, wages." In other words, value is price. Or rather, so as not to do Herr Dühring an injustice and in order to give the absurdity of his definition as far as possible in his own words: value are prices. For he says on page 19: "value and the prices expressing it in money"— thus himself stating that the same value has very different prices and consequently also equally many different values. If Hegel had not died long ago, he would hang himself; with all his theology he could not have conceived this value which has as many different values as it has prices. It requires once again someone with the audacity of Herr Dühring to begin laying a new and deeper founda-

tion for economics with the declaration that there is no other difference between price and value but that one is expressed in money and
the other is not.

But all this still does not tell us what value is, and still less by
what it is determined. Herr Dühring has therefore to come forward
with further explanations. "In general, the basic law of comparison
and evaluation, on which value and the prices expressing it in
money depend, belongs in the first place to the sphere of pure production, apart from distribution, which only afterwards introduces
a second element into the concept of value. The greater or lesser
obstacles which the variety of natural conditions places in the way
of efforts directed to procuring things, necessitating a greater or
lesser expenditure of economic force, determine also ... the greater
or lesser value" and this is appraised according to "the resistance
opposed by Nature and circumstances to the procuring of things. ...
The extent to which we put our own force into them (things) is
the immediate determining cause of the existence of value in general
and of its particular magnitude."

In so far as there is a meaning in this, it is: The value of a
product of labour is determined by the labour time necessary for its
production; and we knew that long ago, even without Herr Dühring.
Instead of stating the fact simply, he has to twist it into an oracular
saying. It is simply false that the extent to which anyone puts his
force into anything (to keep to the bombastic style) is the immediate
determining cause of value and of the magnitude of value. In the
first place, it makes a difference what thing the force is put into, and
secondly, how the force is put into it. If our "anyone" makes a thing
which has no use value for other people, his whole force does not
produce an atom of value; and if he insists on producing by hand
an object which a machine produces twenty times cheaper, nineteen-
twentieths of the force he puts into it produces neither value in
general nor any determinate magnitude of value.

Moreover it is an absolute distortion to transform productive
labour, which creates positive products, into a merely negative overcoming of a resistance. In order to get a shirt we should then have to
set about it somewhat as follows: Firstly we overcome the resistance
of the cotton-seed to being sown and to growing, then the resistance

of the ripe cotton to being picked and packed and transported, then its resistance to being unpacked and carded and spun, further the resistance of the yarn to being woven, then the resistance of the cloth to being bleached and sewn, and finally the resistance of the completed shirt to being put on.

Why all this childish perversion and nonsense? In order, by means of the "resistance" to pass from the "production value," the true but hitherto only ideal value, to the "distribution value," the value falsified by force which has been the sole form in existence in past history: "In addition to the resistance offered by Nature ... there is yet another, a purely social obstacle. ... An obstructing power steps in between man and Nature, and this power is once again man. Man, conceived as alone and isolated, faces Nature as a free being. ... The situation is different as soon as we think of a second man who, sword in hand, holds the approaches to Nature and its resources and demands a price, whatever form it may take, for allowing access. This second man ... so to speak, puts a tax on the other and is thus the cause of the value of the object striven for being greater than it might have been but for this political and social obstacle to the procuring or production of the object. ... The particular forms of this artificially enhanced value of things are extremely manifold, and they have their natural accompaniment in a corresponding forcing down of the value of labour. ... It is therefore an illusion to attempt to regard value in advance as an equivalent in the proper sense of this term, that is, as something which is of equal worth, or as a relation of exchange arising from the principle that service and counterservice are equal. ... On the contrary, the criterion of a correct theory of value will be that the most general principle of evaluation conceived in the theory does not correspond with the special form of worth which rests on the constraint of distribution. This form varies with the social system, while economic value proper can only be a production value measured in relation to Nature and in consequence of this will only change with changes in the obstacles to production of a purely natural and technical kind."

The value which a thing has in practice, according to Herr Dühring, therefore consists of two parts: first, the labour contained in it, and secondly, the additional tax imposed "sword in hand." In other words, value in practice today is a monopoly price. Now if, in accordance with this theory of value, all commodities have such a monopoly price, there are only two possible alternatives. Either each individual loses again as a buyer what he gained as a seller; in this case the prices have changed their names, but in reality—in their mutual relationship—have remained the same; everything remains as before, and the far-famed distribution value is a mere illusion. Or, on the other hand, the alleged additional tax represents a real sum of value, namely, the sum of value produced by the labouring, value-producing class but appropriated by the monopolist class, and then this sum of value consists merely of unpaid labour; in this case, in spite of the man with the sword in his hand, in spite of the alleged additional tax, we come once again to the Marxian theory of *surplus value*.

But let us look at some examples of the famous "distribution value." On page 125 and the following pages we find:

"The determination of prices by means of individual competition must also be regarded as a form of economic distribution and of the mutual imposition of tribute... if the stock of any necessary commodity is suddenly reduced to a considerable extent, this gives the sellers a disproportionate power of exploitation... what a colossal increase in prices this may produce is shown particularly by those abnormal situations in which the supply of necessary articles is cut off for a more or less lengthy period" and so on. Moreover, even in the normal course of things virtual monopolies exist which make possible arbitrary price increases, as for example with the railway companies, the companies for supplying towns with water and gas, etc.—It has long been known that such opportunities for monopolistic exploitation occur. But that the monopoly prices these produce are not to rank as exceptions and special cases, but precisely as classical examples of the determination of values in operation today—this is new. How are the prices of the necessaries of life determined? Herr Dühring replies: Go into a beleaguered city from which supplies have been cut off, and ask for yourself! What effect has competition on the determination of market prices? Ask the monopolists—they will tell you all about it!

For that matter, even in the case of these monopolies, the man with the sword in his hand who is supposed to stand behind them is not discoverable. On the contrary: in beleaguered cities as a rule the man with the sword, the commandant, if he does his duty, very soon puts an end to the monopoly and requisitions the monopolised supplies for the purpose of equal distribution. For the rest, the men with the sword, when they have tried to fabricate a "distribution value," have reaped nothing but bad business and financial loss. With their monopolisation of the East Indian trade, the Dutch brought both their monopoly and their trade to ruin. The two strongest governments which have ever existed, the North American revolutionary government and the French National Convention, had the audacity to attempt to fix maximum prices, and they failed miserably. For some years now, the Russian government has been trying to raise in London the exchange rate of Russian paper money, which it is lowering in Russia by the continual emission of irredeemable banknotes, by the equally continual purchase of bills of exchange on Russia. It has had to pay for this pleasure in the last few years some sixty million rubles, and the ruble now stands at under two marks instead of over three. If the sword has the magic economic power ascribed to it by Herr Dühring, why is it that no government has been able to succeed in permanently compelling bad money to have the "distribution value" of good money, or *assignats* the "distribution value" of gold? And where is the sword which is in command of the world market?

There is also, we are told, another principal form in which distribution value facilitates the appropriation of other peoples' services without any counter-service: this is possession-rent, that is to say, ground rents and the profits of capital. For the moment we merely record this, to enable us to state that this is all that we learn of this famous "distribution value." All? No, not quite all. Listen to this:

"In spite of the twofold standpoint which appears in the recognition of a production value and a distribution value, there is nevertheless always underlying these *something in common, that thing owing to which all values exist* and by which they are therefore measured. The immediate, natural measure is the expenditure of force, and the simplest unit is human force in the crudest sense of the term. This latter depends again on the existence-time whose *self*-maintenance in turn represents the overcoming of a certain sum of obstacles to nutrition and life. Distribution or appropriation value is only present in pure and exclusive form where the power to dispose of unproduced things, or, to use a simpler expression, these things themselves, are exchanged for products or things of real production value. The identical element which is indicated and represented in every expression of value, and therefore also in the portions of value which are appropriated through distribution without counter-service consists therefore in the expenditure of human force, which ... finds embodiment in each commodity."

Now what have we to say to this? If all commodity values are measured by the expenditure of human force embodied in them, what becomes of the distribution value, the price surcharge, the additional tax? It is true that Herr Dühring tells us that even unproduced things—things which consequently cannot have a real value—can be given a distribution value and exchanged against things which have been produced and have value. But at the same time he tells us that *all values*—consequently even pure and exclusive distribution values—consist in the expenditure of force embodied in them. Unfortunately we are not told how an expenditure of force can find embodiment in an unproduced thing. In any case one point seems to emerge clearly from all this criss-cross of values; that distribution value, the price surcharge on commodities imposed as a result of social position, and the tax levied by virtue of the sword, all once more amount to nothing; the values of commodities are determined solely by the expenditure of human force, *vulgo* labour, which finds embodiment in them. So, apart from ground rent and the few monopoly prices, Herr Dühring says the same, though in vaguer and more confused terms, as the much-decried Ricardo-Marxian theory of value said long ago in a clearer and more precise form.

He says it, and in the same breath he says the opposite. Marx. taking Ricardo's investigations as his starting-point, says: The value of commodities is determined by the socially necessary general human labour embodied in them, and this in turn is measured by its duration. Labour is the measure of all values, but labour itself has no value. Herr Dühring, after likewise putting forward, in his slovenly way, labour as the measure of value, continues: "This depends again on the existence-time whose self-maintenance in turn represents the overcoming of a certain sum of obstacles to nutrition and life." Let us ignore the confusion, due purely to his desire to be original, between labour time, which is the only thing that matters here, and existence-time, which has never yet created or measured values. Let us also ignore the false "socialitarian" impression which the *"self*-maintenance" of this existence-time is intended to create; so long as the world has existed and so long as it continues to exist every individual must maintain himself in the sense that he *himself* consumes the means of subsistence. Let us assume that Herr Dühring might have expressed himself precisely and in economic terms, and then the sentence quoted either means nothing at all or it must mean: The value of a commodity is determined by the labour time embodied in it, and the value of this labour time by the means of subsistence required for the maintenance of the labourer for this time. And, in its application to present-day society, this means: the value of a commodity is determined by the *wages* contained in it.

And this brings us at last to what Herr Dühring is really trying to say. The value of a commodity is determined, in the phraseology of vulgar economics, by the cost of production; Carey, on the contrary, "brought out the truth that it is not the costs of production, but the costs of reproduction, which determine value" (*Critical History*, p. 401). We shall deal later with these production or reproduction costs; at the moment we only note that as is well known, they consist of wages and profit on capital. Wages represent the "expenditure of force" embodied in commodities, the production value. Profit represents the tax or price-increment imposed by the capitalist through his monopoly, by virtue of the sword in his hand —the distribution value. And so the whole contradictory confusion of the Dühring theory of value is ultimately resolved into the most beautiful harmonious clarity.

The determination of the value of commodities by wages, which in Adam Smith still frequently appeared side by side with its determination by labour time, has been discarded from scientific economics since Ricardo, and nowadays only survives in vulgar economics. It is precisely the shallowest sycophants of the existing capitalist order of society who preach the determination of value by wages, and along with this, describe capitalist profit also as a higher form of wages, as the wages of abstinence (reward to the capitalist for not playing ducks and drakes with his capital), as the premium on risk, as the wages of management, etc. Herr Dühring only differentiates himself from these by declaring that profit is robbery. In other words, Herr Dühring bases his socialism directly on the doctrines of the worst sort of vulgar-economics. And his socialism is worth just as much as this vulgar-economics; they both stand and fall together.

It is however clear that what a labourer produces and what he costs are just as much different things as what a machine produces and what it costs. The value created by a labourer in a twelve-hour working day has nothing in common with the value of the means of subsistence which he consumes in this working day and the corresponding period of rest. In these means of subsistence there may be embodied three, four or seven hours of labour time, varying with the stage of development reached in the productivity of labour. If we assume that seven hours of labour were necessary for their production, then the theory of value of vulgar economics which Herr Dühring has accepted proves that the product of twelve hours of labour has the value of the product of seven hours of labour, that twelve hours of labour are equal to seven hours of labour or that twelve = seven. To put it even more plainly: a labourer working on the land, no matter under what social relationships, produces in a year a certain quantity of grain, say sixty bushels of wheat. During this time he consumes a sum of value which can be expressed as forty-five bushels of wheat. Then the sixty bushels of wheat have the same value as the forty-five bushels, and that on the same market and with other conditions remaining absolutely identical; in other words, sixty = forty-five. And this styles itself political economy!

The whole development of human society beyond the stage of brute savagery begins from the day when the labour of the family created more products than were necessary for its maintenance, from the day when one portion of labour could be devoted to the production no longer of the mere means of subsistence, but of means of production. A surplus of the product of labour over and above the costs of maintenance of the labour, and the formation and enlargement, by means of this surplus, of a social production and reserve fund, was and is the basis of all social, political and intellectual progress. In history up to the present, this fund has been the possession of a privileged class, on which also devolved, along with this possession, political supremacy and intellectual leadership. The coming social revolution will for the first time make this social production and reserve fund—that is, the total mass of raw materials, instruments of production and means of subsistence—a really social fund, by taking it out of the hands of that privileged class and transferring it to the whole of society as its common property.

Of two alternatives, one. Either the value of commodities is determined by the costs of maintenance of the labour necessary for their production—that is, in present-day society, by wages. In this case each labourer receives *in his wages the value of the product of his labour;* and then the exploitation of the wage-earning class by the capitalist class is an impossibility.

Let us assume that the costs of maintenance of a labourer in a given society can be expressed by the sum of three shillings. Then the product of a day's labour, according to the above cited theory of the vulgar economists, has the value of three shillings. Let us assume that the capitalist who employs this labourer, adds a profit to this product, a tribute of one shilling, and sells it for four shillings. The other capitalists do the same. But from that moment the labourer can no longer cover his daily needs with three shillings, but also requires four shillings for this purpose. As all other conditions are presumed to have remained unchanged, the wages expressed in means of subsistence must remain the same, while the wages expressed in money must rise, in fact from three shillings to four shillings a day. What the capitalists take from the working class in the form of profit, they must give back to it in the form of wages. We are just where we were at the beginning: if wages determine value, no exploitation of labour by the capitalists is possible. But the formation of a surplus of products is also impossible, for, on the basis of the assumption from which we started, the labourers consume just as much value as they produce. And as the capitalists produce no value, it is impossible to see how they are even to live. And if such a surplus of production over consumption, such a production and reserve fund, nevertheless exists, and exists indeed in the hands of the capitalists, no other possible explanation remains but that the labourers consume for their self-maintenance merely the *value* of the commodities, and have handed over the commodities themselves to the capitalist for further use.

Or, on the other hand, if this production and reserve fund does in fact exist in the hands of the capitalist class, if it has in fact arisen through the accumulation of profit (for the moment we leave ground rent out of account) then it necessarily consists of the accumulated surplus of the product of labour handed over to the capitalist class by the working class, over and above the sum of wages paid to the working class, by the capitalist class. In this case, however, it is not wages that determine value, but the quantity of labour; the working class hands over to the capitalist class in the product of labour a greater quantity of value than it receives from it in the payment of wages; and then the profit on capital is explained, like all other forms of the appropriation without payment of the labour product of others, as a simple component part of this surplus value discovered by Marx.

Incidentally, in the whole *Course of Political Economy* there is no mention of that great and epoch-making discovery with which Ricardo opens his most important work: "The value of a commodity ... depends on the relative quantity of labour which is necessary for its production, and not on the greater or less compensation which is paid for that labour." * In the *Critical History* it is dismissed with the oracular phrase: "It is not considered (by Ricardo) that the greater or lesser proportion in which wages can be an indication of the necessaries of life (!) must also involve ... different forms of the value of relationships!"—a phrase into which the reader can read what he pleases, and is on safest ground if he reads into it nothing at all.

And now let the reader select for himself, from the five sorts of value served up to us by Herr Dühring, the one that he likes best;

*Ricardo: *Principles of Political Economy.—Ed.*

the production value, which comes from Nature; or the distribution value, which man's wickedness has created and is distinguished by the fact that it is measured by the expenditure of force, which is not contained in it; or thirdly, the value which is measured by labour time; or fourthly, the value which is measured by the costs of re-production; or lastly, the value which is measured by wages. The selection is wide, the confusion complete, and the only thing left for us to do is to exclaim with Herr Dühring: "The theory of value is the touchstone of the genuineness of economic systems!"

VI. SIMPLE AND COMPOUND LABOUR

Herr Dühring has discovered in Marx an absolutely gross blunder in economics, a blunder which at the same time contains a very dangerous socialist heresy. The Marxian theory of value is "nothing but the ordinary ... theory that labour is the source of all values and labour time is their measure. But the question of how the specific value of so-called skilled labour is to be conceived is left in complete unclarity. It is true that on our theory also only the labour-time expended can be the measure of the natural cost of production and therefore of the absolute value of economic things; but our starting point is that the labour-time of all individuals must be considered absolutely equal, and it is only necessary to examine how far, in skilled production, the labour time of other persons ... for example in the tool used, is added to the separate labour time of the individual. Therefore the position is not, as in Herr Marx's nebulous conception, that the labour time of one person is in itself more valuable than that of another, because more average labour time is as it were condensed within it, but all labour time is in its essence and without exception—and therefore without any need to take an average—absolutely equal in value; and in regard to the work done by a person, as also in every finished product, all that requires to be ascertained is how much of the labour time of other persons may be concealed in what appears to be the labour time of only one individual. Whether it is a hand tool for production, or the hand, or even the head itself, which could not have acquired its special characteristics and utility without the labour time of others, is of not the slightest importance in the strict application of the theory. In his lucubrations on value, however, Herr Marx never rids himself of the ghost of a skilled labour time which lurks in the background. He was unable to do this because he was hampered by the traditional mode of thought of the educated classes, to whom it necessarily appears monstrous to recognize the labour time of a

porter and that of an architect as of absolutely equal value from
the standpoint of economics."

The passage in Marx which calls forth this "mighty wrath" on
Herr Dühring's part is very brief. Marx is examining what it is
that determines the value of *commodities* and gives the answer: the
human labour embodied in them. This, he continues, "is the expenditure of simple labour power which, on an average, apart from
any special development, exists in the organism of every ordinary individual. . . . Skilled labour counts only as simple labour intensified, or rather, as multiplied simple labour, a given quantity of
skilled labour being considered equal to a greater quantity of simple
labour. Experience shows that this reduction is constantly being
made. A commodity may be the product of the most skilled labour,
but its value, by equating it to the product of simple unskilled
labour, represents a definite quantity of the latter labour alone. The
different proportions in which different sorts of labour are reduced
to unskilled labour as their standard, are established by a special
process that goes on behind the backs of the producers and, consequently, appears to be fixed by custom." *

Marx is dealing here directly only with the determination of the
value of *commodities, i.e.,* of objects which, within a society composed of private producers, are produced and exchanged against
each other by these private producers for their private account. In
this passage therefore there is no question whatever of "absolute
value"—wherever this may have its existence—but of the value
which is current in a definite form of society. This value, in this
definite historical sense, is shown to be created and measured by
the human labour embodied in the individual commodities, and
this human labour is further shown to be the expenditure of simple
labour power. But not all labour is a mere expenditure of simple
human labour power; very many sorts of labour involve the use
of capabilities or knowledge acquired with the expenditure of greater
or lesser effort, time and money. Do these kinds of compound labour produce, in the same interval of time, the same commodity
values as simple labour, the expenditure of mere simple labour

---

* *Capital*, Vol. I, pp. 51-52 (Kerr edition).

power? It is obvious that they do not. The product of one hour of compound labour is a commodity of a higher value—perhaps double or treble—in comparison with the product of one hour of simple labour. The value of the products of skilled labour is expressed in this comparison in the form of a definite quantity of simple labour; but this reduction of compound labour is established by a social process which goes on behind the backs of the producers, by a process which at this point, in the development of the theory of value, has only to be stated but not as yet explained.

It is this simple fact, taking place daily before our eyes in present-day capitalist society, which is here noted by Marx. This fact is so indisputable that even Herr Dühring does not venture to dispute it either in his *Course* or in his *History of Economics;* and the Marxian presentation is so simple and lucid that no one but Herr Dühring "is left in complete unclarity" by it. Because of his complete unclarity he mistakes the value of the commodity which alone Marx was concerned with investigating, for "the natural costs of production," which makes the unclarity still more complete, and even for the "absolute value," which so far as our knowledge goes has never before had currency in economics. But whatever Herr Dühring may understand by the natural costs of production, and whichever of his five kinds of value may have the honour to represent absolute value, this much at least is sure: that Marx is not discussing any of these things, but only the value of commodities; and that in the whole section of *Capital* which deals with value there is not even the slightest indication of whether or to what extent Marx considers this theory of the value of commodities applicable also to other forms of society.

"Therefore the position is not," Herr Dühring proceeds, "as in Herr Marx's nebulous conception, that the labour time of one person is in itself more valuable than of another, because more average labour time is as it were condensed within it, but all labour time is in its essence and without exception—and therefore without any need to take an average—absolutely equal in value." It is fortunate for Herr Dühring that fate did not make him a manufacturer, and thus preserved him from fixing the value of his products on the basis of this new rule and thereby running inevitably into the arms of

bankruptcy. What! Are we here still in the society of manufacturers? No, far from it. With his natural costs of production and
absolute value Herr Dühring has made us take a leap, a veritable
salto mortale, out of the present evil world of exploiters into his
own economic commune of the future, into the pure air of equality
and justice; and so we must now, even though prematurely, take a
glance at this new world.

It is true that, on Herr Dühring's theory, only the labour time
expended can measure the value of economic things even in the
economic commune; but the starting point is that the labour time
of each individual must be considered absolutely equal, and all
labour time is in its essence and without exception absolutely equal
in value, without any need to take an average. And now compare
with this radical equalitarian socialism the nebulous Marxian conception that the labour time of one person is in itself more valuable
than that of another, because more average labour time is condensed
within it—a conception to which Marx was restricted by the traditional mode of thought of the educated classes, to whom it necessarily appears monstrous that the labour time of a porter and that
of an architect should be recognised as of absolutely equal value
from the standpoint of economics!

Unfortunately Marx put a short footnote to the passage cited
above: "The reader must note that we are not speaking here of the
wages or value that the labourer *gets* for a given labour time, but
of the *value of the commodity* in which that labour time *is materialised*." Marx, who seems here to have had a presentiment of his
Dühring in advance, therefore guards himself against his statements
quoted above being applied to the wages which may be paid even
in existing society for compound labour. And if Herr Dühring, not
content with doing this, presents these statements as the principles
on which Marx would like to see the distribution of the necessaries
of life regulated in organised socialist society, he is guilty of a
shameless imposture, the like of which is only to be found in the
blackmailing press.

But let us look a little more closely at the theory of equality in
values. All labour time is completely equal in value, the porter's
and the architect's. So labour time, and therefore labour itself, has

a value. But labour is the creator of all values. It alone gives the natural products which exist a value in the economic sense. Value itself is nothing more than the expression of the socially necessary human labour materialised in an object. Labour *can* therefore have no value. It would be just as possible to speak of the value of labour and to try to determine it, as to speak of the value of value, or to try to determine the weight, not of a body, but of heaviness itself. Herr Dühring dismisses people like Owen, Saint Simon and Fourier by calling them social alchemists. By his subtilising over the value of labour time, that is, of labour, he shows that he is a long way below the real alchemists. And now let the reader judge Herr Dühring's audacity in making Marx responsible for asserting that the labour time of one person is in itself more valuable than that of another's, that labour time, and therefore labour, has a value—Marx, who first disclosed that labour *can* have no value, and why it cannot!

For socialism, which will emancipate human labour power from its position as a *commodity*, the discovery that labour has no value and can have none is of great importance. With this discovery all attempts—such as have been inherited by Herr Dühring from natural working-class socialism—to regulate the future distribution of the necessaries of life as a kind of more exalted wages, necessarily fall to the ground. And from it too comes the further understanding that distribution, in so far as it is governed by purely economic considerations, is regulated by the interests of production, and production is most encouraged by a mode of distribution which allows *all* members of society to develop, maintain and exert their capacities in all possible directions. It is true that, to the mode of thought of the educated classes which Herr Dühring has inherited, it must seem monstrous that in time to come there will no longer be any professional porters or architects, and that the man who for half an hour gives instructions as an architect will also push a barrow for a period, until his activity as an architect is once again required. It is a fine sort of socialism which perpetuates the professional porter!

If the equality of value of labour time means that each labourer produces equal values in equal periods of time, without there being any need to take an average, then this is obviously false. If we have two workers, even in the same branch of industry, the value they produce in one hour of labour time will always vary with the intensity of their labour and their skill—and not even an economic commune, at any rate not on our globe, can remedy this inconvenience—which, however, is only an inconvenience for people à la Dühring. What then remains of the complete equality of value of any and every labour? Nothing but the purely braggart phrase, which has no other economic foundation than Herr Dühring's incapacity to distinguish between the determination of value by labour and determination of value by wages—nothing but the ukase, the basic law of the new economic commune: Equal wages for equal labour time! The old French Communist workers and Weitling had much better reasons for the equality of wages which they advocated.

How then are we to solve the whole important question of the higher wages paid for compound labour? In a society of private producers, private individuals or their families pay the costs of training the skilled worker; hence the higher price paid for trained labour power also comes first of all to private individuals; the clever slave is sold for a higher price, and the clever wage earner is paid higher wages. In a socialistically organised society, these costs are born by society, and to it therefore belong also the fruits, the greater values produced by skilled labour. The labourer himself has no claim to extra payment. And from this, incidentally, also follows the moral that there is frequently a drawback to the popular demand of the workers for "the full proceeds of labour."

VII. CAPITAL AND SURPLUS VALUE

"To begin with, Herr Marx does not hold the accepted economic view of capital, namely, that it is means of production already produced; on the contrary, he attempts to elevate it into a more special, dialectical-historical idea, subject to the metamorphoses of concepts and history. According to him, capital is born of money; it forms a historical phase opening with the sixteenth century, that is with the first beginnings of a world market which, on his hypothesis, appeared at that period. It is obvious that the sharpness of economic analysis is lost in such a conception. In such barren conceptions, which are represented as half historical and half logical, but which in fact are only bastards of historical and logical phantasy, the capacity of the mind to distinguish between things disappears, together with all honesty in the use of concepts"—and so he blusters along for a whole page.... "The Marxist definition of the concept of capital can only cause confusion in strict economic theory... trivialities which are offered as profound logical truths... the weakness of the basic principles"—and so forth.

So according to Marx, we are told, capital was born of money at the beginning of the sixteenth century. This is like saying that fully three thousand years ago metal money was born of cattle, because once upon a time cattle, among other things, functioned as money. Only Herr Dühring is capable of such a crude and inept mode of expression. In the analysis which Marx makes of the economic forms in which the process of the circulation of commodities takes place, money appears as the final form. "This final product of the circulation of commodities is the *first form in which capital appears*. As a matter of history, capital, as opposed to landed property, invariably takes the form at first of money; it appears as moneyed wealth, as the capital of the merchant and of the usurer.... We can see it daily under our very eyes. All new capital, to commence with, comes on the stage, that is, on the market, whether of

commodities, labour, or money, even in our days, in the shape of
money that by a definite process has to be transformed into capital." *

Here once again Marx is stating a fact. Unable to dispute it, Herr
Dühring distorts it. Capital is born of money!

Marx then investigates the processes by which money is transformed into capital, and finds, first, that the form in which money
circulates as capital is the inversion of the form in which it circulates
as the general equivalent of commodities. The simple owner of commodities sells in order to buy; he sells what he does not need, and
with the money thus procured he buys what he does need. The embryo capitalist starts by buying what he does *not* himself need; he
buys in order to sell, and to sell at a higher price, in order to get
back the value of the money originally thrown into the transaction,
expanded by an increment in money; and Marx calls this increment
surplus value.

Whence comes this surplus value? It cannot come either from the
buyer buying the commodities under their value, or from the seller
selling them above their value. For in both cases the gains and the
losses of each individual cancel each other out, as each individual
is in turn buyer and seller. Nor can it come from cheating, for
though cheating can enrich one person at the expense of another,
it cannot increase the total sum possessed by both, and therefore
also it cannot augment the sum of the values in circulation: "The
capitalist class, as a whole, in any country, cannot overreach themselves." **

And yet we find that the capitalist class as a whole, in each country, is continuously enriching itself before our eyes, by selling
dearer than it had bought, by appropriating to itself surplus value.
We are therefore just where we were at the beginning: whence comes
this surplus value? This problem must be solved, and it must be
solved in a *purely economic* way, excluding all cheating or the intervention of any force—the problem being, how is it possible
constantly to sell dearer than one has bought, even on the hypothesis
that equal values are always exchanged against equal values?

The solution of this problem was the most epoch-making achieve-

* *Capital*, Vol. I, pp. 163-64 (Kerr edition).
** *Ibid.*, p. 181 (Kerr edition).

ment of Marx's work. It spread the clear light of day through economic domains in which socialists no less than bourgeois economists previously groped in utter darkness. Scientific socialism dates from the discovery of this solution and has been built up around it.

This solution is as follows: The increase of value that occurs in the case of money intended to be converted into capital cannot take place in this *money* itself, nor can it originate in the *act of purchase*, as in it this money does no more than realise the price of the commodity, and this price, inasmuch as we took as our starting point the exchange of equivalents, is not different from its value. For the same reason, the increase of value that occurs cannot originate in the *sale* of the commodity. The change must, therefore, take place in the *commodity* bought: not however in its *value*, as it is bought and sold at its value, but in its *use-value* as such, that is, the change of value must originate in the consumption of the commodity. "In order to be able to extract value from the consumption of a commodity, our friend, Moneybags, must be so lucky as to find ... in the market, a commodity whose use value possesses the peculiar property of being a source of value, whose actual consumption, therefore, is itself an embodiment of labour, and, consequently, a *creation of value*. The possessor of money does find on the market such a special commodity in capacity for labour or *labour power*." * Though, as we saw, labour as such can have no value, this is by no means the case with labour *power*. This acquires a value from the moment that it becomes a *commodity*, as it is in fact at the present time, and this value is determined "as in the case of every other commodity, by the labour time necessary for the production, and consequently also the reproduction, of this special article," ** that is to say, by the labour time necessary for the production of the means of subsistence which the labourer requires for his maintenance in a fit state to work and for the perpetuation of his race. Let us assume that these means of subsistence represent six hours of labour time daily. Our embryo capitalist who buys labour power for carrying on his business, *i.e.*, hires a labourer, consequently pays this labourer the full value of his day's labour power if he

* *Capital*, Vol. I, p. 186 (Kerr edition).
** *Ibid.*, p. 189 (Kerr edition).

pays him a sum of money which also represents six hours of labour. And as soon as the labourer has worked six hours in the employment of the embryo capitalist, he has fully reimbursed the latter for his outlay, for the value of the day's labour power which he had paid. But so far the money would not have been converted into capital; it would not have produced any surplus value. And for this reason the buyer of labour power has quite a different notion of the nature of the transaction he has carried out. The fact that only six hours' labour is necessary to keep the labourer alive for twenty-four hours, does not in any way prevent him from working twelve hours out of the twenty-four. The value of the labour power, and the value which that labour power creates in the labour process, are two different magnitudes. The owner of the money has paid the value of a day's labour power; his, therefore, is the use of it for a day—a whole day's labour. The circumstance that the value which the use of it during one day *creates* is double its own value for a day is a piece of especially good luck for the buyer, but on the basis of the laws of exchange of commodities by no means an injustice to the seller. On our assumption, therefore, the labourer each day *costs* the owner of money the value of the product of six hours' labour, but he *hands over to him* each day the value of the product of twelve hours' labour. The difference in favour of the owner of the money is—six hours of unpaid surplus labour, a surplus produce for which he does not pay and in which six hours' labor is embodied. The trick has been performed. Surplus value has been produced; money has been converted into capital.

In thus showing how surplus value arises, and how alone surplus value can arise under the domination of the laws regulating the exchange of commodities, Marx exposed the mechanism of the existing capitalist mode of production and of the mode of appropriation based on it; he revealed the core around which the whole existing social order has crystallised.

Nevertheless, this creation of capital has one essential pre-condition: "For the conversion of his money into capital, the owner of money must meet in the market with the *free labourer*, free in the double sense, that as a free man he can dispose of his labour power as his own commodity, and that on the other hand he has no other commodity for sale, is short of everything necessary for the realisation of his labour power." * But this relation between the owners of money or of commodities on the one hand, and those who possess nothing beyond their own labour-power on the other, is not a relation belonging to natural history nor is it one that is common to all historical periods: "It is clearly the result of a past historical development, the product...of the extinction of a whole series of older forms of social production." And in fact this free labourer first appears on a mass scale in history towards the end of the fifteenth and the beginning of the sixteenth century, as a result of the dissolution of the feudal mode of production. With this, however, and with the bringing into being of world trade and the world market dating from the same epoch, the basis was given on which the mass of the existing movable wealth was necessarily more and more converted into capital, and the capitalist mode of production, based on the creation of surplus value, necessarily became more and more exclusively the prevailing mode.

Up to this point, we have been following the "barren conceptions" of Marx, these "bastards of historical and logical phantasy" in which "the capacity of the mind to distinguish between things disappears, together with all honesty in the use of concepts." Let us contrast these "trivialities" with the "profound logical truths" and the "definitive and most strictly scientific treatment in the sense of the exact disciplines" such as Herr Dühring offers us.

So Marx "does not hold the accepted economic view of capital, namely, that it is means of production already produced"; he says, rather, that a sum of values is only converted into capital when it *creates value,* when it forms surplus value. And what does Herr Dühring say? "Capital is a branch of instruments of economic power for the continuation of production *and for the formation of shares in the fruits of the general labour-power.*" However oracularly and carelessly this too is expressed, this much at least is clear: the branch of economic instruments of force may continue production to eternity, but Herr Dühring's own words show that it will not become capital so long as it does not form "shares in the fruits of the general labour power"—that is to say, form surplus value or at

* *Capital,* Vol. I, p. 188 (Kerr edition).

least surplus product. Herr Dühring therefore not only himself
commits the sin with which he charges Marx—of not holding the
accepted economic view of capital—but in addition he commits yet
another clumsy plagiarism of Marx, "badly concealed" by high-
sounding phrases.

On page 262 this is further developed: "Capital in the social
sense" (and Herr Dühring still has to discover a capital in the sense
which is not social) "is in fact specifically different from the mere
means of production; for while the latter have only a technical
character and are necessary under all conditions, the former is distinguished by its social power of appropriation and division. It is
true that social capital is to a great extent identical with the technical means of production *in their social function;* but it is also precisely this function which ... must disappear." When we reflect
that it was precisely Marx who first drew attention to the "social
function" by virtue of which alone a sum of values becomes capital,
it will certainly "almost at once be clear to every attentive observer
that the Marxian definition of the concept of capital can only cause
confusion"—not, however, as Herr Dühring thinks, in exact political economic theory, but as the example shows simply and solely
in the head of Herr Dühring himself, who in the *Critical History*
has already forgotten how much use he made of the said concept of
capital in his *Course.*

However, Herr Dühring is not content with borrowing from Marx
the latter's definition of capital, though in a "purified" form. He is
obliged to follow Marx also in the "metamorphoses of concepts and
history," in spite of his own better knowledge that nothing could
come of it but "barren conceptions," "trivialities," "weakness of
the basic principles" and so forth. Whence comes this "social function" of capital, which enables it to appropriate the fruit of others'
labour and through which alone it is distinguished from mere
means of production? Herr Dühring says that it does not depend
"on the nature of the means of production and their technical in-
dispensability." It therefore arose historically, and on page 252
Herr Dühring only tells us again what we have heard ten times before, when he explains its origin by means of the familiar adventures of the two men, one of whom at the dawn of history converted

his means of production into capital by subjugating the other. But not content with ascribing a historical beginning to the social function through which alone a sum of values becomes capital, Herr Dühring also prophesies that it will also have a historical end. It is "precisely this which will necessarily disappear." In ordinary language, it is cutomary to describe a phenomenon which arose in history, and disappears again in history, as "a historical phase." Capital, therefore, is a historical phase not only according to Marx but also according to Herr Dühring, and we are consequently forced to the conclusion that we are among Jesuits here. When two people do the same thing, then it is not the same. When Marx says that capital is a historical phase, that is a barren conception, a bastard of historical and logical phantasy, in which the capacity of the mind to distinguish between things disappears, together with all honesty in the use of concepts. When Herr Dühring likewise presents capital as a historical phase, that is proof of the acuteness of his economic analysis and of his definitive and most strictly scientific treatment in the sense of the exact disciplines.

What is it then that distinguishes the Dühring conception of capital from the Marxian?

"Capital," says Marx, "has not invented surplus labour. Wherever a part of society possesses the monopoly of the means of production, the labourer, free or not free, must add to the working time necessary for his own maintenance an extra working time in order to produce the means of subsistence for the owners of the means of production." * Surplus labour, labour beyond the time required for the labourer's own maintenance, and appropriation by others of the product of this surplus labour, the exploitation of labour, is therefore common to all past forms of society, in so far as these moved in class antagonisms. But it is only when the product of this surplus labour assumes the form of surplus value, when the owner of the means of production finds the free labourer—free from social fetters and free from possessions of his own—as an object of exploitation, and exploits him for the purpose of the production of *commodities*, it is only then, according to Marx, that the means of production assume the specific character of capital. And this first

* *Capital*, Vol. I, p. 259 (Kerr edition).

took place on a large scale from the end of the fifteenth and the beginning of the sixteenth centuries.

Herr Dühring on the contrary declares that *every* sum of means of production is capital, which forms "shares in the fruits of the general labour power," that is, produces surplus labour in any form. In other words, Herr Dühring annexes the surplus labour discovered by Marx, in order to use it to kill the surplus value, likewise discovered by Marx, which for the moment does not suit his purpose. According to Herr Dühring, therefore, not only the movable and immovable wealth of the Corinthian and Athenian citizens, built on a slave economy, but also the wealth of the large Roman landowners of the period of the emperors, and equally the wealth of the feudal barons of the Middle Ages, in so far as it in any way served production—all these forms of wealth without distinction are capital.

So that Herr Dühring himself holds a view of capital which "is not the accepted economic view, namely, that it is means of production already produced," but is rather the very opposite of this; a view which includes in capital even means of production which have not been produced, the earth and its natural resources. The idea, however, that capital is simply "means of production already produced" is once again the accepted view only in vulgar economics. Outside of this vulgar economics which Herr Dühring holds so dear, the "means of production already produced," or any sum of values whatever, only becomes capital by producing profit or interest, *i.e.*, by appropriating the surplus product of unpaid labour in the form of surplus value, and, moreover, by appropriating it in these two definite subforms of surplus value. It is of absolutely no importance that the whole of bourgeois economics is still labouring under the idea that the property of producing profit or interest is inherent in every sum of value which is utilised under normal conditions in production or in exchange. In classical economics, capital and profit, or capital and interest, are just as inseparable, stand in the same reciprocal relations to each other, as cause and effect, father and son, yesterday and today. The word "capital" in its modern economic meaning, however, first comes to light at the time when the thing itself makes its appearance, when movable wealth acquires, to a greater and greater extent, the function of capital, in exploiting the surplus labour of free labourers for the production of commodities; and in fact it was introduced by the first nation of capitalists in history, the Italians of the fifteenth and sixteenth centuries. And if Marx was the first to make a fundamental analysis of the mode of appropriation characteristic of modern capital; if he brought the concept of capital into harmony with the historical facts from which, in the last analysis, it had been abstracted, and to which it owed its existence; if by so doing Marx cleared this economic concept of those obscure and vacillating ideas which still clung to it even in classical bourgeois political economy and among the socialists prior to his time—then it was Marx who exhibited that "definitive and most strictly scientific treatment" about which Herr Dühring is so constantly talking and which is so painfully absent from his works.

In actual fact, Herr Dühring's treatment is quite different from this. He is not content with first inveighing against the presentation of capital as a historical phase on the ground that this is a "bastard of historical and logical phantasy" and then himself presenting it as a historical phase. He also roundly declares that *all* economic means of power, *all* means of production which appropriate "shares in the fruits of the general labour power"—and therefore also landed property in all class societies—are capital; which, however, does not in the least prevent him, in the further course of his work, from separating landed property and ground rent, quite in the traditional way, from capital and profit, and distinguishing as capital only those means of production which produce profit or interest, as he does at considerable length on page 116 and the following pages of his *Course*. With equal justice Herr Dühring might first include under the name "locomotive" also horses, oxen, asses and dogs, on the ground that these also can be used as means of transport, and reproach modern engineers with limiting the name locomotive to the modern steam engine, setting it up as a historical phase, using barren conceptions, bastards of historical and logical phantasy and so forth; and then finally declare that horses, asses, oxen and dogs are however excluded from the term locomotive, and that this term is only applicable to the steam engine. And so once more we are compelled to say that it is precisely the Dühring conception of capital in which all sharpness of economic analysis is lost and the capacity of the mind to distinguish between things disappears, together with all honesty in the use of concepts; and that the barren conceptions, the confusion, the trivialities, which are served out as profound logical truths and the weakness of the basic principles are to be found in full bloom precisely in Herr Dühring's work.

But all that is of no consequence. For to Herr Dühring belongs the glory of having revealed the axis about which all past economics, all politics and jurisprudence, in a word, all past history, has revolved. Here it is: "Force and labour are the two principal factors which come into play in the formation of social relationships."

In this one sentence we have the complete constitution of the economic world up to the present day. It is extremely short, and runs:

Article One: Labour produces.

Article Two: Force distributes.

And this, "speaking plainly and as man to man," also sums up the whole of Herr Dühring's economic wisdom.

VIII. CAPITAL AND SURPLUS VALUE (CONCLUSION)

"In Herr Marx's view, wages represent only the payment of that labour time in which the labourer is actually working to make his own existence possible. But only a small number of hours is required for this purpose; all the rest of the working day, often so prolonged, yields a surplus in which is contained what our author calls 'surplus value,' or, expressed in everyday language, the earnings of capital. If we leave out of account the labour time which at each stage of production is already contained in the instruments of labour and in the raw material of this stage, this surplus part of the working day is the share which falls to the capitalist employer. The prolongation of the working day is consequently a pure exploitation profit for the benefit of the capitalist."

According to Herr Dühring, therefore, Marx's surplus value would be nothing more than what, expressed in everyday language, is known as the earnings of capital, or profit. Let us see what Marx says himself. On page 229 of *Capital* * surplus value is explained by the following words placed in brackets after it: "interest, profit, rent." On page 244, Marx gives an example in which a total surplus value of £3. 11. 0. appears in the different forms in which it is distributed: tithes, rates and taxes, 21s.; rent 28s.; farmer's profit and interest, 22s.; together making a total surplus value of £3. 11. 0. On page 574, Marx points out as one of Ricardo's main errors that he has not investigated "surplus value as such, *i.e.*, independently of its particular forms, such as profit, rent, etc.," and that he therefore confounds the laws of the rate of surplus value with the laws of the rate of profit: in connection with this Marx says: "I shall show in Book III that, with a given rate of surplus value, we may have any number of rates of profit, and that various rates of surplus value may, under given conditions, express themselves in a single rate of profit." On pages 618 and 619 we find: "The capitalist who pro-

* *Capital*, Vol. I (Kerr edition).

233

duces surplus value, *i.e.*, who extracts unpaid labour directly from the labourers, and fixes it in commodities, is, indeed, the first appropriator, but by no means the ultimate owner, of this surplus value. He has to share it with capitalists who fulfil other functions in the complex of social production, with landowners, etc. Surplus value, therefore, splits up into various parts. Its fragments fall to various categories of persons, and take various forms, independent the one of the other, such as profit, interest, merchants' profits, rent, etc. It is only in Book III that we can take in hand these modified forms of surplus value." And there are many other similar passages.

It is impossible to express oneself more clearly. On each occasion Marx calls attention to the fact that his surplus value must not be confounded with profit or the earnings of capital; that this latter is rather a sub-form and frequently even only a fragment of surplus value. And if in spite of this Herr Dühring asserts that Marxian surplus value, "expressed in everyday language, is the earnings of capital"; and if it is a fact that the whole of Marx's book turns on surplus value—then there are only two possible alternatives: Either Herr Dühring does not know any better, and then it is an unparalleled act of impudence to attack a book of whose main content he is ignorant; or he does not know better, and in that case he has committed a deliberate act of falsification.

To proceed:

"The venomous hatred which Herr Marx bestows on this type of exploitation is only too understandable. But an even mightier wrath and an even fuller recognition of the exploitation character of the economic form which is based on wage labour is possible without accepting the theoretical position expressed in the Marxian doctrine of surplus value."

The well-meant but erroneous theoretical position taken up by Marx gives him a venomous hatred against exploitation; but in consequence of his false "theoretical position" the emotion, in itself moral, receives an immoral expression, manifesting itself in dishonourable hatred and low venomousness, while the definitive and most strictly scientific treatment of Herr Dühring expresses itself in moral emotion of a correspondingly more honourable nature, in wrath which even in form is morally superior and in venomous hatred is also quantitatively superior, is a mightier wrath. While Herr Dühring is enjoying himself in this way, let us see what is the origin of this mightier wrath.

We read on:

"Now the question arises, how are the competing manufacturers able constantly to realise the full product of the given labour, including the surplus product, at a price so far above the natural costs of production as is indicated by the relation, already mentioned, of the surplus labour hours. No answer to this is to be found in Marx's doctrine, and indeed for the simple reason that there could be no place in it for even the raising of the question. The luxury character of the production which is based on hired labour is not seriously dealt with at all, and the social constitution with its opportunities of spoilation is in no way recognised as the ultimate basis of the slavery of whites. On the contrary, the political and social conditions have always to be explained by the economic conditions."

Now we have seen from the passages quoted above that Marx does not at all assert that the industrial capitalist, who first appropriates the surplus product, sells it in all circumstances and on the average at its full value, as is here assumed by Herr Dühring. Marx says expressly that merchant's profit also forms a part of surplus value, and on the assumptions made this is only possible when the manufacturer sells his product to the merchant *below* its value, and thus relinquishes to him a part of the booty. When the question is put in this way, clearly there could be no place in Marx for even raising it. Stated in a rational way, the question is: How is surplus value transformed into its sub-forms: profit, interest, merchant's profit, ground rent, and so forth? And Marx indeed promises to settle this question in the third book. But if Herr Dühring cannot wait until the second volume of *Capital* appears, he should in the meantime take a closer look at the first volume. In addition to the passages already quoted, he would then see, for example on p. 347, that according to Marx the immanent laws of capitalist production assert themselves in the external movements of masses of capital as coercive laws of competition, and in this form come to the consciousness of the individual capitalist as the directing motives of his operations; that therefore a scientific analysis of competition is not possible before we have a conception of the inner nature of capital, just as the apparent motions of the heavenly bodies can only be understood by the man who is acquainted with their real motions, which are not directly perceptible by the senses; and then Marx gives an example to show how in a definite case, a definite law, the law of value, manifests itself and exercises its motive power in competition. Herr Dühring might see from this alone that competition plays a leading part in the distribution of surplus value, and a little reflection should suffice to show that the indications given in the first volume are in fact enough to make clear, at least in its main features, the transformation of surplus value into its secondary forms.

But competition is precisely what absolutely prevents Herr Dühring from understanding the process. He cannot comprehend how the competing manufacturers are able constantly to realise the full product of the given labour, including the surplus product, at prices so far above the natural costs of production. Here again we find his customary "strictness" of expression, which in fact is simply slovenliness. *In Marx,* the surplus product as such has *absolutely no costs of production;* it is the part of the product which *costs nothing* to the capitalist. If therefore the competing manufacturer desired to realise the surplus product at its natural costs of production, they would have simply *to give it away.* But do not let us waste time on such "micrological details." Are not the competing manufacturers every day selling the product of labour above its natural costs of production? According to Herr Dühring, the natural costs of production consist "in the expenditure of labour or force and this in turn, in the last analysis, can be measured by the expenditure of nourishment"; that is, in present-day society, these costs consist in the outlays really expended on raw materials, instruments of labour, and wages as distinguished from the "additional tax," the profit, the surcharge levied sword in hand. Now everyone knows that in the society in which we live the competing capitalists do *not* realise their commodities at the natural costs of production, but that they reckon on to these—and as a rule also receive—the so-called surcharge, the profit. The question which Herr Dühring thinks he has only to raise to blow down the whole Marxian structure—as Joshua once blew down the walls of Jericho—this question also exists for Herr Dühring's economic theory. Let us see how he answers it.

"Capital-property," he says, "has no practical meaning, and cannot be realised, unless the indirect power over human material is also incorporated in it. The product of this power is the capital-profit, and the size of the latter will therefore depend on the range and intensity in which this power is exercised. . . . Profit on capital is a political and social institution which has a more powerful influence than competition. In relation to this the manufacturers act as an 'estate,' and each one of them maintains his position. A certain measure of profit on capital is a necessity for the mode of economy which is prevalent at each period."

Unfortunately even now we do not know how the competing manufacturers are able constantly to realise the product of labour at a price above the natural costs of production. It cannot be that Herr Dühring thinks so immeasurably little of his public as to fob it off with the phrase that profit on capital is above competition, as the King of Prussia used to be above the law. We know the manoeuvres by which the King of Prussia attained his position above the law; the manoeuvres by which the profit on capital succeeds in being more powerful than competition are precisely what Herr Dühring should explain to us, but what he obstinately refuses to enlighten us on. And it is of no avail, if, as he tells us, in this connection the manufacturers act as an estate, and each one of them maintains his position. We surely cannot be expected simply to take his word for it that a number of people only need to act as an estate for each one of them to maintain his position? Everyone knows that the guildsmen of the Middle Ages and the French nobles in 1789 acted very definitely as an estate and yet were wiped out. The Prussian army at Jena also acted as an estate, but instead of maintaining their position they had on the contrary to take to flight and afterwards even to capitulate in sections. Just as little can we be satisfied with the assurance that a certain rate of profit on capital is a necessity for the mode of economy prevalent at each period; for the issue that has to be settled is to show *why* this is so. We do not get a step nearer to the goal when Herr Dühring informs us: "The domination of capital arose as a sequence of domination over land. A part of the agricultural serfs was transformed into the craftsmen of the towns, and ultimately into factory material. After ground rent, the profit on capital developed as a second form of rent of possession." Even if we ignore the historical inexactitude of this assertion, it nevertheless remains a mere assertion, and is restricted to assuring us over and over again of precisely what should have been explained and proved. We can therefore come to no other conclusion but that Herr Dühring is unable to answer his own question; how the competing manufacturers are able constantly to sell the product of labour at a price above the natural costs of production; that is to say, he is unable to explain the genesis of profit. He can only bluntly lay down: profit on capital is the product of *force*—which, it is true, is in complete agreement with Article 2 of the Dühring constitution of society: Force distributes. Certainly this is very nicely expressed; but now "the question arises": Force distributes—what? There must surely be something to distribute, or even the most omnipotent force, with the best will in the world, can distribute nothing. The profit pocketed by the competing manufacturers is something very solid and tangible. Force can *seize* it, but cannot *produce* it. And if Herr Dühring obstinately refuses to explain to us *how* force seizes the profit of manufacturers, the question of *whence* force takes it he meets only with silence, the silence of the grave. Where there is nothing, the emperor, like any other force, loses his rights. Out of nothing comes nothing, and certainly not profit. If capital-property has no practical meaning, and cannot be realised, unless indirect force over human material is embodied in it, then once again the question arises, first, how capital-wealth got this force—a question which is not answered in any way by the couple of historical assertions cited above; secondly, how this force is transformed into the realisation of capital, into profit; and thirdly, whence it obtains this profit.

From whatever side we approach the Dühring economics, we do not make one step forward. For everything that he does not like—profit, ground rent, starvation wages, the enslavement of the workers—he has only *one* word of explanation: Force, and ever again force, and Herr Dühring's "mightier wrath" finally resolves itself into wrath at force. We have seen, first, that this invocation of force is a rotten subterfuge, a relegation of the problem from the sphere of economics to that of politics, which cannot provide an explanation of any single economic fact; and secondly, that it leaves unexplained the origin of force itself—and very prudently, for otherwise it would have been forced to come to the conclusion that all social power and all political force have their source in economic conditions, in the mode of production and exchange historically given for each society at each period.

But let us see whether we cannot wrest from the inexorable builder of "deeper foundations" some further disclosures about profit. Perhaps we shall meet with success if we apply ourselves to his treatment of wages. On page 158 we find:

"Wages are pay for the maintenance of labour-power, and first come under consideration only as the basis for ground rent and profit on capital. In order to get absolute clarity as to the relationships obtaining in this field, we must imagine ground rent, and subsequently also profit on capital, as first appearing in history without wages, that is to say, on the basis of slavery or serfdom. . . . Whether it is a slave or a serf, or on the other hand a wage labourer, who has to be maintained, only gives rise to a difference in the kind and mode of imposition of the cost of production. *In every case the net proceeds obtained by the utilisation of the labour-power constitutes the income of the employer of labour.* . . . It can therefore be seen that . . . the chief contradiction, in virtue of which there exists on the one hand some form of *rent of possession* and on the other hand propertyless wage labour, is not to be found exclusively in one of its members, but always only in both at the same time." Rent of possession, however, as we learn on page 188, is a phrase which covers both ground rent and profit on capital. Further, we find on page 174: "The characteristic of profit on capital is that it is *an appropriation of the most important part of the proceeds of labour-power.* It cannot be conceived except in correlation with some form of directly or indirectly subjected labour." And on page 174: Wages "are in all circumstances nothing more than the pay by means of which, generally speaking, the labourer's maintenance and possibility of perpetuation must be assured." And finally, on page 195: "The portion that falls to rent of possession must be lost to wages, and *vice versa*, the portion of the general productive capacity (!) that reaches labour must necessarily be taken from the revenue of possession."

Herr Dühring leads us from surprise to surprise. In his theory of value and the following chapters up to and including the theory of competition, that is from page 1 to page 155, the prices of commodities or values were first divided into natural costs of production or the production value (*i.e.*, the outlays on raw materials, instruments of labour and wages); and secondly, into the surcharge or distribution value, the tribute levied sword in hand for the benefit of the monopolist class; an impost which, as we have seen, could not in reality make any difference to the distribution of wealth— for what it took with one hand would have to be given back with the other—and which, in so far as Herr Dühring enlightens us as to its origin and nature, arose out of nothing and therefore also consists of nothing. In the two succeeding chapters, which dealt with the form of revenue, that is, from pages 156 to 217, there is no further mention of the surcharge. Instead of this, the value of every product of labour, that is, of every commodity, is now divided into two portions: first, the production costs, in which the wages paid are included; and secondly the "*net proceeds* obtained by the utilisation of the labour power," which constitute the employer's income. And these net proceeds have a very well-known physiognomy, which no tattooing and no artistic painting can conceal. "In order to get absolute clarity as to the relationships obtaining in this field," let the reader imagine the passages just cited from Herr Dühring printed opposite the passages previously cited from Marx, dealing with surplus labour, surplus product and surplus value, and he will find that Herr Dühring is here, though in his own style, *directly copying* from *Capital*.

Surplus labour, in any form, whether slavery, serfdom or wage labour, is recognised by Herr Dühring as the source of the revenues of all ruling classes up to now: this is taken from the much-quoted passage in *Capital*, page 259: Capital has not invented surplus labour, and so on. And the "net proceeds" which constitute "the income of the employer of labour"—what is this but the surplus of the labour product over and above the wages paid, which, even for Herr Dühring, in spite of his quite superfluous disguise of it in the term "pay," must assure, generally speaking, the labourer's maintenance and possibility of perpetuation? How can the "appropriation of the most important part of the proceeds of labour power" be carried out except in so far as the capitalist, as Marx shows, extorts from the labourer more labour than is necessary for the reproduction of the means of subsistence consumed by the latter; that is to say, by the capitalist making the labourer work a longer time than is necessary for the replacement of the value of the wages paid to the labourer? Thus the prolongation of the working day beyond the time necessary for the reproduction of the labourer's means of subsistence—Marx's surplus labour—this, and nothing but this, is what is concealed behind Herr Dühring's "utilisation of labour power"; and his "net proceeds" falling to the employer of labour—how can this manifest itself otherwise than in the Marxian surplus product and surplus labour? And what, apart from its inexact formulation, is there to distinguish the Dühring rent of possession from the Marxian surplus value? For the rest, Herr Dühring has taken the name "rent of possession" from Rodbertus, who included both ground rent and the rent of capital, or profit on capital, under the one term *rent*, so that Herr Dühring had only to add "possession" to it.* And so that no doubt should be left of his plagiarism, Herr Dühring sums up, in his own way, the laws of the changes of magnitude in the price of labour power and in surplus value which are developed by Marx in Chapter XVI (page 557 of *Capital*), as follows: that which falls to the rent of possession must be lost to wages, and *vice versa;* thereby reducing the particular Marxian laws so rich in content, to a tautology without content—for it is self-evident that in a given magnitude falling into two parts, one part cannot increase unless the other is reduced. And so Herr Dühring

* And not even this. Rodbertus says (*Social Letters,* Letter 2, page 59): "Rent, according to this (his) theory, is all income obtained without personal labour, purely *on the ground of possession.*" [*Note by F. Engels.*]

has succeeded in appropriating the ideas of Marx in such a way that the "definitive and most strictly scientific treatment in the sense of the exact disciplines"—which is certainly present in Marx's development of the theory—is completely lost.

We therefore cannot avoid the conclusion that the astonishing din which Herr Dühring makes in the *Critical History* in connection with *Capital,* and the dust he raises with the famous question which arises in connection with surplus value (a question which he had better have left unasked, since he cannot answer it himself)—that all this is only a military ruse, a sly manoeuvre to cover up the gross plagiarism of Marx which he has committed in his *Course.* Herr Dühring had in fact every reason for warning his readers not to give any attention to "the intricate maze which Herr Marx calls capital," the bastards of historical and logical phantasy, the confused and nebulous Hegelian conceptions and jugglery, etc. The Venus against whom this faithful Eckart warns the German youth had been taken by him stealthily from the Marxian preserves and brought to a safe place for his own use. We must congratulate him on this "net proceeds" derived from the utilisation of Marx's labour power, and on the peculiar light thrown by his annexation of Marxian surplus value under the name of rent of possession on the motives for his obstinate (it was repeated in two editions) and false assertion that by the term surplus value Marx meant only profit or earnings of capital.

And so we should have to portray Herr Dühring's achievements in Herr Dühring's own words somewhat as follows: "In Herr" (Dühring's) "view wages represent only the payment of that labour time in which the labourer is actually working to make his own existence possible. But only a small number of hours is required for this purpose; the whole remaining balance of the working day, often so prolonged, yields a surplus in which is contained what our author calls"—rent of possession. "If we leave out of account the labour time which at each stage of production is already contained in the instruments of labour and in the raw material of this stage, this surplus part of the working day is the share which falls to the capitalist employer. The prolongation of the working day is consequently a profit of pure extortion for the benefit of the capitalist. The venomous hatred which Herr" (Dühring) "bestows on this type of exploitation is only too understandable...." But what is less understandable is how he will now arrive at his "mightier wrath."

IX. NATURAL LAWS OF ECONOMICS. GROUND RENT

Up to this point we have been unable, with the best will in the world, to discover how Herr Dühring, in the domain of economics, can "come forward with the claim to a new *system* which is not merely adequate for the epoch but *authoritative for the epoch.*" However, what we have not been able to discover in his force theory and his theories of value and capital, may perhaps be as clear as daylight to us when we consider the "Natural Laws of National Economy" put forward by Herr Dühring. For, as he puts it with his usual originality and precision, "the triumph of the higher scientific method consists in passing beyond the mere description and classification of apparently static matter and attaining living intuitions which explain the genesis of things. Knowledge of laws is therefore the most perfect form of knowledge, for it shows us how one process is conditioned by another."

The very first natural law of all economics has been specially discovered by Herr Dühring. Adam Smith "curiously enough, not only did not bring out the leading part played by the most important factor in all economic development, but even completely failed to give it its distinctive formulation, and thus unintentionally reduced to a subordinate role the force which played its stamp on the development of modern Europe." This "fundamental law, to which the leading role must be assigned, is that of the technical equipment, one might even say the armament, of the natural economic force of man." This "fundamental law" discovered by Herr Dühring runs as follows:

Law No. 1. "The productivity of the economic instruments, natural resources and human force, is increased *by inventions and discoveries.*"

We are overcome with astonishment. Herr Dühring treats us as Molière's newly created nobleman is treated by the wag, who announces to him the news that all through his life he has been speaking prose without knowing it. That in many cases the productive power of labour is increased by inventions and discoveries (but also that in very many cases it is not increased, as is proved by the mass of waste paper in the archives of every patent office in the world) we knew long ago; but we owe to Herr Dühring the enlightening information that this banality which is as old as the hills, is the fundamental law of all economics. If "the triumph of the higher scientific treatment" in economics, as in philosophy, only consists in giving a highsounding name to the first commonplace that comes to one's mind, and trumpeting it forth as a natural law or even a fundamental law, then indeed it becomes possible for anyone, even the editor of the Berlin *Volkszeitung*, to "lay more basic foundations" and to revolutionise science. We should then "in all rigour" be forced to apply to Herr Dühring himself Herr Dühring's judgment on Plato: "If that is supposed to be economic wisdom, then the author of"—the critical foundations—"shares it with every person who ever conceives an idea"—or even ever says anything—"about whatever occurs to him at the moment." If, for example, we say animals eat, we are saying quite calmly, in our innocence, something of great importance; for we only have to say that eating is the fundamental law of all animal life, and we have revoltionised the whole of zoology.

Law No. 2. Division of Labour. "The separation of trades and the division of activities raises the productivity of labour." In so far as this is true, it also has been a commonplace since Adam Smith. *How* far it is true will be shown in Part III.

Law No. 3. "*Distance and transport* are the chief causes which hinder and facilitate the co-operation of the productive forces."

Law No. 4. "The industrial state has an incomparably greater population capacity than the agricultural state."

Law No. 5. "In economics nothing takes place without a material interest."

These are the "Natural Laws" on which Herr Dühring founds his new economics. He remains faithful to his method already seen in his Philosophy. In economics too a few self-evident statements of the utmost banality—moreover often very ineptly expressed—form the axioms which need no proof, the fundamental principles, the natural laws. Under the pretext of developing the content of these laws, which have no content, he seizes the opportunity to pour out a wordy stream of economic twaddle on the various themes whose *names* appear in these so-called laws—on inventions, division of labour, means of transport, population, interests, competition, and so forth—twaddle whose commonplace platitudinousness is only seasoned by oracular grandiloquence, and here and there by inept formulations or pretentious word-spinning over all kinds of casuistical subtleties. Then finally we reach ground rent, profit on capital and wages, and as we have only dealt with the two latter forms of appropriation in the preceding sections, we propose now in conclusion to make a brief examination of the Dühring conception of ground rent.

In doing this we shall not deal with those points where Herr Dühring has merely copied his predecessor Carey; we are not concerned with Carey, nor with defending Ricardo's views on ground rent against Carey's distortions and stupidities. We are only concerned with Herr Dühring, and he defines ground rent as "that income which the proprietor *as such* draws from the land." The economic concept of ground rent, which is what Herr Dühring is to explain, is straightway transferred by him into the juridical sphere, so that we are no wiser than we were before. Our constructor of deeper foundations must therefore, whether he likes it or not, condescend to give some further explanation. He then compares the lease of a farm to a farmer with the loan of capital to a manufacturer, but soon finds that the comparison, like many others, is not satisfactory. For, he says, "if we wanted to press the analogy further, the profit left to the farmer after payment of ground rent must correspond to the balance of profit on capital left with the manufacturer who uses the capital, after he has paid interest. But *it is not customary* to regard farmers' profits as the main income and ground rent as a balance. . . . A proof of this difference of conception is the *fact* that in the theory of ground rent the case in which the land is worked by the owner is not separately treated, and no special weight is laid on the difference between the amount of rent in the case of a lease and where the owner produces the rent himself. *At any rate no one has found occasion to conceive* the rent resulting from the owner's cultivation of land as divided in such a way that one portion represents as it were the interest on the property and the other portion the surplus profit of enterprise. Apart from the capital which the farmer himself brings into the business, it would *seem* that his specific *profit* is *generally regarded* as a kind of wages. It is however *dangerous* to assert anything on this subject, as the question has never been raised in this definite form. Wherever we are dealing with fairly large farms it will be easily seen that what are specifically farming profits cannot be treated as wages. For this profit is itself dependent on the contradiction with the labour power of agricultural labourers, through whose exploitation that form of income is alone made possible. It is clearly *a part of the rent* which remains in the hands of the farmer and through which the *full rent*, which the owner cultivating his own land would expect, is reduced."

The theory of ground rent is a part of economics which is specifically English, and necessarily so, because it was only in England that there existed a mode of production in which rent had in fact been separated from profit and interest. In England, as is well known, the predominant form is large landed estates and large-scale agriculture. The landlords lease their land in large, often very large, farms, to farmers who are provided with sufficient capital to work them and do not work themselves, as our peasants do, but employ the labour of farm servants and day labourers on the lines of capitalist enterprise proper. Here, therefore, we have the three classes of bourgeois society and the form of income peculiar to each: the ground landlord, drawing rent; the capitalist, drawing profit; and the labourer drawing wages. It has never occurred to any English economist to regard the farmers' profit as a kind of wages, as *seems* to Herr Dühring to have been the case; even less could it be *dangerous* for an English economist to assert that farming profit is what it indisputably, obviously and tangibly is, namely, profit on capital. It is perfectly ridiculous to say that the question of what the farmer's profit actually is has never been raised in this definite form. In England there has never been any necessity even to raise this question; both the question and the answer have long existed in the facts themselves, and since Adam Smith there has never been any doubt about them.

The case of the owner cultivating his own land—or rather, the management of farms by bailiffs for the landowner's account, as is the actual case in the greater part of Germany—does not alter the matter. If the landowner also provides the capital and has the farm run for his own account, he pockets the profit on capital in addition to the ground rent, as is obvious and cannot be otherwise on the basis of the existing mode of production. And if Herr Dühring asserts that up to now no one has found occasion to conceive the rent (he should say revenue) resulting from the owner's cultivation as divided into two parts, this is simply untrue, and at best only once again proves his own ignorance. For example:

"The revenue derived from labour is called wages. That derived from stock, by the person who manages or employs it, is called profit. . . . The revenue which proceeds altogether from land is called rent, and belongs to the landlord. . . . When those three different sorts of revenue belong to different persons, they are readily distinguished; but when they belong to the same, they are sometimes confounded with one another, at least in common language. A gentleman *who farms a part of his own estate*, after paying the expense of cultivation, *should gain both the rent of the landlord and the profit of the farmer*. He is apt to denominate, however, his whole gain, profit, and thus confounds rent with profit, at least in common language. The greater part of our North American and West Indian planters are in this situation. They farm, the greater part of them, their own estates, and accordingly we seldom hear of the rent of a plantation, but frequently of its profit. . . . A gardener who cultivates his own garden with his own hands unites in his own person the three different characters of landlord, farmer, and labourer. His produce, therefore, should pay him the rent of the first, the produce of the second, and the wages of the third. The whole, however, is commonly considered as the earnings of his labour. Both rent and profit are, in this case, confounded with wages."

This passage is from the sixth chapter of Book I of *Adam Smith*.*

* *The Wealth of Nations.—Ed.*

The case of the landowner cultivating his own land was therefore investigated a hundred years ago, and the doubts and uncertainties which are such a source of worry to Herr Dühring in this connection are merely due to his own ignorance.

He eventually saves himself from his quandary by an audacious trick: The farmer's profit comes from the exploitation of "the labour power of the agricultural labourers," and is therefore obviously a "part of the rent," by which the "full rent," which should flow into the landowner's pocket, is "reduced." From this we learn two things. Firstly, that the rent of the landowner is "reduced" by the farmer, so that, according to Dühring, it is not, as imagined hitherto, the farmer who plays rent to the landowner, but the *landowner who pays rent to the farmer*—certainly a "view which is original from the foundation upwards." And secondly, we eventually learn what Herr Dühring imagines is covered by the term ground rent: namely, the whole surplus product obtained in farming by the exploitation of agricultural labour. But as this surplus product in all economics hitherto—save for the works of a few vulgar economists—has been divided into ground rent and profit on capital, we are compelled to note that Herr Dühring's view of ground rent also is "not the accepted one."

According to Herr Dühring, therefore, the only difference between ground rent and profit on capital is that the former is obtained in agriculture and the latter in industry or commerce. And Herr Dühring necessarily arrived at such an uncritical and confused view of the matter. We saw that his starting-point was the "really historical conception," that domination over the land could only be based on domination over men. As soon, therefore, as land is cultivated by means of any form of subjugated labour, a surplus for the landlord arises, and this surplus is in fact the rent, just as in industry the surplus labour product beyond what the labourer earns is the profit on capital. "Thus it is clear that ground rent exists on a considerable scale whenever and wherever agriculture is carried on by means of any of the forms of subjugation of labour." In this presentation of rent as the whole surplus product obtained in agriculture, Herr Dühring comes up against both English farming profit and the division, based on English farming and recognised by all the classical economists, of that surplus product into ground rent and farming profit, and hence the *pure*, precise conception of rent. What does Herr Dühring do? He pretends not to have ever heard the very faintest whisper of the division of the surplus product of agriculture into farmer's profit and ground rent, and therefore of the whole rent theory of the classical economists; he pretends that the question of what farming profit really is has never yet been raised "in this definite form," that he is dealing with a subject which has never yet been investigated and about which there is no knowledge but only illusion and uncertainty. And he flees from fatal England—where, without the intervention of any theoretical school, the surplus product of agriculture is so remorselessly divided into its elements: ground rent and profit on capital—to the country so beloved by him, where the Prussian *Landrecht* is in force, where farming by the owner of the land still flourishes in its full patriarchal bloom, where "the landlord understands by rent the income from his farm" and the *junkers'* views on rent still claim to govern science—where, therefore Herr Dühring can still hope to slip through with his confused ideas of rent and profit and even to find credence for his latest discovery: that ground rent is paid not by the farmer to the landlord but by the landlord to the farmer.

X. FROM THE *CRITICAL HISTORY*

Finally, let us take a glance at the *Critical History of Political Economy*, at "this enterprise" of Herr Dühring's which, as he says, "is absolutely without precedent." It may be that here at last we shall find the definitive and most strictly scientific treatment which he has so often promised us.

Herr Dühring makes a great deal of noise over his discovery that "economic science" is "a colossally modern phenomenon" (page 12).

In fact, Marx says in *Capital:* "Political economy... as an autonomous science, first makes its appearance in the period of manufacture"; and in the *Critique of Political Economy*, page 56,* that *"the classical school of political economy... dates from William Petty in England and Boisguillebert in France, and closes with Ricardo in the former country and Sismondi in the latter."* Herr Dühring follows the path thus laid down for him; but in his view *higher* economics begins only with the wretched trash produced by bourgeois science after the close of its classical period. On the other hand, he is fully justified in triumphantly proclaiming at the end of his introduction: "But though this enterprise, in its externally appreciable characteristics and in the more novel portion of its content, is absolutely without precedent, in its inner critical approaches and its general standpoint, it is even more peculiarly mine" (page 9). It is a fact that, on the basis of both its external and its internal features, he might very well have announced his "enterprise" (the industrial term is not badly chosen) as: *The Ego and His Own.*

Since political economy, as it makes its appearance in history, is in fact nothing but the scientific insight into the economics of the period of capitalist production, statements and theorems relating to it (for example, in the writings of ancient Greek society) can

* Kerr edition.

only be found to the extent that certain phenomena—such as commodity production, trade, money, interest-bearing capital, etc.—are common to both societies. In so far as the Greeks make occasional excursions into this sphere, they show the same genius and originality as in all other spheres. Because of this, their views form, historically, the theoretical starting point of the modern science. Let us now listen to what Herr Dühring, with his world-historical approach, has to say.

"We have properly speaking (!) nothing positive to report of a scientific character in the economic theory of antiquity, and the completely unscientific mediæval period gives still less occasion for this (for this—for reporting *nothing!*). As however those who proudly display the appearance of erudition ... have defiled the true character of modern science, attention must be called to at least a few examples." And Herr Dühring then produces examples of a criticism which is in truth free from even the "appearance of erudition."

Aristotle states that "the use of any property is twofold—one is peculiar to the thing as such and the other is not; as for example a sandal, which may be used as footwear and also for exchange; both are modes of use of the sandal, for whoever exchanges the sandal for what he lacks, money or food, uses the sandal as a sandal; but not in its natural function, for it is not there for the purpose of exchange." Herr Dühring maintains that this statement is "not only expressed in a really platitudinous and pedantic way"; but those who see in it a "distinction between use value and exchange value" also fall into the "ridiculous frame of mind" of forgetting that "in the earliest period" and "in the framework of the most advanced system"—which of course is Herr Dühring's own system—use value and exchange value have vanished.

"In Plato's writings on the state, people ... have claimed to find the *modern* category of the economic division of labour." This seems to be intended to refer to the passage in *Capital*,* where however, the views of classical antiquity on the division of labour are on the contrary referred to as "in most striking contrast" with the modern view.—Herr Dühring—has only sneers and nothing besides for Plato's presentation—one which, for his time, was full of genius

* Vol. I, p. 401 (Kerr edition).

—of the division of labour as the natural basis of the city (which for the Greeks was identical with the state); and this on the ground that he did not mention—though the Greek Xenophon did, Herr Dühring—the "limit set by the contemporary extent of the market to the further differentiation of professions and the technical subdivision of special operations . . . only when this limit is realised have we such knowledge as transforms what can hardly be termed a scientific idea into an important economic truth."

It was in fact "Professor" Roscher (of whom Herr Dühring is so contemptuous) who set up this "limit" at which the idea of the division of labour is supposed first to become "scientific," and who therefore expressly pointed to Adam Smith as the discoverer of the laws of the division of labour. In a society in which commodity production is the predominant form of production, "the market"—to adopt Herr Dühring's style for once—was always a "limit" which was very well known to "business people." But more than "the knowledge and instinct of routine" is needed to realise that it was not the market that created the capitalist division of labour, but that on the contrary, it was the dissolution of former social connections, and the division of labour resulting from this, that created the market. (See *Capital*, Vol. 1, Ch. XXX: *Creation of the Home Market for Industrial Capital*).*

"The role of money has at all times provided the main stimulus to economic (!) ideas. But what did an Aristotle know of this role? No more, clearly, than was contained in the idea that exchange through the medium of money had followed the primitive exchange by barter."

But when "an" Aristotle presumes to discover the two different *forms of the circulation* of money—the one in which it operates as a mere medium of circulation, and the other in which it operates as money capital—in this he is only—according to Herr Dühring— "expressing a moral antipathy." And when "an" Aristotle carries his audacity so far as to attempt an analysis of money in its "role" *as a measure of value,* and indeed states this problem, which has such decisive importance for the theory of money, correctly—then "a"

* Kerr edition, p. 817.

Dühring prefers (and for very good private reasons) to say nothing about such impermissible temerity.

And the final outcome is: Greek antiquity, as mirrored in the Dühring "attention" to it, in fact had "only quite ordinary ideas" (page 25), if indeed such "buffoonery" (page 29) has anything in common with ideas, whether ordinary or extraordinary.

It would be better to read Herr Dühring's chapter on Mercantilism in the "original," that is, in F. List's *National System*, Chapter 29: *The Industrial System, incorrectly called the Mercantile System by the School*. How carefully Herr Dühring manages to avoid any "appearance of erudition" on this subject also is shown by the following passage, among others:

List, Chapter 28: *The Italian Political Economists*, says: "Italy was in advance of all modern nations both in the practice and in the theory of political economy," and then he cites as "the first work which deals with political economy, particularly in Italy, the book written by Antonio Serra, of Naples, on *How to Secure for the Kingdoms an Abundance of Gold and Silver* (1613)." Herr Dühring confidently accepts this, and is therefore able to regard Serra's *Breve trattato* "as a kind of inscription at the entrance of the more recent pre-history of economics." His treatment of the *Breve trattato* is in fact limited to this "literary buffoonery." Unfortunately, the real position was somewhat different: in 1609, that is, four years before the *Breve trattato*, Thomas Mun's *A Discourse of Trade, etc.*, had appeared. The particular significance of this book was that, even in its first edition, it was directed against the original *monetary system* which was then still defended in England as being the policy of the state; that is, it represented the conscious *self-separation* of the mercantile system from the system which gave it birth. Even in the form in which it first appeared the book had several editions and exercised a direct influence on legislation. In the edition of 1664 (*England's Treasure, etc.*), which had been completely rewritten by the author and was published after his death, it continued to be the mercantilist gospel for another hundred years. If mercantilism therefore has an epoch-making work "as a kind of inscription at the entrance," it is this book, and for this very reason it simply does not exist for Herr Dühring's "history which most carefully observes the distinctions of rank."

Of *Petty*, the founder of modern political economy, Herr Dühring tells us that he had "a somewhat superficial mind" and also "he had no sense of the intrinsic and nicer distinctions between concepts," while he had "a versatility which knows a great deal but skips lightly from one thing to another without taking root in any idea of a more profound character;"... his "economic methods are still very crude," and he "achieves *naïvetés* whose contrasts ... a serious thinker may well find amusing." What illimitable condescension, therefore, for the "serious thinker" Herr Dühring to deign to take any notice at all of "a Petty"! And what notice does he take of him?

Petty's statements on "labour and even labour time as a measure of value, of which *imperfect traces* can be found in his writings," are not mentioned again apart from this sentence. Imperfect traces! In his *Treatise on Taxes and Contributions* (first edition, 1662), Petty gives a perfectly clear and correct analysis of the magnitude of value of commodities. In illustrating this at the outset by the equal value of precious metals and corn on which the same quantity of labour has been expended, he says the first and the last "theoretical" word on the value of the precious metals. But he also states definitely and as a general law that the values of commodities are measured by *"equal labour."* He applies his discovery to the solution of various problems, some of which are very complex, and on various occasions and in various works he draws important conclusions from this law, even where he does not repeat the fundamental proposition. And in his very first work he says:

"This (estimation of value by equal labour), I say, *to be the foundation of equalising and balancing of values;* yet in the superstructures and practices hereupon, I *confess* there is much variety and intricacy." * Petty was thus conscious equally of the importance of his discovery as of the difficulty of applying it in detail. He therefore tried to find another way of reaching certain conclusions of a detailed nature. He thought that "a natural par" could be discovered between land and labour, so that value might be expressed "by

* The Economic Writings of Sir William Petty, Vol. I, p. 44 (Cambridge University Press edition, 1899).—*Ed.*

either of them alone as well or better than by both." Even this error
has genius.

Herr Dühring makes this penetrating observation on Petty's theory
of value: "Had his thought been more penetrating, it would not have
been possible to find, in other passages, traces of a contrary view-
point, to which we have previously referred"; that is to say, to
which no "previous" reference has been made except that we have
been told the "traces" are "imperfect." This is very characteristic
of Herr Dühring's method—to allude to something "previously" in
a meaningless phrase, in order "subsequently" to make the reader
believe that he had "previously" been made acquainted with an
important point, which in fact Herr Dühring has slid over both
"previously" and "subsequently."

In Adam Smith we can certainly find not only "traces" of "contradictory views" on the concept of value, not only two but even three,
and strictly speaking even four sharply contradictory views on value,
running quite happily side by side and after each other. But what
is quite natural in a writer who is laying the foundations of political
economy and is necessarily feeling his way, experimenting and
struggling with a chaos of ideas which are only just taking shape,
may seem strange to a writer who is surveying and summarising
more than a hundred and fifty years of investigations whose results
have already partly passed from books into the general consciousness
of society. And, to pass from great things to small: as we have seen,
Herr Dühring himself likewise gives us five different kinds of value
to select from at will, and with them, an equal number of contradictory conceptions. Certainly, "if his own thought had been more
penetrating," he would not have expended so much effort in trying
to throw his readers back from Petty's perfectly clear conception of
value into the uttermost confusion.

A very finished work of Petty's, which is as it were cast in a single
block, is his *Quantulumcunque Concerning Money,* published in
1682, ten years after his *Anatomy of Ireland* (this "first" appeared
in 1672, not 1691 as stated by Herr Dühring, who takes it second-
hand from the "most current text-book compilations"). In this book
the last vestiges of mercantilist views, found in his other writings,
have completely disappeared. In content and form it is a little

masterpiece, and for this very reason Herr Dühring does not even mention its title. It is quite in the order of things that, in relation to the most able and original of economic investigators, our vainglorious and pedantic mediocrity should only express his snarling displeasure, and should only take offence at the fact that the flashes of theoretical insight are not set out proudly in ordered ranks as ready-made "axioms," but merely rise to the surface here and there from the depths of "crude" practical material, for example, of taxation.

Petty's founding of "Political Arithmetic," *vulgo* statistics, is treated by Herr Dühring in the same way as Petty's specially economic works. He shrugs his shoulders spitefully at the peculiar methods used by Petty! Considering the grotesque methods used on this field even a century later by Lavoisier, and in view of the great distance that separates even contemporary statistics from the goal which Petty assigned to them in broad outline, such self-satisfied superiority two centuries *post festum* stands out in all its undisguised stupidity.

Petty's most important ideas—which receive such scant attention in Herr Dühring's "enterprise"—are, in the latter's view, nothing but useless conceits, chance thoughts, incidental comments, to which in our day a significance is given, which in themselves they have not got, only by the use of extracts torn from their context; which therefore also play no part in the *real* history of political economy, but only in modern books below the standard of Herr Dühring's deep-rooted criticism and "historical treatment in the grand style." In his "enterprise" he seems to have had in view a circle of readers who would have implicit faith and would never dream of asking for proof of his assertions. We shall return to this point soon (when dealing with Locke and North), but must first take a brief glance at Boisguillebert and Law.

In connection with the former, we must draw attention to the sole discovery made by Herr Dühring: he has discovered a connection between Boisguillebert and Law which had hitherto been missed. Boisguillebert asserts that the precious metals could be replaced, in the normal monetary functions which they fulfill in commodity production, by credit money (*un morceau de papier*). Law on the other hand imagines that any "increase" whatever in the number of these "pieces of paper" increases the wealth of the nation. Herr Dühring draws from this the conclusion that Boisguillebert's idea "already embodied a new idea of mercantilism"—in other words, already included Law. This is made as clear as daylight in the following: "All that was necessary was to attribute to the 'simple pieces of paper' the same role which the precious metals *should* have played, and a metamorphosis of mercantilism was thereby at once accomplished." In the same way it is possible to accomplish at once the metamorphosis of an uncle into an aunt. It is true that Herr Dühring adds appeasingly: "Of course Boisguillebert had no such purpose in mind." But, in the devil's name, how could he have in mind the purpose of replacing his own rationalist conception of the money function of the precious metals by the superstitious conception of the mercantilists, because he holds the view that this role of the precious metals can be played by paper money?—Nevertheless, Herr Dühring continues in his serio-comic style, "nevertheless it may be conceded that here and there our author succeeded in making a really pertinent comment" (page 83).

In reference to Law, Herr Dühring succeeded in making only "the really pertinent comment": "Law too, naturally, was never able completely to *eliminate* the ultimate basis (namely, "the basis of the precious metals"), but he pushed the issue of notes to its extreme limit, that is to say, to the collapse of the system" (page 94). In reality, however, these paper butterflies, mere money tokens, fly round among the public, not to "eliminate" the basis of the precious metals, but to attract them from the pockets of the public into the depleted treasures of the state.

To return to Petty and the insignificant role in the history of economics attributed to him by Herr Dühring, we must first listen to what we are told about Petty's immediate successors, Locke and North. Locke's *Considerations on Lowering of Interest and Raising of Money,* and North's *Discourse upon Trade,* appeared in the same year, 1691.

"What he (Locke) writes on interest and money does not go beyond the range of the reflections which were current, under the dominion of mercantilism, on the events of political life" (page 64). The reader of this "report should now see quite clearly why Locke's

Lowering of Interest had such an important influence, in more than one direction, on political economy in France and Italy during the second half of the eighteenth century.

"Many business men thought the same (as Locke) on free play for the rate of interest, and the developing social relations also produced the tendency to regard legal restrictions on interest as ineffective. At a period when a Dudley North could write his *Discourses upon Trade*, directed towards free trade, there must already have been as it were a great deal in the air which made the theoretical opposition to restrictions on interest rates not seem something extraordinary" (page 64).

So Locke had to copy the ideas of some of his contemporary "business men," or to breathe in a great deal of what was "as it were in the air," before he could develop any theory of free play for the rate of interest without saying anything "extraordinary"! In fact, however, as early as 1662, in his *Treatise on Taxes and Contributions*, Petty had contrasted interest, as "rent of money which we call usury," with "rent of land and houses," and lectured the landlords who wished to keep down by legislation not of course land rent, but the rent of money, on "the vanity and fruitlessness of making civil positive law against the law of nature." In his *Quantulumcunque* (1682) he therefore declared that legislative regulation of the rate of interest was as stupid as regulation of exports of precious metals or of exchange rates. In the same work he made statements on the "raising of money" which have settled this point once and for all—for example, the attempt to give sixpence the name of one shilling, by doubling the number of shillings coined from one ounce of silver.

As regards this last point, Locke and North did little more than copy his theory. In regard to interest, however, Locke follows Petty's parallel between interest on money and land rent, while North goes further and contrasts interest as "rent of stock" with land rent, and the stocklords with the landlords. And while Locke accepts only with reservations free play for the rate of interest as demanded by Petty, North accepts it unconditionally.

Herr Dühring—himself a bitter mercantilist in the "more subtle" sense—surpasses himself when he dismisses Dudley North's *Discourses upon Trade* with the comment that they were written "in the direction of free trade." It is rather like saying of Harvey that he wrote "in the direction" of the circulation of the blood. North's work—apart from its other merits—is a classical exposition, driven home with relentless logic, of the doctrine of free trade both for foreign and internal trade—certainly "something extraordinary" in 1691!

Herr Dühring, by the way, informs us that North was a "merchant" and a rogue at that, also that his work "met with no success." How could a book of this sort have met with any "success" among the dominant mob at the moment of the final triumph of protectionism in England? But this did not prevent it from having an immediate effect on theory, as can be seen from a whole series of economic works published in England shortly after it, some of them even before the end of the seventeenth century.

Locke and North provide examples of how the first bold strokes which Petty made in almost every sphere of political economy were taken up one by one by his English successors and further developed. The traces of this process during the period 1691 to 1752 are obvious even to the most superficial observer from the very fact that all the more important economic writings of that period refer to Petty, either in confirmation of his views or to refute them. This period, which contained many original thinkers, is therefore the most significant for the investigation of the gradual genesis of political economy. The "historical treatment in the grand style," which charges Marx with the unpardonable sin of making so much commotion about Petty and the writers of that period, simply strikes it right out of history. From Locke, North, Boisguillebert and Law it jumps straight to the Physiocrats, and then, at the entrance to the real temple of political economy, appears—David Hume. With Herr Dühring's permission, however, we must restore the real chronological order, putting Hume before the Physiocrats.

Hume's economic *Essays* appeared in 1752. In the essays contained in this volume: *Of Money, Of the Balance of Trade, Of Commerce,* Hume follows step for step, and in many passages even in mere idiosyncrasies, Jacob Vanderlint's *Money Answers All Things,* published in London in 1734. However unknown this Vanderlint may have been to Herr Dühring, references to him can be found in

English economic works even at the end of the eighteenth century, that is to say, even in the period after Adam Smith.

Like Vanderlint, Hume treated money as a mere token of value; he copied almost word for word (and this is important, as he might have taken the theory of money as a token of value from many other sources) Vanderlint's argument on why the balance of trade cannot be permanently either favourable or unfavourable to a country; like Vanderlint, he teaches that the equilibrium of trade balances is brought about naturally, through the differing economic situation in the various countries; like Vanderlint, he preaches free trade, but not so boldly or consistently; like Vanderlint, though with less profundity, he emphasizes human needs as the motive forces of production; he follows Vanderlint in the influence on commodity prices which he wrongly attributes to bank money and public paper issues in general; like Vanderlint, he opposes fiduciary money; like Vanderlint, he makes commodity prices dependent on the price of labour, that is, on wages; he even copies Vanderlint's fanciful notion that a large treasure keeps commodity prices down, etc., etc.

At a much earlier point Herr Dühring made an oracular allusion to how other writers had misunderstood Hume's monetary theories, with a particularly denunciatory reference to Marx, who in *Capital* had also, in a positively subversive way, pointed to the secret connections of Hume with Vanderlint and with J. Massie, who will be mentioned later.

As for this misunderstanding, the facts are as follows. In regard to Hume's real theory of money (that money is a mere token of value, and, therefore, if other conditions remain unaltered, commodity prices fall in proportion to the increase in the volume of money in circulation, and rise in proportion to its decrease), with the best will in the world—though in his own luminous way—Herr Dühring can only repeat the errors made by his predecessors. Hume, however, after stating the theory cited above, himself raises the objection (as Montesquieu, starting from the same premises, had done previously) that it is nevertheless "certain" that since the discovery of the mines in America "industry has increased in all the nations of Europe, except in the possessors of those mines," and that this "may justly be ascribed, among other reasons, to the increase of gold and silver."

His explanation of this phenomenon is that "though the high prices of commodities be a necessary consequence of the increase of gold and silver, yet it follows not immediately upon that increase; but some time is required before the money circulates through the whole state and makes its effect be felt on all ranks of people." In this intermediate period it has a beneficial effect on industry and trade. At the end of this analysis Hume also tells us why this is so, although in a less comprehensive way than many of his predecessors and contemporaries: "It is easy to trace the money in its progress through the whole commonwealth; where we shall find, that it must first quicken the diligence of every individual before it *increases the price of labour.*"

In other words, Hume is here describing the effect of a revolution in the value of the precious metals, in fact a depreciation, or, which is the same thing, a revolution in the *measure of value* of the precious metals. He makes the correct discovery from this that, in the slow process of price equalisation, this depreciation only in the last instance "increases the price of labour"—*vulgo,* wages; that is to say, it increases the profit made by merchants and industrialists at the cost of the labourer (which he thinks just as it should be), and thus "quickens diligence." But he does not raise the problem which is of real interest to science, namely, whether and in what way an increase in the supply of the precious metals, if their value remains unchanged, affects the prices of commodities; and he confuses *every* "increase of the precious metals" with their depreciation. Hume therefore does precisely what Marx says he does (*Critique of Political Economy,* page 220). We shall have to make another reference to this point, but we must first turn to Hume's essay on *Interest.*

Hume's proof, expressly directed against Locke, that the rate of interest is not regulated by the existing volume of money but by the rate of profit, and his other explanations of the causes which determine rises or falls in the rate of interest, are all to be found, much more exactly though not so brilliantly stated, in *An Essay on the Governing Causes of the Natural Rate of Interest, Wherein the Sentiments of Sir W. Petty, and Mr. Locke, on That Head, are Considered.* This work appeared in 1750, two years before Hume's essay; its author was J. Massie, a writer with very varied interests, who had a wide public, as can be seen from contemporary English literature. Adam Smith's discussion of the rate of interest is closer to Massie than to Hume. Neither Massie nor Hume know or say anything at all regarding the nature of "profit," which plays a role in the theories of both.

"In general," Herr Dühring sermonises to us, "the attitude of most of Hume's commentators has been very prejudiced, and ideas have been attributed to him which were not his." And Herr Dühring himself gives us more than one striking example of his "attitude."

For example, Hume's *Essay on Interest* begins with the following: "Nothing is esteemed a more certain sign of the flourishing condition of any nation than the lowness of interest: and with reason, though I believe the cause is somewhat different from what is commonly apprehended." In the very first sentence, therefore, Hume cites the view that the lowness of the rate of interest is the surest indication of the flourishing condition of a nation as a commonplace which had already become trivial in his day. And in fact this "idea" had already had a hundred years, since Child, to become generally current. But we are told: "Among Hume's views on the rate of interest *we must particularly draw attention to the idea* that it is the true barometer of conditions (conditions of what?) and that its lowness is an almost infallible indication of the prosperity of a nation" (page 130). Who is the "prejudiced" and biased "commentator" who says this? No other than Herr Dühring.

What arouses the naïve astonishment of our "critical historian" is the fact that Hume, in connection with some felicitous idea or other, "does not even claim to have originated it." This would certainly not have happened to Herr Dühring.

We have seen how Hume confuses any increase of the precious metals with an increase of them which is accompanied by a depreciation, a revolution in their own value, *i.e.*, in the measure of value of commodities. This confusion was inevitable with Hume because he had not the slightest understanding of the function of the precious metals as *the measure of value*. And he could not have it, because he had absolutely no knowledge of value itself. The word itself is to be found perhaps only once in his essays, where, in attempting to correct Locke's erroneous idea that the precious metals had "only an imaginary value," he makes it even worse by saying that they had "chiefly a fictitious value."

In this he is much inferior not only to Petty but to many of his English contemporaries. He shows the same "backwardness" in still proclaiming the old-fashioned notion that the "merchant" is the chief mainspring of production—an idea which Petty had long passed beyond. As for Herr Dühring's assurance that in his *Essays* Hume concerned himself with the "chief economic relationships," if the reader only compares Cantillon's book (quoted by Adam Smith) which appeared the same year as Hume's essays, 1752, but many years after its author's death, he will be astonished at the narrow field covered by Hume's economic writings. Hume, as we have said, in spite of the letters-patent issued to him by Herr Dühring, is nevertheless quite a respectable figure even in the economic field, but in this field he is anything but an original investigator, and even less an epoch-making one. The influence of his economic essays on the educated circles of his day was due, not merely to his brilliant exposition, but also and principally to the fact that the essays were a progressive and optimistic glorification of industry and trade, which were then flourishing—in other words, of the capitalist society which at that time was rapidly developing in England, and which was bound to provide the *Essays* with a "success." One indication of this suffices here. Everyone knows the passionate fight that the masses of the English people were waging, just in Hume's period, against the system of indirect taxes which was being systematically exploited by the notorious Robert Walpole for the relief of the landlords and of the rich in general. In his essay *Of Taxes,* in which, without mentioning his name, Hume polemises against his ever-present authority Vanderlint—the stoutest opponent of indirect taxation and the most determined advocate of a land tax —we find: "They (taxes on consumption) must be very heavy taxes indeed and very injudiciously levied, which the artisan will not, of himself, be enabled to pay by superior industry and frugality, *without raising the price of his labour.*" It is almost as if Robert Walpole himself were speaking, especially if we also take into consideration the passage in the essay on *Public Credit* in which, referring to the difficulty of taxing the state's creditors, Hume says: "The diminution of their revenue would not be *disguised* under the appearance of a branch of excise or customs."

As might have been expected of a Scotsman, Hume's admiration of bourgeois industry was by no means purely platonic. Starting as a poor man, he worked up to a yearly income of some very, very heavy thousand pounds; which Herr Dühring (as he is not here dealing with Petty) tastefully expresses in this way: "Starting with very small means he succeeded, by good *domestic economy*, in reaching the position of not having to write to please anyone." Herr Dühring further says: "He had never made the slightest concession to the influence of parties, princes or universities." There is certainly no evidence that Hume ever shared literary enterprises with a "Wagener," but it is well known that he was an indefatigable partisan of the Whig oligarchy, that he thought highly of "*Church* and State," and that in reward for these services he was given first a secretaryship in the Embassy in Paris and subsequently the incomparably more important and better-paid post of an Under-Secretary of State. "In politics Hume was and always remains conservative and strongly monarchist in his views. For this reason he was never so bitterly denounced as Gibbon by the supporters of the established church," the old Schlosser says. "The selfish Hume, this lying historian" reproaches the fat English monks who live by begging and have neither wife nor family; but "he himself never had a family or a wife, and was a great, fat fellow, fed, in considerable part, out of public money, without having merited it by any real public services"—this is what the "rude" plebeian Cobbett says. Herr Dühring says that Hume was "in many essential respects superior to a Kant in the *practical* management of life."

But why is Hume given such an exaggerated position in the *Critical History?* Simply because this "serious and subtle thinker" has the honour to be the Dühring of the eighteenth century. The example of a Hume shows that "the creation of this whole branch of science (economics) was the achievement of a more enlightened philosophy"; and the precedent of Hume is the best guarantee that this whole branch of science will be closed, for the immediately foreseeable future, in that phenomenal man who has transformed the merely "more enlightened" philosophy into the absolutely luminous philosophy of reality, and with whom, just as with Hume, "as never before in Germany . . . the study of philosophy in the narrow sense of the word is combined with scientific attempts to investigate political economy." Accordingly we find Hume, in any case respectable as an economist, inflated into an economic star of the first magnitude, whose importance has hitherto been denied only by the same envious people who have hitherto also been so obstinately silent on Herr Dühring's "epoch-making" achievements.

*   *   *

The *physiocratic school* left us in *Quesnay's Tableau Economique*, as everyone knows, a riddle on which all former critics and historians of political economy have up to now broken their teeth in vain. This *Tableau*, which was intended to bring out clearly the physiocrats' conception of the production and circulation of a country's total wealth, remained obscure enough for the economic world which succeeded it. On this, too, Herr Dühring comes at last to give us light. "What this economic image of the relations of production and distribution *means even for Quesnay himself*," he says, can only be seen if we have "*first carefully examined* the leading ideas which are peculiar to him. All the more because these have hitherto only been stated with 'wavering indefiniteness,' and their essential features cannot be recognised," even in Adam Smith. Herr Dühring will now once for all put an end to these traditional "superficial accounts." He then proceeds to pull the reader's leg through five whole pages, five pages in which all kinds of pretentious phrases, constant repetitions and calculated confusion are designed to conceal the fatal fact that, in regard to Quesnay's "leading ideas," Herr Dühring has hardly as much to tell us as "the most current text-book compilations" against which he warns us so untiringly. It is "one of the most dubious sides" of this introduction that here too the *Tableau*, which up to that point had only been mentioned by name, is only just casually snuffled at, and is then lost sight of in all sorts of "reflections," such as, for example, "the difference between effort and result." Though the latter, "it is true, is not to be found completed in Quesnay's ideas," Herr Dühring will give us a fulminating example of it as soon as he comes from his lengthy introductory "effort" to his remarkably short-winded "result," that is to say, to his elucidation of the *Tableau* itself. We will now give all, *literally all* that he feels it right to tell us of Quesnay's *Tableau.*

In his "effort" Herr Dühring says: "It seemed to him (Quesnay) self-evident that the proceeds (Herr Dühring had just spoken of the net product) must be thought of and treated as a *value in money* ... he applied his deliberations (!) immediately to the *values in money* which he assumed as the results from the sale of all agricultural products by the actual producer. In this way (!) he operates in the columns of his *Tableau* with several milliards" (that is, of values in money). We have therefore learnt three times over that, in his *Tableau*, Quesnay operates with the "values in money" of agricultural products," including the money values of the "net product" or "net proceeds." Further on in the text we find: "Had Quesnay considered things from a really natural standpoint, and had he rid himself not only of regards for the precious metals and the amount of money, but also of regards for *money values....* But as it is he reckons solely with *sums of value,* and imagined (!) the net product in advance as a *money value.*" So for the fourth and fifth time: there are only money values in the *Tableau!*

"He (Quesnay) obtained it (the net product) by deducting the expenses and *thinking* (!) principally" (not the traditional account but for that reason all the more superficial) "of that value which came to the landlord as rent."—We have still not advanced a step; but now it is coming: "on the other hand, *however, now also*"—this "however, now also" is a gem!—"the net product, as a natural object, enters into circulation, and in this way becomes an element which serves to maintain the class which is described as sterile. In this the confusion can *at once* (!) be seen—the confusion arising from the fact that in one case it is the money value, and in the other the thing itself, which determines the course of his ideas."—In general, it appears, *all* circulation of commodities suffers from the confusion that commodities enter into circulation simultaneously as "natural objects" and as "money values." But we are still moving in a circle about "money value," for "Quesnay wishes to avoid a double application of the economic proceeds."

With Herr Dühring's permission: in Quesnay's "analysis" at the foot of the *Tableau,* the various kinds of products figure as "natural objects" and up above, in the *Tableau* itself, in their money values. Subsequently Quesnay even made his pupil, the Abbé Baudeau, write in the natural objects in the *Tableau* itself, *by the side of* their money values.

After all this "effort," at last we get the "result," which the reader will be astonished to hear: "Nevertheless, the inconsequence" (referring to the role assigned by Quesnay to the landlords) *"at once* becomes clear when we enquire *what becomes of the net product, which has been appropriated as rent, in the course of the economic circulation?* In regard to this the physiocrats and the *Tableau Economique* could offer nothing but confused and arbitrary conceptions, increasing to mysticism."

All's well that ends well. So Herr Dühring does not know "what becomes of the net product, which has been appropriated as rent, in the course of the economic circulation" (represented in the *Tableau*). To him the *Tableau* is the "squaring of the circle." By his own confession, he does not understand the A.B.C. of the physiocrats. After all the beating about the bush, the empty antics, the jumping hither and thither, the harlequinades, episodes, diversions, repetitions and stupefying confusions whose sole purpose is to prepare us for the imposing conclusion, "what the *Tableau* means for Quesnay himself"—after all this, we come finally to Herr Dühring's shamefaced confession that *he himself does not know.*

Once he has shaken off this painful secret, this Horatian "black care" which was seated behind him during his ride through the land of the physiocrats, our "serious and subtle thinker" blows another merry blast on his trumpet, as follows: "The lines which Quesnay draws here and there" (in all there are just six of them!) "in his otherwise fairly simple (!) *Tableau,* and which are meant to represent the circulation of the net product," make one wonder whether "these strange combinations of columns" may not be based on some mathematical phantasy; they are reminiscent of Quesnay's attempts to square the circle—and so forth. As Herr Dühring, by his own admission, was unable to understand these lines in spite of their simplicity, he had to follow his favourite procedure of *throwing suspicion* on them. And now he can confidently deliver the death blow to the vexatious *Tableau:* "We have considered the net product in this *its most doubtful aspect,*" etc. So the despairing confession that he does not understand the first word about the *Tableau Economique* and the role played by the net product which figures in it—this is what Herr Dühring calls "the most doubtful aspect of the net product"! What grim humour!

But so that our readers may not be left in the same cruel uncertainty about Quesnay's *Tableau* as those necessarily are who take their economic wisdom "at first hand" from Herr Dühring, we will explain it briefly as follows:

As is known, the physiocrats divide society into three classes: (1) the productive, *i.e.*, the class which is really active in agriculture, farmers and agricultural labourers; they are called productive, because their labour yields a surplus: rent. (2) The class which appropriates this surplus, including the landowners and their dependents, the princes and all officials paid by the state, and finally also the Church in its special character as appropriator of tithes. For the sake of brevity, in what follows we call the first class simply "farmers," and the second class "landlords." (3) The industrial or sterile (unfruitful) class; sterile because, in the view of the physiocrats, it adds to the raw materials delivered to it by the productive class only the same quantity of value as it consumes in the means of subsistence provided for it by that same class. Quesnay's *Tableau* was intended to portray how the total annual product of a country (in fact, France) circulates between these three classes and enables annual reproduction to take place.

The first hypothesis of the *Tableau* is that the farming system and with it large-scale agriculture such as existed in Quesnay's time had been generally introduced; he took as examples, Normandy, Picardy, Ile de France and a few other French provinces. The farmer therefore appears as the real leader of agriculture, representing in the *Tableau* the whole productive (agricultural) class and paying the landlord a rent in money. An invested capital or inventory of ten milliard *livres* is attributed to the farmers as a whole; of this sum, one-fifth, or two milliards, is the working capital which has to be replaced every year—this figure also was estimated on the basis of the best-managed farms in the provinces mentioned above.

Quesnay also presupposes (1) constant prices and simple reproduction, for the sake of simplicity; (2) that all circulation which takes place merely within one class is excluded, and that only circulation between class and class is taken into account; (3) that all purchases and sales taking place between class and class in the course of the industrial year are combined in a single total sum. Finally, it must be borne in mind that in Quesnay's time in France, as was more or less the case throughout Europe, the home industry of the peasant families provided far the greater portion of their needs, other than food, and this home industry is therefore taken as an integral part of agriculture.

The starting point of the *Tableau* is the total harvest, the gross product of the annual yield of the soil, which is consequently placed as the first item—the "total reproduction" of the country, in this case France. The total value of this gross product is estimated on the basis of the average prices of agricultural products among the trading nations. It comes to five milliard *livres*, a sum which roughly expresses the money value of the gross agricultural production of France on the basis of such statistical estimates as were then possible. This, and nothing but this, is the reason why in this *Tableau* Quesnay "operates with several milliards," to be precise, with five milliards, and not with five *livres tournois*.

The whole gross product, of a value of five milliards, is therefore in the hands of the productive class, that is, in the first place the farmers who have produced it by advancing an annual working capital of two milliards, which corresponds to an invested capital of ten milliards. The agricultural products—means of subsistence, raw materials, etc.—which are required for the replacement of working capital, including therefore the maintenance of all persons directly engaged in agriculture, are taken *in natura* [in kind] from the total harvest, and again expended for the purpose of new agricultural production. As we have seen, constant prices and simple reproduction at a given level are assumed; and because of this, the money value of the portion which is thus taken from the total gross product is equal to two milliard *livres*. This portion, therefore, does not enter into general circulation. For, as we have noted, circulation which takes place only *within* a particular class, and not between one class and another, is excluded from the *Tableau*.

After the replacement of working capital out of the gross product there remains a surplus of three milliards, of which two are in food-stuffs and one in raw materials. The rent which the farmers have to pay to the landlords is however only two-thirds of this sum, equal to two milliards. It will soon be seen why it is only these two mil-liards which figure under the heading of "net product" or "net income."

In addition, however, to the "total reproduction" of agriculture amounting in value to five milliards, of which three milliards enter into general circulation, there is also, *before* the movements de-scribed in the *Tableau* begin, the whole "pécule" [hoard] of the nation, two milliards of actual cash, in the hands of the farmers. This comes about in the following way.

As the starting point of the *Tableau* is the total harvest, this also forms the closing point of an economic year, for example, of the year 1758, from which point a new economic year begins. During the course of this new year, 1759, the portion of the gross product destined to enter into circulation is distributed among the two other classes through the medium of a number of individual payments, purchases and sales. These movements, separated, following each other in succession, and continuing through a whole year, are, how-ever, (as was unavoidable in the *Tableau*) combined into a few characteristic transactions each of which embraces a whole year's operations in one figure. This, then, is how at the close of the year 1758 there has flowed back to the farming class the money paid by it to the landlords as rent for the year 1757 (the *Tableau* itself will show how this comes about), amounting to two milliards; so that the farming class can again throw this sum into circulation in 1759. As, however, this sum, as Quesnay observes, is much larger (since payments in instalments constantly repeat themselves) than is re-quired in reality for the total circulation of the country (France), the two milliards in the hands of the farmers represent the total money in circulation in the nation.

The class of landlords drawing rent first appears, as is accidentally the case even today, in the role of receivers of payments. On the basis of Quesnay's assumptions the actual landlords receive only four-sevenths of the two milliards of rent: two-sevenths go to the government, and one-seventh to the receivers of tithes. In Quesnay's day the Church was the greatest landlord in France and in addition received the tithes on all other landed property.

The working capital (*avances annuelles*) advanced by the "sterile" class in the course of a whole year consists of raw materials to the value of one milliard—only raw materials, because tools, machinery, etc., are included among the products of that class itself. The many roles, however, played by such products in the industrial enterprises of this class, do not concern the *Tableau*, any more than the circulation of commodities and money which takes place exclusively within that class. The wages for the labour through which the sterile class transforms the raw materials into manufactured goods is equal to the value of the means of subsistence which it receives, in part directly from the productive class, and in part indirectly through the landlords. Although it is itself divided into capitalists and wage-earners, on Quesnay's basic presupposition it forms a total class which is in the pay of the productive class and of the landlords. The total industrial production, and consequently also its total circulation, which is distributed over the year following the harvest, is likewise combined into a single whole. It is therefore assumed that at the beginning of the movement set out in the *Tableau* the annual commodity production of the sterile class is entirely in its hands, and consequently that its whole working capital, consisting of raw materials to the value of one milliard, has been converted into goods to the value of two milliards, one-half of which represents the price of the means of subsistence consumed during the process. An objection might be raised here: Surely the sterile class also uses industrial products for its domestic needs; where are these shown, if its own total product passes through circulation to the other classes? This is the answer we are given: The sterile class not only itself consumes a portion of its own commodities, but in addition to this portion it also strives to retain as much of the rest as possible. It therefore sells the commodities thrown into circulation above their real value, and must do this, as we have entered these commodities

at the total value of its production. This, however, does not affect
the figures of the *Tableau* for the two other classes receive manufactured goods only to the value of their total production.

Now, therefore, we know the economic position of the three separate classes at the beginning of the movement set out in the *Tableau*.
The productive class, after its working capital has been replaced
in kind, still has three milliards of the gross product of agriculture
and two milliards in money. The landlord class first appears with
its rent claim of two milliards on the productive class. The sterile
class has two milliards in manufactured commodities. Circulation
passing between only two of these three classes is called by the
physiocrats, imperfect; circulation which takes place between all
three classes is called perfect.

Now for the economic *Tableau* itself.

First (imperfect) *Circulation:* The farmers pay the landlords,
without receiving anything in return, the rent due to them, with two
milliards of money. With one of these two milliards the landlords
buy means of subsistence from the farmers, to whom one-half of the
money expended by them in the payment of rent thus returns.

In his *Analyse du Tableau Economique* Quesnay does not make
further mention of the state, which receives two-sevenths, and of the
Church, which receives one-seventh, of the ground rent, as their
social roles are generally known. In regard to the landlord class
proper, however, he says that its expenditure (in which that of all its
retainers is included) is, at least as regards the great bulk of it,
unfruitful expenditure, with the exception of that small portion
which is used "for the maintenance and improvement of their properties and the raising of their standard of cultivation." But by "natural law" their proper function consists precisely in "provision for
the good management and expenditure for the maintenance of their
heritage," or, as this is developed further on, in the *avances foncières*,
that is, outlays for the preparation of the soil and provision of
equipment needed by the farms, which enable the farmer to devote
his whole capital exclusively to the business of actual cultivation.

Second (perfect) *Circulation:* With the second milliard of money
still remaining in their hands, the landlords purchase manufactured
goods from the sterile class, and the latter, with the money thus ob-

tained, purchases from the farmers means of subsistence for its own maintenance.

Third (imperfect) *Circulation:* The farmers buy from the sterile class, with one milliard of money, manufactured goods for their own use; a large part of these goods consists of agricultural implements and other means of production required in agriculture. The sterile class returns the same money to the farmers, buying with it one milliard of raw materials with which to replace its own working capital. With this transaction the two milliards expended by the farmers in the payment of rent have flowed back to them, and the account is closed. And therewith also the great riddle is solved: "What becomes of the net product, which has been appropriated as rent, in the course of the economic circulation?"

We saw above that at the starting point of the process there was a surplus of three milliards in the hands of the productive class. Of these, only two were paid as net product in the form of rent to the landlords. The third milliard of the surplus constitutes the interest for the total invested capital of the farmers, that is, ten per cent on ten milliards. They do not receive this interest—this should be carefully noted—from circulation; it exists *in natura* [in kind] in their hands, and they realise it only in circulation, by replacing it, through circulation, with manufactured goods of equal value.

If it were not for this interest, the farmer—the chief agent in agriculture—would not advance the capital for investment. Already from this standpoint, according to the physiocrats, the appropriation by the farmer of that portion of the agricultural *surplus product* which represents interest is consequently as necessary a condition of the reproductive process as the farming class itself; and this element therefore cannot be put in the category of the national "net product" or "net income"; for the latter is characterised precisely by the fact that it is consumable without any regard to the immediate needs of national reproduction. This fund of one milliard, however, according to Quesnay, serves for the most part to cover the repairs which become necessary in the course of the year, and the partial renewals of invested capital; further, as a reserve fund against accidents, and finally, where possible, for the enlargement of the invested and working capital, as well as the improvement of the soil and extension of cultivation.

The whole process is certainly "fairly simple." There enter into circulation: from the farmers, two milliards in money for the payment of rent, and three milliards in products, of which two-thirds are means of subsistence and one-third, raw materials; from the sterile class, two milliards in manufactured commodities. Of the means of subsistence amounting to two milliards, one half is consumed by the landlords and their retainers, the other half by the sterile class in payment for its labour. The raw materials to the value of one milliard replace the working capital of this latter class. Of the manufactured goods in circulation, amounting to two milliards, one half goes to the landlords and the other to the farmers, for whom it is only a converted form of the interest, which arises at first hand out of agricultural reproduction, on their invested capital. The money thrown into circulation by the farmer in payment of rent, however, flows back to him through the sale of his products, and thus the same process can take place again in the next economic year.

And now we must admire Herr Dühring's "really critical" exposition, which is so infinitely superior to the "traditional superficial account." After mysteriously telling us five times in succession how unsatisfactory it was of Quesnay to operate with mere money values —which moreover turned out not to be true—he finally reaches the result that, when he asks: "What becomes of the net product, which has been appropriated as rent, in the course of the economic circulation?"—the *Tableau* "could offer nothing but confused and arbitrary conceptions, increasing to mysticism." We have seen that the *Tableau*—this both simple and, for its time, inspired representation of the annual process of reproduction through the medium of circulation—gives a very exact answer to the question of what becomes of this net product in the course of economic circulation, and therefore once again the "mysticism" and the "confused and arbitrary conceptions" are left simply and solely with Herr Dühring, as "the most doubtful aspect" and the sole "net product" of his studies of the physiocrats.

Herr Dühring is just as familiar with the historical influence of the physiocrats as with their theories. "With Turgot," he teaches us, "the physiocrats in France came to an end both in practice and in theory." If, however, Mirabeau was essentially a physiocrat in his economic views; if he was the leading economic authority in the Constituent Assembly of 1789; if in its economic reforms this Assembly translated into practice a substantial portion of the physiocrats' principles, and in particular even laid a heavy tax on ground rent, the net product appropriated by the landowners "without any payment in return"—all this does not exist for "a" Dühring.

Just as the long stroke drawn through the years from 1691 to 1752 removes all Hume's predecessors, so another stroke obliterates Sir James Steuart, who came between Hume and Adam Smith. There is not a syllable in Herr Dühring's "enterprise" on Steuart's great work, which, apart from its historical importance, permanently enriched the domain of political economy. But, instead, Herr Dühring applies to him the most abusive epithet in his dictionary, and says that he was "a *professor*" in Adam Smith's time. Unfortunately this charge is a pure invention. Steuart was in fact a large landowner in Scotland, who was banished from Great Britain for alleged complicity in the Stuart plots and through long residence and his journeys on the continent made himself familiar with economic conditions in various countries.

In a word: according to the *Critical History* the value of all earlier economists was only to serve either as "rudiments" of Herr Dühring's authoritative and more deeply laid foundation, or by their worthlessness to serve as a foil to the latter. In economics, however, there are also some heroes who represent not only "rudiments" of the "more deeply laid foundation," but "theses" from which the foundation, as was prescribed in his *Natural Philosophy*, is not "developed" but in fact "composed": for example, the "incomparably great and eminent" *List*, who, for the benefit of German manufacturers, puffed up the "more subtle" mercantile teachings of a Ferrier and others in "mightier" words; also *Carey*, who reveals the true essence of his wisdom in the following sentence: "Ricardo's system is one of discords ... its whole tends to the production of hostility among classes ... his book is the true manual of the demagogue, who seeks power by means of agrarianism, war, and plunder"; and finally the Confucius of the City of London, MacLeod....

People who want to study the history of political economy in the present and immediately foreseeable future would certainly be on much safer ground if they make themselves acquainted with the "watery products," "commonplaces" and "beggars' soup" of the "most current text-book compilations," rather than rely on Herr Dühring's "historical treatment in the grand style."

*   *   *

What then is the final result of our analysis of Dühring's "very own" system of political economy? Nothing except the fact that with all the great words and the still more mighty promises we are just as much led into the dark as we were in the *Philosophy*. His theory of value, this "touchstone of the genuineness of economic systems," amounts to the fact that by value Herr Dühring understands five totally different and directly contradictory things, and, therefore, to put it at its best, himself does not know what he means. The "natural laws of all economics," ushered in with such pomp, prove to be merely universally familiar and often not even properly understood platitudes of the worst description. The sole explanation of economic facts which his "very own" system can give is that they are the result of "force," a phrase with which the philistine of all nations has for thousands of years consoled himself for everything unpleasant that happens to him, and which leaves us just where we were. Instead however of investigating the origin and effects of this force, Herr Dühring tells us to remain gratefully content with the mere *word* "force" as the final cause and ultimate explanation of all economic phenomena. Compelled to give further elucidation of the capitalist exploitation of labour, he first represents it in a general way as based on tribute and additions to price, in this completely appropriating the Proudhon "deduction" (*prélèvement*), then proceeding to explain it in detail by means of the Marxian theory of surplus labour, surplus product and surplus value. In this way he contrives successfully to reconcile two totally contradictory points of view, by copying down both without taking breath. And just as in philosophy he could not find hard words enough for the very Hegel whom he was so constantly exploiting and at the same time emasculating, so in the *Critical History* the most baseless calumniation of Marx only serves to conceal the fact that everything in the *Course* about capital and labour which has any sense in it at all is likewise an emasculated plagiarism of Marx. The ignorance which, in the *Course*, puts the "large landowners" at the beginning of the history of civilised peoples, and knows not a word of the common ownership of land in the tribal and village communities, which is the real starting point of history—this ignorance, at the present day almost incomprehensible, is almost surpassed by the ignorance which, in the *Critical History*, puts itself forward with no little pride on the basis of "the breadth of its historical survey," and of which we have given only a few awful examples. In a word: first the colossal "effort" of self-admiration, of charlatan blasts on his own trumpet, of promises each surpassing the other; and then the "result"— which is equal to zero.

I. HISTORICAL

We saw in the introduction * how the French philosophers of the eighteenth century, who paved the way for the revolution, appealed to reason as the sole judge of all that existed. A rational state, a rational society were to be established; everything that ran counter to eternal reason was to be relentlessly set aside. We saw also that in reality this eternal reason was no more than the idealised intellect of the middle class, just at that period developing into the bourgeoisie. When, therefore, the French Revolution had realised this rational society and this rational state, it became apparent that the new institutions, however rational in comparison with earlier conditions, were by no means absolutely rational. The rational state had suffered shipwreck. Rousseau's Social Contract had found its realisation in the Reign of Terror, from which the bourgeoisie, who had lost faith in their own political capacity, had sought refuge first in the corruption of the Directorate, and ultimately in the protection of the Napoleonic despotism. The promised eternal peace had changed to an endless war of conquest. The rational society had fared no better. The antithesis between rich and poor, instead of being resolved in general well-being, had been sharpened by the abolition of the guild and other privileges, which had bridged it over, and of the benevolent institutions of the Church, which had mitigated its effects; the impetuous growth of industry on a capitalist basis raised the poverty and suffering of the working masses into a vital condition of society's existence. The number of crimes increased from year to year. And if the feudal depravities, formerly shamelessly flaunting in the light of day, though not abolished, were yet temporarily forced into the background, on the other hand the bourgeois vices, until then cherished only in privacy, now bloomed all the more luxuriantly. Trade developed more and more into swindling. The "fraternity" of the revolutionary motto was realised in the chi-

* Cf. Philosophy; I [Note by F. Engels.]
281

canery and envy of the competitive struggle. Corruption took the place of violent oppression, and money replaced the sword as the chief lever of social power. The "right of the first night" passed from the feudal lords to the bourgeois manufacturers. Prostitution assumed proportions hitherto unknown. Marriage itself remained, as before, the legally recognised form, the official cloak of prostitution, and was also supplemented by widespread adultery. In a word, compared with the glowing promises of the prophets of the Enlightenment, the social and political institutions established by the "victory of reason" proved to be bitterly disillusioning caricatures. The only thing still lacking was people to voice this disillusionment, and these came with the turn of the century. In 1802 Saint-Simon's *Geneva Letters* appeared; Fourier's first work was published in 1808, although the groundwork of his theory dated from 1799; on the first of January, 1800, Robert Owen took over the management of New Lanark.

At this period, however, the capitalist mode of production, and with it the antagonism between bourgeoisie and proletariat, was as yet very undeveloped. Large-scale industry, which had only just arisen in England, was still unknown in France. But it is large-scale industry that on the one hand first develops the conflicts which make a revolution in the mode of production an urgent necessity—conflicts not only between the classes born of it, but also between the very productive forces and forms of exchange which it creates; and on the other hand it develops, precisely in these gigantic productive forces, also the means through which these conflicts can be resolved. If, therefore, about 1800, the conflicts arising from the new social order were only just beginning to develop, this is even more true of the means through which they were to be resolved. Though during the Reign of Terror the propertyless masses of Paris had been able to win the mastery for a moment, by doing so they had only proved how impossible their rule was in the then existing conditions. The proletariat, only then just separating itself from these propertyless masses as the nucleus of a new class, as yet quite incapable of independent political action, appeared as an oppressed, suffering estate of society, to which, in its incapacity to help itself, help could at most be brought from outside, from above.

This historical situation also dominated the founders of socialism. To the immature stage of capitalist production and the immature class position, immature theories corresponded. The solution of social problems, a solution which still lay hidden in the undeveloped economic conditions, was to be produced out of men's heads. Society presented nothing but abuses; it was the task of the thinking intellect to remove them. What was required was to discover a new and more perfect social order and to impose this on society from without, by propaganda and where possible by the example of model experiments. These new social systems were from the outset doomed to be utopias; the more their details were elaborated, the more they necessarily receded into pure phantasy.

This once established, we shall not dwell a moment longer on this aspect, now belonging wholly to the past. We can leave it to literary retailers à la Dühring to puzzle their brains solemnly over these phantasies, which today are only diverting, and to prove the superiority of their own sober mode of thought over such "absurdity." We, on the contrary, delight in the inspired ideas and germs of ideas which everywhere emerge through their covering of phantasy, and to which those philistines are blind.

In his *Geneva Letters*, Saint-Simon already laid down the principle that "all men should work." When he wrote these letters he already knew that the Reign of Terror was the reign of the propertyless masses. "See," he tells them, "what happened in France when your comrades were masters there; they created famine." But to conceive the French Revolution as a class war between nobility, bourgeoisie and the propertyless masses was, indeed, in the year 1802, a discovery of genius. In 1816 he declared that politics was the science of production, and predicted the complete absorption of politics in economics. And if the recognition that economic conditions are the basis of political institutions here shows itself only in embryo, nevertheless the transformation of political government over men into the administration of things and the direction of production processes —that is, the abolition of the state about which so much noise has recently been made everywhere—is already clearly stated. With equal superiority over his contemporaries, in 1814, immediately after the entry of the Allies into Paris, and again in 1815, during the Hundred

Days' War, he proclaimed the alliance of France with England, and
in the second line, of these two countries with Germany, as the sole
guarantee of the prosperous development and the peace of Europe.
To preach to the French in 1815 an alliance with the victors of
Waterloo certainly required more courage than to declare a war of
tittle-tattle on German professors.

If in Saint-Simon we find the breadth of view of a genius, thanks
to which almost all the ideas of later socialists which are not strictly
economic are contained in his works in embryo, in Fourier we find a
critique of existing social conditions, which, typically French in its
wit, is none the less penetrating. Fourier takes the bourgeoisie at their
word—both their enthusiastic prophets before the revolution and
their interested sycophants after it. He mercilessly lays bare the material and moral poverty of the bourgeois world, contrasting it both
with the glittering promises made by the philosophers of the Enlightenment of a society only ruled by reason, of a civilisation which
would yield universal happiness, of the illimitable perfectibility of
man; and with the highly coloured phraseology of his contemporary
bourgeois ideologists, showing how everywhere the most pitiable
reality corresponds to the most fine-sounding phrase, and over-
whelming with his mordant satire this hopeless fiasco of phrases.
Fourier is not only a critic; his irrepressible gaiety makes him a
satirist, and indeed one of the greatest satirists of all time. He depicts
with the touch of a master, and at the same time in a most diverting
way, the speculative swindles which flourished on the downfall of
the revolution, and also the shopkeeping outlook which was characteristic of the French merchants of that period. His criticism of the
bourgeois form of relations between the sexes, and of the position of
woman in bourgeois society, is even more masterly. He was the first
to declare that in a given society the degree of emancipation of
women is the natural measure of the general emancipation. But it is
in his conception of the history of society that Fourier appears at his
greatest. He divides its whole past course into four stages of development: savagery, barbarism, the patriarchate, civilisation, the last of
which coincides with what is now called bourgeois society; and he
shows "that the civilised stage raises every vice, practised by barbarism in a simple way, into a complex, ambiguous, hypocritical

mode of existence"; that civilisation moves in a "vicious circle," in contradictions which it constantly reproduces but is never able to overcome, so that it constantly attains the opposite of what it wants or pretends that it wants to achieve. So that, for example, "in civilisation, *poverty springs from superabundance itself.*" Fourier, as we see, handles dialectics in the same masterly way as his contemporary Hegel. With the same use of dialectics he brings out the fact, in opposition to the talk about the illimitable perfectibility of man, that each historical phase has its ascending, but also its descending curve, and applies this conception also to the future of the whole human race. As Kant introduced into natural science the ultimate destruction of the earth, so Fourier introduced into historical thought the ultimate extinction of humanity.

While in France the hurricane of the revolution swept through the land, in England a quieter, but none the less mighty, revolutionising process was developing. Steam and the new tool-making machinery were transforming manufacture into modern large-scale industry, and thereby revolutionising the whole basis of bourgeois society. The sluggish march of development in the manufacturing period had changed to a real period of storm and stress in production. The division of society into big capitalists and propertyless proletarians was taking place with ever-increasing rapidity; and between these two classes, instead of the former stable middle-class, there was now an unstable mass of artisans and small shopkeepers leading a precarious existence—the most fluctuating section of the population. The new mode of production was still only at the beginning of its ascending curve; it was still the normal, in existing conditions the sole possible mode of production. But even at that time it was producing crying social abuses: the crowding together of a homeless population in the worst quarters of great cities—the rupture of all traditional bonds based on descent, of patriarchal subordination, of the family—excessive labour, especially of women and children, on an appalling scale—widespread demoralisation of the working class, suddenly hurled into completely new conditions. Then a twenty-nine year old manufacturer came on the scene as a reformer, a man of almost sublimely child-like simplicity of character and at the same time a born leader of men such as is rarely seen. Robert Owen had adopted the teachings of the materialist philosophers of the Enlightenment, that man's character is the product on the one hand of his hereditary constitution, and on the other, of his environment during his lifetime, and particularly during the period of his development. In the industrial revolution most of his class saw only confusion and chaos, enabling them to fish in troubled waters and get rich quickly. He saw in it the opportunity to put his favourite theory into practice, and thereby to bring order out of chaos. He had already tried it out with success in Manchester, as manager of a factory with over five hundred workers; from 1800 to 1829 he directed the great cotton-spinning mill of New Lanark in Scotland, as managing partner, along the same lines but with greater freedom of action, and with a success which won him European fame. He transformed a population which rose gradually to 2,500 persons, and was originally composed of the most diverse and for the most part extremely demoralised elements, into an absolutely model colony, in which drunkenness, police, magistrates, lawsuits, poor law institutions and any need of charity were things unknown. And in fact he did so simply by placing the people in conditions more worthy of human beings, and especially by having the rising generation carefully brought up. He was the inventor of infant schools, and first introduced them here. From two years of age the children came to school, where they enjoyed themselves so much that they could hardly be got home again. While his competitors worked thirteen to fourteen hours a day, in New Lanark only ten and a half hours was worked. When a cotton crisis made a four months' stoppage necessary, full wages were paid to the idle workers. And with all this the concern had more than doubled its value and to the end brought in substantial profits to the proprietors.

In spite of it all, Owen was not content. The existence which he had contrived for his workers in his eyes fell far short of being worthy of human beings; "the people were my slaves": the relatively favourable conditions in which he had set them were still far removed from allowing them an all-round and rational development of character and mind, and much less a free life. "And yet, the working part of this population of 2,500 persons was daily producing as much real wealth for society as, less than half a century before, it would have required the working part of a population of 600,000 to create. I asked myself: what became of the difference between the wealth consumed by 2,500 persons and that which would have been consumed by 600,000?" The answer was clear. It had been used to pay the owners of the concern five per cent interest on their invested capital and in addition a profit of more than £300,000 sterling. And what was true of New Lanark held good in still greater measure of all the factories in England. "Without this new wealth created by machinery, the wars for the overthrow of Napoleon, and for maintaining the aristocratic principles of society, could not have been carried through. And yet this new power was the creation of the working class." To them, therefore, also belonged the fruits. To Owen, the new mighty productive forces, which until then had served only for the enrichment of individuals and the enslavement of the masses, offered the basis for a reconstruction of society, and were destined, as the common property of all, to work only for the common welfare of all.

The Owenite communism arose in this purely business way, as the result, so to speak, of commercial calculation. It retained this practical character throughout. Thus in 1823 Owen put forward a scheme to end the distress in Ireland by means of communist colonies; attached to the scheme were comprehensive estimates of the initial costs, the annual expenditure and the revenue which could be expected. Thus, too, in his definite plan for the future the technical elaboration of details shows such practical knowledge that, once the Owenite method of social reform is accepted, from an expert's standpoint there is little to be said against the actual detailed arrangements.

His advance to communism was the turning-point in Owen's life. As long as he merely played the part of a philanthropist he had reaped nothing but wealth, applause, honour and glory. He was the most popular man in Europe. Not only those of his own class, but statesmen and princes listened to him with approval. But when he came forward with his communist theories, the situation was entirely changed. There were three great obstacles which above all seemed to him to block the path to social reform: private property, religion and marriage in its present form. He knew what confronted him if he attacked them: complete outlawry from official society and the loss of his whole social position. But he did not let anything hold him back from attacking them regardless of the consequences, and what he had foreseen came to pass. Banished from official society, banned by the press, impoverished by the failure of communist experiments in America in which he sacrificed his whole fortune, he turned directly to the working class and worked among them for another thirty years. All social movements, all real advances made in England in the interests of the working class were associated with Owen's name. Thus in 1819, after five years' effort, he was successful in securing the first law limiting the labour of women and children in the factories. He presided at the first Congress at which the trade unions of all England united in a single great trades association. As transition measures to the complete communist organisation of society he introduced on the one hand the co-operative societies (both consumers' and productive), which have since at least given practical proof that it is very well possible to dispense with both merchants and manufacturers; and on the other hand, the labour bazaars, institutions for the exchange of the products of labour by means of labour notes with the labour hour as unit. These institutions were necessarily bound to fail, but they completely anticipated the Proudhon exchange bank of a much later period, and only differed from it in that they did not represent the panacea for all social ills, but only the first step towards a far more radical transformation of society.

These are the men on whom the sovereign Herr Dühring looks down, from the height of his "final and ultimate truth," with a contempt of which we have given a few examples in the introduction. And in one respect this contempt was not devoid of adequate reason: for its basis is, in essence, a really terrifying ignorance of the works of the three utopians. Thus Herr Dühring says of Saint-Simon that "his basic idea was, in essentials, correct, and apart from some one-sided aspects, even today provides the directing impulse towards real changes." But although Herr Dühring does actually seem to have had some of Saint-Simon's works in his hands, our search through the twenty-seven relevant pages for Saint-Simon's "basic idea" is just as fruitless as our earlier search for what Quesnay's *Tableau Economique* "meant for Quesnay himself," and in the end we have to allow ourselves to be put off with the phrase "that imagination and philanthropic fervour ... along with the extravagant phantasy that goes with it, dominated the whole of Saint-Simon's thought!" As regards Fourier, all that Herr Dühring knows or takes into account is his phantasies of the future, painted in romantic detail; which of course "is far more important" from the standpoint of proving Herr Dühring's infinite superiority over Fourier than an examination of how the latter "attempts *incidentally* to criticise actual conditions." Incidentally! In fact, almost every page of his works scintillates with sparkling satire and criticism aimed at the wretchedness of our vaunted civilisation. It is like saying that Herr Dühring only "incidentally" declares Herr Dühring to be the greatest thinker of all time. And as for the twelve pages devoted to Robert Owen, Herr Dühring has absolutely no other source for this than the miserable biography of the philistine Sargant, who also did not know Owen's most important works—on marriage and the communist system. This ignorance makes it possible for Herr Dühring to go the length of boldly asserting that we should not "attribute any clear-cut communism" to Owen. Had Herr Dühring even fingered Owen's *Book of the New Moral World,* he would most assuredly have found clearly expressed in it not only the most clear-cut communism possible, with equal obligation to labour and equal rights in the product—equal according to age, as Owen always adds—but also the most comprehensive project of the future communist community, with its ground-plan, elevation and bird's-eye view. But a man who, like Herr Dühring, limits his "first-hand study of the writings of the representatives of socialist opinion" to a knowledge of the title and at most the *motto* of a small number of these works, naturally cannot do anything but make such a stupid and purely phantastic assertion. Owen did not only preach "clear-cut communism"; for five years (at the end of the 'thirties and beginning of the 'forties) he put it into practice in the Harmony Hall Colony in Hampshire, whose communism left nothing to be desired in definiteness. I myself was acquainted with several former members of this communist model experiment. But Sargant knew absolutely nothing of all this, or of any of Owen's activity between 1836 and 1850, and consequently Herr Dühring's "more profound historical treatment" is also left in pitch-black ignorance. Herr

Dühring calls Owen "in all aspects a veritable monster of importunate philanthropy." But when this same Herr Dühring starts to
give us information about the contents of books whose title and
inscription he hardly knows, we must not on any account say that
he is "in all aspects a veritable monster of importunate ignorance,"
for on *our* lips this would certainly be "abuse."

The utopians, we saw, were utopians because they could be nothing else at a time when capitalist production was as yet so little
developed. They necessarily had to construct the outlines of a new
society out of their own heads, because within the old society the elements of the new were not as yet generally apparent; for the basic
plan of the new edifice they could only appeal to reason, just because
they could not as yet appeal to contemporary history. But when
now, almost eighty years after their time, Herr Dühring steps on to
the stage and puts forward his claim to an "authoritative" system of
a new social order—not evolved out of the historically developed
material at his disposal, as its inevitable result—oh, no!—but constructed out of his sovereign head, out of his ·mind, pregnant with
ultimate truths—then he, who scents epigones everywhere, is himself
nothing but the epigone of the utopians, the latest utopian. He calls
the great utopians "social alchemists." That may be. Alchemy was
necessary in its epoch. But since that time large-scale industry has
developed the contradictions lying dormant in the capitalist mode of
production into such crying antagonisms that the imminent collapse
of this mode of production is, so to speak, palpable; that the new
productive forces themselves can only be maintained and further
developed by the introduction of a new mode of production corresponding to their present stage of development; that the struggle
between the two classes engendered by the former mode of production and constantly reproduced in ever sharper antagonism has affected all civilised countries and is daily becoming more violent;
and that this historical process, the conditions of the social transformation which it makes necessary, and the basic features of this
transformation likewise determined by it, have already also been
understood. And if Herr Dühring produces a new utopian social
order out of his sovereign brain instead of from the economic material ready to his hand, he is not practising mere "social alchemy."

On the contrary, he is acting like a person who, after the discovery and establishment of the laws of modern chemistry, attempts to restore the old alchemy and to use atomic weights, molecular formulæ, the quantivalence of atoms, crystallography and spectral analysis for the sole purpose of discovering the *Philosopher's Stone*.

II. THEORETICAL

The materialist conception of history starts from the principle that production, and with production the exchange of its products, is the basis of every social order; that in every society which has appeared in history the distribution of the products, and with it the division of society into classes or estates, is determined by what is produced and how it is produced, and how the product is exchanged. According to this conception, the ultimate causes of all social changes and political revolutions are to be sought, not in the minds of men, in their increasing insight into eternal truth and justice, but in changes in the mode of production and exchange; they are to be sought not in the *philosophy* but in the *economics* of the epoch concerned. The growing realisation that existing social institutions are irrational and unjust, that reason has become nonsense and good deeds a scourge is only a sign that changes have been taking place quietly in the methods of production and forms of exchange with which the social order, adapted to previous economic conditions, is no longer in accord. This also involves that the means through which the abuses that have been revealed can be got rid of must likewise be present, in more or less developed form, in the altered conditions of productions. These means are not to be *invented* by the mind, but *discovered* by means of the mind in the existing material facts of production.

Where then, on this basis, does modern socialism stand?

The existing social order, as is now fairly generally admitted, is the creation of the present ruling class, the bourgeoisie. The mode of production peculiar to the bourgeoisie—called, since Marx, the capitalist mode of production—was incompatible with the local privileges and privileges of birth as well as with the reciprocal personal ties of the feudal system; the bourgeoisie shattered the feudal system, and on its ruins established the bourgeois social order, the realm of free competition, freedom of movement, equal rights for

292

commodity owners, and all the other bourgeois glories. The capitalist mode of production could now develop freely. From the time when steam and the new tool-making machinery had begun to transform the former manufacture into large-scale industry, the productive forces evolved under bourgeois direction developed at a pace that was previously unknown and to an unprecedented degree. But just as manufacture, and the handicraft industry which had been further developed under its influence, had previously come into conflict with the feudal fetters of the guilds, so large-scale industry, as it develops more fully, comes into conflict with the barriers within which the capitalist mode of production holds it confined. The new forces of production have already outgrown the bourgeois form of using them; and this conflict between productive forces and mode of production is not a conflict which has risen in men's heads, as for example the conflict between original sin and divine justice; but it exists in the facts, objectively, outside of us, independently of the will or purpose even of the men who brought it about. Modern socialism is nothing but the reflex in thought of this actual conflict, its ideal reflection in the minds first of the class which is directly suffering under it—the working class.

In what, then, does this conflict consist?

Previous to capitalist production, that is to say, in the Middle Ages, small-scale production was general, on the basis of the private ownership by the workers of their means of production; the agricultural industry of the small peasant, freeman or serf, and the handicraft industry of the towns. The instruments of labour—land, agricultural implements, the workshop and tools—were the instruments of labour of individuals, intended only for individual use, and therefore necessarily puny, dwarfish, restricted. But just because of this they belonged, as a rule, to the producer himself. To concentrate and enlarge these scattered, limited means of production, to transform them into the mighty levers of production of the present day, was precisely the historic role of the capitalist mode of production and of its representative, the bourgeoisie. In Part IV of *Capital* Marx gives a detailed account of how, since the fifteenth century, this process has developed historically through the three stages of simple co-operation, manufacture and large-scale industry.

But as Marx also points out, the bourgeoisie was unable to transform those limited means of production into mighty productive forces except by transforming them from individual means of production into *social* means of production, which could be used only *by a body of men as a whole*. The spinning wheel, the hand loom and the blacksmith's hammer were replaced by the spinning machine, the mechanical loom and the steam hammer; and the factory, making the co-operation of hundreds and thousands of workers necessary, took the place of the individual work-room. And, like the means of production, production itself changed from a series of individual operations into a series of social acts, and the products from the products of individuals into social products. The yarn, the cloth and the metal goods which now came from the factory were the common product of many workers through whose hands it had to pass successively before it was ready. No individual can say of such products: I made it, that is *my* product.

But where the natural spontaneous division of labour within society is the basic form of production, it imprints upon the products the form of *commodities*, the mutual exchange, purchase and sale of which enables the individual producers to satisfy their manifold needs. And this was the case during the Middle Ages. The peasant, for example, sold agricultural products to the artisan and purchased from him in exchange the products of his craft. Into this society of individual producers, producers of commodities, the new mode of production thrust itself, setting up, in the midst of the spontaneous *planless* division of labour which then existed throughout society, the *planned* division of labour organised in the individual factory; alongside of *individual* production, *social* production made its appearance. The products of both were sold on the same market, and consequently at prices which were at least approximately the same. But the planned organization was stronger than the natural division of labour; the factories in which labour was socially organised produced their commodities more cheaply than the separate small producers. Individual production was vanquished on one field after another; social production revolutionised the whole former mode of production. But this, its revolutionary character, was so little understood that, on the contrary, it was introduced as a means of stimulating and accelerating the production of commodities. In its origin, it was directly linked with certain levers of commodity production and exchange which were already in existence: merchant's capital, handicraft, wage labour. Inasmuch as it itself came into being as a new form of commodity production, the forms of appropriation characteristic of commodity production remained in full force also for it.

In commodity production as it had developed in the Middle Ages, the question could never arise of who should be the owner of the product of labour. The individual producer had produced it, as a rule, from raw material which belonged to him and was often produced by himself, with his own instruments of labour, and by his own manual labour or that of his family. There was no need whatever for the product to be appropriated by him; it belonged to him as an absolute matter of course. His ownership of the product was therefore based *upon his own labour*. Even where outside help was used, it was as a rule subsidiary, and in many cases received other compensation in addition to wages; the guild apprentice and journeyman worked less for the sake of their board and wages than to train themselves to become master craftsmen. Then came the concentration of the means of production in large workshops and manufactories, their transformation into means of production that were in fact social. But the social means of production and the social products were treated as if they were still, as they had been before, the means of production and the products of individuals. Hitherto, the owner of the instruments of labour had appropriated the product because it was as a rule his own product, the auxiliary labour of other persons being the exception; now, the owner of the instruments of labour continued to appropriate the product, although it was no longer *his* product, but exclusively the product of *other's labour*. Thus, therefore, the products, now socially produced, were not appropriated by those who had really set the means of production in motion and really produced the products, but by the *capitalists*. Means of production and production itself had in essence become social. But they were subjected to a form of appropriation which has as its presupposition private production by individuals, with each individual owning his own product and bringing it on to the market. The mode of production is subjected to this form of appropriation, although it removes the presuppositions on which the latter was based.* In this contradiction, which gives the new mode of production its capitalist character, *the whole conflict of today is already present in germ*. The more the new mode of production gained the ascendancy on all decisive fields of production and in all countries of decisive economic importance, supplanting individual production except for insignificant relics, the *more glaring necessarily became the incompatibility of social production with capitalist appropriation*.

The first capitalists found, as we have said, the form of wage labour already in existence; but wage labour as the exception, as an auxiliary occupation, as a supplementary, as a transitory phase. The agricultural labourer who occasionally went to work as a day labourer had a few acres of his own land, from which if necessary he could get his livelihood. The regulations of the guilds ensured that the journeyman of today became the master craftsman of to-morrow. But as soon as the means of production had become social and were concentrated in the hands of capitalists, this situation changed. Both the means of production and the products of the small, individual producer lost more and more of their value; there was nothing left for him to do but to go to the capitalist, and work for wages. Wage labour, hitherto an exception and subsidiary, became the rule and the basic form of all production; hitherto an auxiliary occupation, it now became the labourer's exclusive activity. The occasional wage worker became the wage worker for life. The number of lifelong wage workers was also increased to a colossal extent by the simultaneous disintegration of the feudal

* There is no need here to explain that although the form of appropriation remains the same, the *character* of the appropriation is revolutionised by the process described above, to no less a degree than production. My appropriation of my own product and my appropriation of another person's product are certainly two very different forms of appropriation. It may be noted in passing that wage labour, in which the whole capitalist mode of production is already present in embryo form, is a very old institution; in isolated and scattered form it developed alongside slavery for centuries. But the germ could only develop into the capitalist mode of production when the necessary historical conditions had come into existence. [*Note by F. Engels.*]

system, the dispersal of the retainers of the feudal lords, the eviction of peasants from their homesteads, etc. The separation between the means of production concentrated in the hands of the capitalists, on the one side, and the producers now possessing nothing but their labour power, on the other, was made complete. *The contradiction between social production and capitalist appropriation became manifest as the antagonism between proletariat and bourgeoisie.*

We saw that the capitalist mode of production thrust itself into a society of commodity producers, individual producers, whose social cohesion resulted from the exchange of their products. But every society based on commodity production has the peculiarity that in it the producers have lost control of their own social relationships. Each produces for himself, with the means of production which happen to be at his disposal and in order to satisfy his individual needs through the medium of exchange. No one knows how much of the article he produces is coming onto the market, or how much demand there is for it; no one knows whether his individual product will meet a real need, whether he will cover his costs or even be able to sell it at all. Anarchy reigns in social production. But commodity production, like all other forms of production, has its own laws, which are inherent in and inseparable from it; and these laws assert themselves in spite of anarchy, in and through anarchy. These laws are manifested in the sole form of social relationship which continues to exist, in exchange, and enforce themselves on the individual producers as compulsory laws of competition. At first therefore, they are unknown even to these producers, and have to be discovered by them gradually only through long experience. They assert themselves therefore apart from the producers and against the producers, as the natural laws of their form of production, working blindly. The product dominates the producers.

In mediæval society, especially in the earlier centuries, production was essentially for the producer's own use; for the most part its aim was to satisfy only the needs of the producer and his family. Where, as in the countryside, personal relations of dependence existed, it also contributed towards satisfying the needs of the feudal lord. No exchange was involved, and consequently the products did not assume the character of commodities. The peasant family produced almost everything it required—utensils and clothing as well as food. It was only when it succeeded in producing a surplus beyond its own needs and the payments in kind due to the feudal lord—it was only at this stage that it also began to produce commodities; these surplus products, thrown into social exchange, offered for sale, became commodities. The town artisans, it is true, had to produce for exchange from the very beginning. But even they supplied the greatest part of their own needs themselves; they had gardens and small fields; they sent their cattle out into the communal woodland, which also provided them with timber and firewood; the women spun flax, wool, etc. Production for the purpose of exchange, the production of commodities, was only in its infancy. Hence, restricted exchange, restricted market, stable methods of production, local isolation from the outside world, and local unity within: the Mark in the countryside, the guild in the town.

With the extension of commodity production, however, and especially with the emergence of the capitalist mode of production, the laws of commodity production, previously latent, also began to operate more openly and more potently. The old bonds were loosened, the old dividing barriers broken through, the producers more and more transformed into independent, isolated commodity producers. The anarchy of social production became obvious, and was carried to further and further extremes. But the chief means through which the capitalist mode of production accentuated this anarchy in social production was the direct opposite of anarchy: the increasing organisation of production on a social basis in each individual productive establishment. This was the lever with which it put an end to the former peaceful stability. In whatever branch of industry it was introduced, it could suffer no older method of production to exist alongside it; where it laid hold of a handicraft, that handicraft was wiped out. The field of labour became a field of battle. The great geographical discoveries and the colonisation which followed on them multiplied markets and hastened on the transformation of handicraft into manufacture. The struggle broke out not only between the individual local producers; the local struggles developed into national struggles, the trade wars of the seventeenth and eighteenth centuries. Finally, large-scale industry and the creation of the world market have made the struggle universal and at the same time given it an unparalleled intensity. Between individual capitalists, as between whole industries and whole countries, advantages in natural or artificial conditions of production decide life or death. The vanquished are relentlessly cast aside. It is the Darwinian struggle for individual existence, transferred from Nature to society with intensified fury. The standpoint of the animal in Nature appears as the last word in human development. The contradiction between social production and capitalist appropriation reproduces itself as *the antithesis between the organisation of production in the individual factory and the anarchy of production in society as a whole.*

The capitalist mode of production moves in these two forms of manifestation of the contradiction immanent in it from its very nature, without hope of escaping from that "vicious circle" which Fourier long ago discovered in it. But what Fourier in his day was as yet unable to see is that this circle is gradually narrowing; that the motion is rather in the form of a spiral and must meet its end, like the motion of the planets, by collision with the centre. It is the driving force of the social anarchy of production which transforms the immense majority of men more and more into proletarians, and it is in turn the proletarian masses who will ultimately put an end to the anarchy of production. It is the driving force of the social anarchy of production which transforms the infinite perfectibility of the machine in large-scale industry into a compulsory commandment for each individual industrial capitalist to make his machinery more and more perfect, under penalty of ruin. But the perfecting of machinery means rendering human labour superfluous. If the introduction and increase of machinery meant the displacement of millions of hand workers by a few machine workers, the improvement of machinery means the displacement of larger and larger numbers of the machine workers themselves, and ultimately the creation of a mass of available wage workers exceeding the average requirements of capital for labour—a complete industrial reserve army, as I called it as long ago as 1845 *—a reserve that would be available at periods when industry was working at high

* *The Condition of the Working Class in England,* p. 109. German edition. [Note by F. Engels.]

pressure, but would be thrown out onto the streets by the crash inevitably following the boom; a reserve that would at all times be like a leaden weight on the feet of the working class in their fight for existence against capital, a regulator to keep wages down to the low level which suits the needs of capital. Thus it comes about that machinery, to use Marx's phrase, becomes the most powerful weapon in the war of capital against the working class, that the instruments of labour constantly tear the means of subsistence out of the hands of the labourer, that the very product of the labourer is turned into an instrument for his subjection. Thus it comes about that the economising of the instruments of labour becomes from the outset a simultaneous and absolutely reckless waste of labour power and robbery of the normal conditions necessary for the labour function; that machinery, "the most powerful instrument for shortening labour time, becomes the most unfailing means for placing every moment of the labourer's time and that of his family at the disposal of the capitalist for the purpose of expanding the value of his capital." *

Thus it comes about that the excessive labour of some becomes the necessary condition for the lack of employment of others, and that large-scale industry, which hunts all over the world for new consumers, restricts the consumption of the masses at home to a starvation minimum and thereby undermines its own internal market. "The law that always equilibrates the relative surplus population, or industrial reserve army, to the extent and energy of accumulation, this law rivets the labourer to capital more firmly than the wedges of Vulcan did Prometheus to the rock. It establishes an accumulation of misery, corresponding with accumulation of capital. Accumulation of wealth at one pole is, therefore, at the same time accumulation of misery, agony of toil, slavery, ignorance, brutality, mental degradation, at the opposite pole, *i.e.*, on the side of the class that *produces its own products in the form of capital.*" **

And to expect any other distribution of the products from the capitalist mode of production is like expecting the electrodes of a battery, while they are in contact with the battery, not to decompose

---

* *Capital*, Vol. I, p. 445 (Kerr edition).
** *Capital*, Vol. I, p. 709 (Kerr edition).

water, not to develop oxygen at the positive pole and hydrogen at the negative.

We have seen how the perfectibility of modern machinery, pushed to an extreme point, through the medium of the anarchy of production in society is transformed into a compulsory commandment for the individual industrial capitalist constantly to improve his machinery, constantly to increase its productive power. The mere possibility of extending his field of production is transformed for him into a similar compulsory commandment. The enormous expanding power of large-scale industry, compared with which the expanding power of gases is mere child's play, now appears to us as a *necessity* for both qualitative and quantitative expansion that laughs at all counteracting pressure. Such counteracting pressure comes from consumption, sale, markets for the products of large-scale industry. But the capacity of the market to expand, both extensively and intensively, is controlled directly by quite other and far less effective laws. The expansion of the market cannot keep pace with the expansion of production. The collision becomes inevitable, and as it can yield no solution so long as it does not burst the capitalist mode of production itself, it becomes periodic. Capitalist production brings into being a new "vicious circle."

And in fact, since 1825, when the first general crisis broke out, the whole industrial and commercial world, the production and exchange of all civilised peoples and of their more or less barbarian dependent people have been dislocated practically once in every ten years. Trade comes to a standstill, the markets are glutted, the products lie in great masses, unsalable, ready money disappears, credit vanishes, the factories are idle, the working masses go short of the means of subsistence because they have produced too much of them, bankruptcy follows upon bankruptcy, forced sale upon forced sale. The stagnation lasts for years, both productive forces and products are squandered and destroyed on a large scale, until the accumulated masses of commodities are at last disposed of at a more or less considerable depreciation, until production and exchange gradually begin to move again. By degrees the pace quickens; it becomes a trot; the industrial trot passes into a gallop, and the gallop in turn passes into the headlong onrush of a complete industrial commercial, credit and speculative steeple-chase, only to land again in the end, after the most breakneck jumps—in the ditch of a crash. And so on again and again. We have now experienced it five times since 1825, and at this moment (1877) we are experiencing it for the sixth time. And the character of these crises is so clearly marked that Fourier hit them all off when he described the first as *crise pléthorique*, a crisis of super-abundance.

In these crises, the contradiction between social production and capitalist appropriation comes to a violent explosion. The circula-tion of commodities is for the moment reduced to nothing; the means of circulation, money, becomes an obstacle to circulation; all the laws of commodity production and commodity circulation are turned upside down. The economic collision has reached its culminating point: *the mode of production rebels against the mode of exchange; the productive forces rebel against the mode of pro-duction, which they have outgrown.*

The fact that the social organisation of production within the factory has developed to the point at which it has become incom-patible with the anarchy of production in society which exists alongside it and above it—this fact is made palpable to the capi-talists themselves by the violent concentration of capitals which take place during crises through the ruin of many big and even more small capitalists. The whole mechanism of the capitalist mode of production breaks down under the pressure of the productive forces which it itself created. It is no longer able to transform the whole of this mass of means of production into capital; they lie idle, and for this very reason the industrial reserve army must also lie idle. Means of production, means of subsistence, available la-bourers, all the elements of production and of general wealth are there in abundance. But "abundance becomes the source of distress and want" (Fourier), because it is precisely abundance that pre-vents the conversion of the means of production and subsistence into capital. For in capitalist society the means of production can-not begin to function unless they have first been converted into capital, into means for the exploitation of human labour power. The necessity for the means of production and subsistence to take on the form of capital stands like a ghost between them and the workers. It alone prevents the coming together of the material and personal levers of production; it alone forbids the means of production to function, the workers to work and to live. Thus on the one hand the capitalist mode of production stands convicted of its own incapacity any longer to control these productive forces. And on the other hand these productive forces themselves press forward with increasing force to put an end to the contradiction, to rid themselves of their character as capital, *to the actual recognition of their character as social productive forces.*

It is this pressure of the productive forces, in their mighty upgrowth, against their character as capital, increasingly compelling the recognition of their social character, which forces the capitalist class itself more and more to treat them as social productive forces, in so far as this is at all possible within the framework of capitalist relations. Both the period of industrial boom, with its unlimited credit inflation, and the crisis itself through the collapse of great capitalist establishments, urge forward towards that form of the socialisation of huge masses of means of production which we find in the various kinds of joint-stock companies. Many of these means of production are from the outset so colossal that, like the railways, they exclude all other forms of capitalist exploitation. At a certain stage of development even this form no longer suffices; the official representative of capitalist society, the state, is constrained to take over their management.* This necessity of conversion into

* I say *is constrained* to. For it is only when the means of production or communication have *actually* outgrown management by share companies, and therefore their transfer to the state has become inevitable *from an economic standpoint*—it is only then that this transfer to the state, even when carried out by the state of today, represents an economic advance, the attainment of another preliminary step towards the taking over of all productive forces by society itself. Recently, however, since Bismarck adopted state ownership, a certain spurious socialism has made its appearance—here and there even degenerating into a kind of flunkeyism—which declares that *all* taking over by the state, even the Bismarckian kind, is in itself socialistic. If, however, the taking over of the tobacco trade by the state was socialistic, Napoleon and Metternich would rank among the founders of socialism. If the Belgian state, for quite ordinary political and financial reasons, constructed its own main railway lines; if Bismarck, without any economic compulsion, took over the state property makes itself evident first in the big institutions for communication: the postal service, telegraphs and railways.

If the crises revealed the incapacity of the bourgeoisie any longer to control the modern productive forces, the conversion of the great organisations for production and communication into joint-stock companies and state property shows that for this purpose the bourgeoisie can be dispensed with. All the social functions of the capitalists are now carried out by salaried employees. The capitalist has no longer any social activity save the pocketing of revenues, the clipping of coupons and gambling on the Stock Exchange, where the different capitalists fleece each other of their capital. Just as at first the capitalist mode of production displaced the workers, so now it displaces the capitalists, relegating them, just as it did the workers, to the superfluous population, even if in the first instance not to the industrial reserve army.

But neither the conversion into joint-stock companies nor into state property deprives the productive forces of their character as capital. In the case of joint-stock companies this is obvious. And the modern state, too, is only the organisation with which bourgeois society provides itself in order to maintain the general external conditions of the capitalist mode of production against encroachments either by the workers or by individual capitalists. The modern state, whatever its form, is an essentially capitalist machine; it is the state of the capitalists, the ideal collective body of all capitalists. The more productive forces it takes over as its property, the more it becomes the real collective body of all the capitalists, the more citizens it exploits. The workers remain wage-earners, proletarians. The capitalist relationship is not abolished; it is rather pushed to an extreme. But at this extreme it is transformed into its opposite. State ownership of the productive forces is not the solution of the

main railway lines in Prussia, simply in order to be better able to organise and use them for war, to train the railway officials as the government's voting cattle, and especially to secure a new source of revenue independent of Parliamentary votes—such actions were in no sense socialist measures, whether direct or indirect, conscious or unconscious. Otherwise, the Royal Maritime Company, the Royal Porcelain Manufacture, and even the regimental tailors in the army, would be socialist institutions. [*Note by F. Engels.*]

conflict, but it contains within itself the formal means, the key to the solution.

This solution can only consist in the recognition in practice of the social nature of the modern productive forces, in bringing, therefore, the mode of production, appropriation and exchange into accord with the social character of the means of production. And this can only be brought about by society, openly and without deviation, taking possession of the productive forces which have outgrown all control other than that of society itself. Thereby the social character of the means of production and of the products— which today operates against the producers themselves, periodically breaking through the mode of production and exchange and enforcing itself only as a blind law of Nature, violently and destructively—is quite consciously asserted by the producers, and is transformed from a cause of disorder and periodic collapse into the most powerful lever of production itself.

The forces operating in society work exactly like the forces operating in Nature: blindly, violently, destructively, so long as we do not understand them and fail to take them into account. But when once we have recognised them and understood how they work, their direction and their effects, the gradual subjection of them to our will and the use of them for the attainment of our aims depends entirely upon ourselves. And this is quite especially true of the mighty productive forces of the present day. So long as we obstinately refuse to understand their nature and their character—and the capitalist mode of production and its defenders set themselves against any such attempt—so long do these forces operate in spite of us, against us, and so long do they control us, as we have shown in detail. But once their nature is grasped, in the hands of the producers working in association they can be transformed from demoniac masters into willing servants. It is the difference between the destructive force of electricity in the lightning of a thunderstorm and the tamed electricity of the telegraph and the arc light; the difference between a conflagration and fire in the service of man. This treatment of the productive forces of the present day, on the basis of their real nature at last recognised by society, opens the way to the replacement of the anarchy of social production by a socially planned regulation of production in accordance with the needs both of society as a whole and of each individual. The capitalist mode of appropriation, in which the product enslaves first the producer, and then also the appropriator, will thereby be replaced by the mode of appropriation of the products based on the nature of the modern means of production themselves: on the one hand direct social appropriation as a means to the maintenance and extension of production, and on the other hand direct individual appropriation as a means to life and pleasure.

By more and more transforming the great majority of the population into proletarians, the capitalist mode of production brings into being the force which, under penalty of its own destruction, is compelled to carry out this revolution. By more and more driving towards the conversion of the vast socialised means of production into state property, it itself points the way for the carrying through of this revolution. *The proletariat seizes the state power, and transforms the means of production in the first instance into state property.* But in doing this, it puts an end to itself as the proletariat, it puts an end to all class differences and class antagonisms, it puts an end also to the state as the state. Former society, moving in class antagonisms, had need of the state, that is, an organisation of the exploiting class at each period for the maintenance of its external conditions of production; that is, therefore, for the forcible holding down of the exploited class in the conditions of oppression (slavery, villeinage or serfdom, wage labour) determined by the existing mode of production. The state was the official representative of society as a whole, its embodiment in a visible corporation; but it was this only in so far as it was the state of that class which itself, in its epoch, represented society as a whole; in ancient times, the state of the slave-owning citizens; in the Middle Ages, of the feudal nobility; in our epoch, of the bourgeoisie. When ultimately it becomes really representative of society as a whole, it makes itself superfluous. As soon as there is no longer any class of society to be held in subjection; as soon as, along with class domination and the struggle for individual existence based on the former anarchy of production, the collisions and excesses arising from these have also been abolished, there is nothing more to be repressed which would make a special repressive force, a state, necessary. The first act in which the state really comes forward as the representative of society as a whole—the taking possession of the means of production in the name of society—is at the same time its last independent act as a state. The interference of the state power in social relations becomes superfluous in one sphere after another, and then ceases of itself. The government of persons is replaced by the administration of things and the direction of the processes of production. The state is not "abolished," *it withers away*. It is from this standpoint that we must appraise the phrase "free people's state"—both its justification at times for agitational purposes, and its ultimate scientific inadequacy—and also the demand of the so-called anarchists that the state should be abolished overnight.

Since the emergence in history of the capitalist mode of production, the taking over of all means of production by society has often been dreamed of by individuals as well as by whole sects, more or less vaguely and as an ideal of the future. But it could only become possible, it could only become a historical necessity, when the material conditions for its realisation had come into existence. Like every other social advance, it becomes realisable not through the perception that the existence of classes is in contradiction with justice, equality, etc., not through the mere will to abolish these classes, but through certain new economic conditions. The division of society into an exploiting and an exploited class, a ruling and an oppressed class, was the necessary outcome of the low development of production hitherto. So long as the sum of social labour yielded a product which only slightly exceeded what was necessary for the bare existence of all; so long, therefore, as all or almost all the time of the great majority of the members of society was absorbed in labour, so long was society necessarily divided into classes. Alongside of this great majority exclusively absorbed in labour there developed a class, freed from direct productive labour, which managed the general business of society: the direction of labour, affairs of state, justice, science, art, and so forth. It is therefore the law of the division of labour which lies at the root of the division into classes. But this does not mean that this division into classes was not established by violence and robbery, by deception and fraud, or that the ruling class, once in the saddle, has ever failed to strengthen its domination at the cost of the working class and to convert its social management into the exploitation of the masses.

But if, on these grounds, the division into classes has a certain historical justification, it has this only for a given period of time, for given social conditions. It was based on the insufficiency of production; it will be swept away by the full development of the modern productive forces. And in fact the abolition of social classes has as its presupposition a stage of historical development at which the existence not merely of some particular ruling class or other but of any ruling class at all, that is to say, of class difference itself, has become an anachronism, is out of date. It therefore presupposes that the development of production has reached a level at which the appropriation of means of production and of products, and with these, of political supremacy, the monopoly of education and intellectual leadership by a special class of society, has become not only superfluous but also economically, politically and intellectually a hindrance to development.

This point has now been reached. Their political and intellectual bankruptcy is hardly still a secret to the bourgeoisie themselves, and their economic bankruptcy recurs regularly every ten years. In each crisis society is smothered under the weight of its own productive forces and products of which it can make no use, and stands helpless in face of the absurd contradiction that the producers have nothing to consume because there are no consumers. The expanding force of the means of production bursts asunder the bonds imposed upon them by the capitalist mode of production. Their release from these bonds is the sole condition necessary for an unbroken and constantly more rapidly progressing development of the productive forces, and therewith of a practically limitless growth of production itself. Nor is this all. The appropriation by society of the means of production puts an end not only to the artificial restraints on production which exist today, but also to the positive waste and destruction of productive forces and products which is now the inevitable accompaniment of production and reaches its zenith in crises. Further, it sets free for society as a whole a mass of means of production and products by putting an end to the senseless luxury and extravagance of the present ruling class and its political representatives. The possibility of securing for every member of society, through social production, an existence which is not only fully sufficient from a material standpoint and becoming richer from day to day, but also guarantees to them the completely unrestricted development and exercise of their physical and mental faculties—this possibility now exists for the first time, but it *does exist.**

The seizure of the means of production by society puts an end to commodity production, and therewith to the domination of the product over the producer. Anarchy in social production is replaced by conscious organisation on a planned basis. The struggle for individual existence comes to an end. And at this point, in a certain sense, man finally cuts himself off from the animal world, leaves the conditions of animal existence behind him and enters conditions which are really human. The conditions of existence forming man's environment, which up to now have dominated man, at this point pass under the dominion and control of man, who now for the first time becomes the real conscious master of Nature, because and in so far as he has become master of his own social organisation. The laws of his own social activity, which have hitherto confronted him as external, dominating laws of Nature, will then be applied by man with complete understanding, and hence will be dominated by man. Men's own social organisation which has hitherto stood in opposition to them as if arbitrarily decreed by Nature and history, will then become the voluntary act of men themselves. The ob-

* A few figures may given an approximate idea of the enormous expansive power of modern means of production, even under the weight of capitalism. According to Giffen's latest estimates, the total wealth of Great Britain and Ireland was as under in round figures:

1814	....	£2,200,000,000
1865	....	6,100,000,000
1875	....	8,500,000,000

An indication of the waste of means of production and products resulting from crises is the estimate given at the Second German Industrial Congress (Berlin, Feb. 21, 1878) that the total loss to the *German iron industry* alone in the last crisis amounted to 455 million marks [£22,750,000]. [*Note by F. Engels.*]

jective, external forces which have hitherto dominated history, will then pass under the control of men themselves. It is only from this point that men, with full consciousness, will fashion their own history; it is only from this point that the social causes set in motion by men will have, predominantly and in constantly increasing measure, the effects willed by men. It is humanity's leap from the realm of necessity into the realm of freedom.

To carry through his world-emancipating act is the historical mission of the modern proletariat. And it is the task of scientific socialism, the theoretical expression of the proletarian movement, to establish the historical conditions and, with these, the nature of this act, and thus to bring to the consciousness of the now oppressed class the conditions and nature of the act which it is its destiny to accomplish.

III. PRODUCTION

After all that has been said above, the reader will not be surprised to learn that the evolution of the principles of socialism described in the two preceding chapters is not at all in accordance with Herr Dühring's view. On the contrary. He has no alternative but to relegate them to the abyss where lie all the other rejected "bastards of historical and logical phantasy," "barren conceptions" and "confused and nebulous conceptions." To Herr Dühring, socialism in fact is not in any sense a necessary product of historical development and still less of the gross material economic conditions of today, in which mere "fodder" is the governing consideration. He knows much better than that. His socialism is a final and ultimate truth; it is "the natural system of society," whose roots are to be found in a "universal principle of justice"; and if he cannot avoid taking notice of the existing state of things, created by the sinful history of the past, in order to remedy it, this must be regarded merely as a misfortune for the pure principle of justice. Herr Dühring creates his socialism, like all his other creations, through the medium of his famous two men. Instead of these marionettes playing the part of master and servant, as they did in the past, all of a sudden, by way of a change, they play at having equal rights— and the foundations of the Dühring socialism have been laid.

It therefore goes without saying that to Herr Dühring the periodical crises in industry have not at all the historical significance which we were compelled to attribute to them. In his view, crises are only accidental deviations from "normality" and at most only serve to occasion "the development of a more regulated order." The "common method" of explaining crises by overproduction is nowise adequate for his "more exact conception of things." Of course such a theory "may be permissible for special crises in special areas." As for example: "a swamping of the book market with editions of works suddenly released for publication and suitable for mass sale."

Herr Dühring can at any rate go to sleep with the beneficent consciousness that his immortal works will never cause any such world disaster. In great crises, however, in his view it is not overproduction, but rather "the lagging behind of national consumption ... artificially produced underconsumption ... the restriction of the *needs of the people* (!) in their natural growth, which ultimately makes the gulf between supply and demand so critically wide." And he has even had the good fortune to find a disciple for this crisis theory of his.

But unfortunately the underconsumption of the masses, the restriction of the consumption of the masses to what is necessary for their maintenance and reproduction, is not a new phenomenon. It has existed as long as there have been exploiting and exploited classes. Even in those periods of history when the situation of the masses was particularly favourable, as for example in England in the fifteenth century, they underconsumed. They were very far from having at their disposal for consumption their own annual total of production. Therefore, while underconsumption has been a constant feature in history for thousands of years, the general shrinkage of the market which breaks out in crises as the result of a surplus of production is a phenomenon only of the last fifty years; and so the whole superficiality of Herr Dühring's vulgar economics is necessary in order to explain the new collision not by the *new* phenomenon of overproduction but by the thousand-year old phenomenon of underconsumption. It is like a mathematician attempting to explain the variation in the relation between two magnitudes, one constant and one variable, not by the variation of the variable but by the fact that the constant magnitude remains unchanged. The underconsumption of the masses is a necessary condition of all forms of society based on exploitation, consequently also of the capitalist form, but it is the capitalist form which first produces crises. The underconsumption of the masses is therefore also a necessary condition of crises, and plays in them a role which has long been recognised; but it tells us just as little why crises exist today as why they did not exist at earlier periods.

Herr Dühring's notions of the world market are in general remarkable. We saw how, like a typical German man of letters, he

seeks to explain real industrial partial crises by means of imaginary
crises on the Leipzig bookmarket—the storm on the ocean by the
storm in a teacup. He also imagines that present-day capitalist
production must "depend for its market mainly on *the circles of the
possessing classes themselves*"; which does not prevent him, only
sixteen pages later, from putting forward in his familiar way, as the
modern industries of decisive importance, the iron and cotton industries—that is, precisely the two branches of production whose
products are consumed only to an infinitesimally small degree within
the circle of the possessing classes and are directed more than any
others to mass use. Wherever we turn in Herr Dühring's works
there is nothing but empty and contradictory chatter. But let us take
an example from the cotton industry. In the relatively small town
of Oldham alone—it is one of a dozen towns round Manchester,
with fifty to a hundred thousand inhabitants, in which cotton is the
main industry—in this town alone, in the four years 1872 to 1875,
the number of spindles spinning only Number 32 yarn increased
from two and a half to five million; so that in one medium-sized
English town there are as many spindles spinning one single count
as the cotton industry of all Germany, including Alsace, possesses.
And the expansion in other branches and areas of the cotton industry in England and Scotland has taken place in approximately the
same proportion. In view of these facts, it requires a strong dose of
deep-rooted effrontery to explain the present complete stagnation in
the yarn and cloth markets by the underconsumption of the English
masses and not by the overproduction carried on by the English
cotton factory owners.*

But enough of arguing with people who are ignorant enough of
economics to regard the Leipzig book market as a market in the
modern industrial sense. We therefore merely note that Herr Dühring has only one more piece of information for us on the subject
of crises: that in crises we have nothing but "the ordinary interplay
of overstrain and relaxation"; that over-speculation "is not only

---

* The "underconsumption" explanation of crises originated with Sismondi,
and in his exposition it has a certain meaning. Rodbertus took it from Sismondi, and Herr Dühring has in turn copied it, in his usual vulgarising fashion,
from Rodbertus. [*Note by F. Engels.*]

due to the planless multiplication of private enterprises," but that "the rashness of individual capitalists and the lack of private circumspection must also be reckoned among the causes which give rise to oversupply." And what is then the "cause which gives rise" to the rashness and lack of private prudence? Just precisely this very planlessness of capitalist production which manifests itself in the planless multiplication of private enterprises. And to misrepresent the translation of an economic fact into moral reprobation as the discovery of a new cause is also a piece of extreme "rashness."

With this let us leave the question of crises. In the preceding section we showed their necessary origin in the capitalist mode of production, and their significance as crises of this mode of production itself, as the necessary means towards the revolutionising of society, and it is not necessary to say another word in reply to Herr Dühring's superficialities on this subject. Let us pass on to his positive creations, to the "natural system of society."

This system, built on a "universal principle of justice" and therefore free from any dependence on troublesome material facts, consists of a federation of economic communes among which there is "freedom of movement and obligatory acceptance of new members on the basis of fixed laws and administrative regulations." The economic commune itself is above all "a comprehensive schematism of human and historical import" which is far superior to the "erroneous half-measures," for example, of a certain Marx. It implies "a community of persons linked together by their public right to dispose of a definite area of land and a group of production establishments, which they use in common, jointly participating in the proceeds." This public right is "a right to the object—in the sense of a *purely publicistic relation to Nature* and to the productive institutions." We leave it to the future jurists of the economic commune to cudgel their brains as to what this means; we give it up. The only thing we gather is that it is not at all the same as the "corporative ownership of associations of workers" which would not exclude mutual competition and even wage exploitation. And in this connection he observes by the way that the conception of a "collective ownership" such as is found in Marx is "to say the least unclear and open to question, as this conception of future society always gives the impression that it means nothing more than a cor-porative ownership by groups of workers." This is one more instance of the many "contemptible mannerisms" of interpolation in which Herr Dühring abounds, "for whose vulgar nature"—to use his own words—"only the vulgar word saucy would be quite appropriate"; it is just as baseless a lie as Herr Dühring's other invention that by "collective ownership" Marx means an ownership "which is at the same time both individual and social."

In any case this much is clear: the publicistic right of an eco-nomic commune in its instruments of labour is an exclusive right of property at least as against every other economic commune and also as against society and the state. But this right is not to entitle the commune "to cut itself off from the outside world, for among the various economic communes there is freedom of movement and compulsory acceptance of new members on the basis of fixed laws and administrative regulations ... like ... belonging to a political organisation at the present time, or participation in the economic affairs of the commune." There will therefore be rich and poor communes, and the levelling out takes place through the crowding of population to the rich communes and away from the poor ones. So that although Herr Dühring would prohibit competition in products between the individual communes by means of the national organi-sation of trade, he allows competition among the producers to con-tinue. Things are removed from the sphere of competition, but men remain under its control.

But we are still very far from clear on the question of this "publicistic right." Two pages further on Herr Dühring explains to us that the trade commune "will at first cover the politico-social area whose inhabitants form a single legal entity and in this char-acter possess the whole of the land, houses and productive insti-tutions." So after all it is not the individual commune at whose disposal these things are, but the whole nation. The "public right," "right in the object," "publicistic relation to Nature" and so forth is therefore not merely "at the very least unclear and open to ques-tion": it is in direct contradiction with itself. It is in fact, at any rate in so far as each individual economic commune is likewise a legal entity, "an ownership which is at the same time both individual and

316 ANTI-DÜHRING: SOCIALISM

social," and this latter "nebulous hybrid" is once again, therefore, only to be met with in Herr Dühring's own works.

In any case the economic commune has at its disposal instruments of labour for the purpose of production. How is this production carried on? In every respect, according to all that Herr Dühring tells us, precisely as in the past, except that the commune takes the place of the capitalists. The most we are told is that everyone will then be free to choose his occupation, and that there will be equal obligation to work.

The basic form of all production hitherto is the division of labour, on the one hand within society as a whole, and on the other within each separate productive establishment. Where does the Dühring "sociality" stand in this question?

The first great division of labour in society is the separation of town and country. This antagonism, according to Herr Dühring, is "inevitable, in the nature of things." But "it is in general doubtful to regard the gulf between agriculture and industry . . . as unbridgable. In fact, there is already a certain measure of constant interconnection which promises to increase considerably in the future." Already, we learn, two industries have penetrated agriculture and rural production: "in the first line, distilling, and secondly, beet-sugar manufacture . . . the production of spirits is already of such importance that it is easier to under-estimate it than to exaggerate it." And "if it were possible, as a result of some inventions, for a large number of industries to develop which were compelled to localise their production in the country in direct association with the production of raw materials"—then this would weaken the antithesis between town and country and "provide the widest possible basis for the development of civilisation." Moreover, "a somewhat similar result might also be brought about in another way. Apart from technical requirements, social needs are coming more and more to the front, and if the latter become the dominant consideration in the grouping of human activities it will no longer be possible to overlook those advantages which ensue from a close and systematic connection between the occupations of the countryside and the technical operations for the working up of raw materials."

Now in the economic commune it is precisely social needs which

are the determining factor; and so we would naturally expect the
commune to hasten to take advantage, to the fullest possible extent,
of the above-mentioned union of agriculture and industry. Herr
Dühring surely does not omit to tell us, at his accustomed length,
his "more exact conceptions" on the attitude of the economic commune to this question? The reader who expected this would be dis-
illusioned. The above-mentioned meagre, hesitating commonplaces,
once again not passing beyond the schnapps-distilling and beet-sugar-
making area of the Prussian *Landrecht,* are all that Herr Dühring
has to say on the antithesis between town and country in the present
and in the future.

Let us pass on to the division of labour in detail. Here Herr Dühring is a little "more exact." He speaks of "a person who has to
devote himself *exclusively* to *one* form of occupation."

If there is a matter of introducing a new branch of production,
the question simply depends on whether a certain number of *existences,* who had to *devote themselves to the production of an article,*
can be provided together with the consumption (!) they require. In
the socialitarian system no branch of production would "*require
many people,*" and there would be "different *economic* varieties of
men distinguished by their mode of living." Accordingly, within the
sphere of production everything remains much the same as under
the old system. In society up to now, however, there has been a "false
division of labour"; but as to what this was, and by what it is to
be replaced in the economic commune, we are only told: "As for the
division of labour itself, we have already said above that this question can be considered solved as soon as account is taken of varying
natural aptitudes and personal capabilities." In addition to capabilities, personal inclinations are taken into account: "The pleasure
felt in rising to types of activity which involve additional capabilities and training would depend entirely on the inclination felt for
the occupation in question and on the joy produced *in the exercise
of precisely this and no other thing*" (exercise of a thing!). But this
will stimulate competition within the socialitarian system, so that
"production itself will become interesting, and the dull pursuit of
it, which sees in it nothing but a means of earning will no longer
be the dominant feature in the system."

In every society in which production has developed spontaneously—and our present society is of this type—it is not the producers who control the means of production, but the means of production which control the producers. In such a society each new lever of production is necessarily transformed into a new means for the subjection of the producers to the means of production. This is most of all true of that lever of production which, prior to the introduction of large-scale industry, was by far the most powerful —the division of labour. The first great division of labour, the separation of town and country, condemned the rural population to thousands of years of degradation, and the people of the towns to subjection to each one's individual trade. It destroyed the basis of the intellectual development of the former and the physical development of the latter. When the peasant appropriates his land, and the citizen his trade, to just the same extent his land appropriates the peasant and his trade the citizen. In the division of labour, man is also divided. All other physical and mental faculties are sacrificed to the development of one single activity. This stunting of man's faculties grows in the same measure as the division of labour, which attains its highest development in manufacture. Manufacture splits up each trade into its separate fractional operations, allots each of these to an individual labourer as his life calling, and thus chains him for life to a particular detail function and a particular tool. "It converts the labourer into a crippled monstrosity, by forcing his detail dexterity at the expense of a world of productive capabilities and instincts. . . . The individual himself is made the automatic motor of a fractional operation" (Marx) *—a motor which in many cases becomes perfect only through the literal physical and mental crippling of the labourer. The machinery of modern industry degrades the labourer from a machine to the mere appendage of a machine. "The life-long speciality of handling one and the same tool, now becomes the life-long speciality of serving one and the same machine. Machinery is put to a wrong use, with the object of transforming the workman, from his very childhood, into a part of a detail-machine" (Marx).** And not only the labourers, but also

* *Capital*, Vol. I, p. 396 (Kerr edition).
** *Capital*, Vol. I, p. 461 (Kerr edition).

the classes directly or indirectly exploiting the labourers are made
subject, through the division of labour, to the tool of their function;
the empty-minded bourgeois to his own capital and his own thirst
for profits; the lawyer to his fossilised legal conceptions, which
dominate him as a power independent of him; the "educated classes"
in general to their manifold local limitations and one-sidedness, to
their own physical and mental short-sightedness, to their stunted
specialised education and the fact that they are chained for life to
this specialised activity itself—even when this specialised activity
is merely to do nothing.

The utopians were already perfectly clear as to the effects of the
division of labour, the stunting on the one hand of the labourer, and
on the other of the labour function, which is restricted to the life-
long, uniform and mechanical repetition of one and the same operation. The abolition of the antithesis between town and country
was demanded by Fourier, as by Owen, as the first prerequisite for
the abolition of the old division of labour as a whole. Both of them
thought that the population should be scattered through the country
in groups of sixteen hundred to three thousand persons; each group
was to occupy a gigantic palace, run on communal lines, in the
centre of their area of land. It is true that Fourier occasionally refers
to towns, but these were only to consist in turn of four or five such
palaces situated near each other. Both writers indicated that each
member of the social group would be occupied both in agriculture
and in industry; with Fourier, industry covers handicrafts and manufacture, while Owen assigns the main role to large-scale industry
and already demands the application of steam power and machinery
to domestic work. But within agriculture and industry both of them
also demand the greatest possible variety of occupation for each
individual, and in accordance with this, the training of young persons for the utmost possible all-round technical functions. Both of
them consider that man should develop in every direction through
universal practical activity and that labour should recover the at-
tractiveness of which the division of labour has deprived it, in the
first place through this variation of occupation, and through the
correspondingly short duration of the "session"—to use Fourier's
expression—devoted to each separate type of work. Both Fourier

and Owen are far in advance of the mode of thought of the exploiting classes inherited by Herr Dühring, according to which the antithesis between town and country is inevitable in the nature of
things; the narrow-minded view that a number of "existences" must
under all conditions be condemned to the production of *a single*
article, the view that desires to perpetuate the "different economic
varieties" of men distinguished by their mode of living—people who
take pleasure in the exercise of precisely this and no other thing, who
have therefore sunk so low that they *rejoice* in their own subjection
and one-sidedness. In comparison with the basic conceptions even of
the "idiot" Fourier's most extravagant phantasies, in comparison
even with the paltriest ideas of the "crude, feeble and paltry" Owen
—Herr Dühring, himself still completely dominated by the division
of labour, is no more than an impertinent dwarf.

In making itself the master of all the means of production, in
order to use them in accordance with a social plan, society puts an
end to the former subjection of men to their own means of production. It goes without saying that society cannot itself be free unless
every individual is free. The old mode of production must therefore
be revolutionised from top to bottom, and in particular the former
division of labour must disappear. Its place must be taken by an
organisation of production in which, on the one hand, no individual
can put on to other persons his share in productive labour, this
natural condition of human existence; and in which on the other
hand, productive labour, instead of being a means to the subjection
of men, will become a means to their emancipation, by giving each
individual the opportunity to develop and exercise all his faculties,
physical and mental, in all directions; in which, therefore, productive labour will become a pleasure instead of a burden.

Today this is no longer a phantasy, no longer a pious wish. The
present development of productive forces is already adequate as
the basis on which the increase in production which must follow
from the very fact of the socialisation of the productive forces—the
abolition of the barriers and disturbing factors and of the waste of
products and means of production resulting from the capitalist
mode of production—can reduce the time required for labour, with

every individual taking his share, to what on our present conceptions would be a small amount.

Nor is the abolition of the former division of labour a demand
which could only be carried through at the cost of the productivity
of labour. On the contrary. Large-scale industry has made it a necessary condition of production itself. "The employment of machinery
does away with the necessity of crystallising this distribution after
the manner of manufacture by the constant annexation of a particular man to a particular function. Since the motion of the whole
system does not proceed from the workman, but from the machinery,
a change of persons can take place at any time without an interrup-
tion of the work. . . . Lastly, the quickness with which machine
work is learnt by young people does away with the necessity of
bringing up for exclusive employment by machinery, a special class
of operatives." * But while the capitalist mode of employment of
machinery necessarily perpetuates the old division of labour with its
fossilized specialisation, although it has become superfluous from a
technical standpoint, the machinery itself rebels against this anachronism. The technical basis of modern industry is revolutionary.
"By means of machinery, chemical processes and other methods, it
is continually causing changes not only in the technical basis of production, but also in the functions of the labourer, and in the social
combinations of the labour process. At the same time, it thereby also
revolutionises the division of labour within the society, and incessantly launches masses of capital and of workpeople from one
branch of production to another. Modern industry, by its very nature, therefore necessitates variation of labour, fluency of function,
universal mobility of the labourer. . . . We have seen how this absolute contradiction . . . vents its rage in the incessant human sacrifices
from among the working class, in the most reckless squandering
of labour power and in the devastation caused by social anarchy.
This is the negative side. But if, on the one hand, variation of work
imposes itself after the manner of an overpowering natural law, and
with the blindly destructive action of a natural law that meets with
resistance at all points, modern industry, on the other hand, through
its catastrophes imposes the necessity of recognising, as a funda-

* *Capital*, Vol. I, p. 460 (Kerr edition).

mental law of production, variation of work, consequently fitness of the labourer for varied work, consequently the greatest possible development of his varied aptitudes. It becomes a question of life and death for society to adapt the mode of production to the normal functioning of this law. Modern industry, indeed, compels society, under penalty of death, to replace the detail worker of today, crippled by life-long repetition of one and the same operation, and thus reduced to the mere fragment of a man, by the fully developed individual, fit for a variety of labours, ready to face any change of production, and to whom the different social functions he performs are but so many modes of giving free scope to his own natural and acquired powers." (Marx, *Capital*.) *

Large-scale industry which has taught us to convert the movement of molecules, which is more or less universally realisable, into the movement of masses for technical purposes, has thereby to a considerable extent freed production from the restrictions of place. Water-power was local; steam-power is free. Though water-power was necessarily confined to the countryside, steam-power is by no means necessarily confined to the towns. It is the capitalist mode of its utilisation which concentrates it mainly in the towns and changes factory villages into factory towns. But in so doing, it at the same time undermines the conditions of its own exploitation. The first necessity for the steam engine, and a main requirement of almost all branches of production, is relatively pure water. The factory town, however, transforms all water into stinking ditch water. However much therefore concentration in the towns is a basic condition of capitalist production, each individual industrial capitalist is constantly striving to get away from the large towns necessarily created by it, and to move towards exploitation in the countryside. This process can be studied in detail in the textile industry districts of Lancashire and Yorkshire; modern capitalist industry is constantly bringing new large towns into being by constantly fleeing from the towns into the country. The position in the engineering industry areas is very similar, where, in part, other causes produce the same effects.

Once more, only the abolition of the capitalist character of mod-

* *Capital*, Vol. I, pp. 533-4 (Kerr edition).

ern industry can do away with this new vicious circle, this contradiction in modern industry, which is constantly reproducing itself.
Only a society which makes possible the harmonious co-operation
of its productive forces on the basis of one single vast plan can allow
industry to settle in whatever form of distribution over the whole
country is best adapted to its own development and the maintenance
of development of the other elements of production.

Accordingly, abolition of the antithesis between town and country
is not merely possible. It has become a direct necessity of industrial
production itself, just as it has become a necessity of agricultural
production and, moreover, of public health. The present poisoning
of the air, water and land can only be put an end to by the fusion of
town and country; and only this fusion will change the situation of
the masses now languishing in the towns, and enable their excre-
ment to be used for the production of plants instead of for the production of disease.

Capitalist industry has already made itself relatively independent
of the local limitations arising from the location of sources of raw
materials. The textile industry, in the main, works up imported raw
materials. Spanish iron ore is worked up in England and Germany
and Spanish and South American copper ores are used in England.
Every coalfield now supplies fuel to an industrial area beyond its
own borders, an area which is widening every year. Along the whole
of the European coast steam engines are driven by English and to
some extent also by German and Belgian coal. Society liberated
from the barriers of capitalist production can go much further still.
By producing a race of producers with an all-round training who
understand the scientific basis of industrial production as a whole,
and each of whom has had practical experience in a whole series of
branches of production from start to finish, this society will bring
into being a new productive force which will fully compensate for
the labour required for the transport of raw materials of fuel from
great distances.

The abolition of the separation between town and country is therefore not utopian, even in so far as it presupposes the most equal
distribution possible of large-scale industry over the whole country.
It is true that in the huge towns civilisation has bequeathed us a

heritage to rid ourselves of which will take much time and trouble. But this heritage must and will be got rid of, however protracted the process may be. Whatever destiny may be in store for the Prussian German Empire, Bismarck can go to his grave with the proud consciousness that the desire of his heart will certainly be fulfilled: the great towns will perish.

And now see how puerile Herr Dühring's notions are—that society can take possession of all means of production without revolutionising from top to bottom the former method of production and in particular putting an end to the old division of labour; that everything will be in order once "natural aptitudes and personal capabilities are taken into account"—that therefore whole masses of existences will remain, as in the past, enslaved to the production of *one single* article; whole "populations" will be required by a single branch of production, and humanity will remain, as in the past, divided into a number of different crippled "economic varieties"; that there will still be "porters" and "architects." Society is to take control of the means of production as a whole, in order that each individual may remain the slave of his means of production, and has only a choice as to *which* means of production are to enslave him. And see also how Herr Dühring considers the separation of the land from the country as "inevitable in the nature of things," and can only find a tiny palliative in schnapps-distilling and beet-sugar manufacturing—two specifically Prussian branches of industry; how he makes the distribution of industry over the country dependent on some future inventions and on the *necessity* to associate industry directly with the winning of its raw materials—raw materials which are already used at an ever-increasing distance from their place of origin! And Herr Dühring finally tries to cover himself by assuring us that the union between agriculture and industry will nevertheless be carried through even *against* economic considerations, as if this would be some economic sacrifice!

Certainly, in order to see that the revolutionary elements which will do away with the old division of labour, along with the separation of town and country, and will revolutionise the whole of production; in order to see that these elements are already contained in embryo in the productive conditions of modern large-scale industry, and that their development is hindered by the existing capitalist mode of production—in order to see these things, it is necessary to have a somewhat wider horizon than the sphere within which the Prussian *Landrecht* holds sway, than the country where schnapps and beet-sugar are the important industrial products, and where commercial crises can be studied on the book market. In order to see these things, it is necessary to have some knowledge of real large-scale industry in its historical growth and in its present actual form, especially in the one country which is its native land where alone it has attained its classical development; and with this knowledge it will not be possible even to think of attempting to vulgarise modern scientific socialism and to degrade it into Herr Dühring's *specifically Prussian socialism.*

IV. DISTRIBUTION

We have already seen that the Dühring economics leads up to the proposition: the capitalist mode of *production* is quite good, and can remain in existence, but the capitalist mode of *distribution* is bad, and must disappear. We now find that Herr Dühring's "socialitarian" system is nothing more than the carrying through of this principle in phantasy. In fact, it turned out that Herr Dühring has practically nothing to take exception to in the mode of production —as such—of capitalist society, that he wants to retain the old division of labour in all its essentials, and that he consequently has hardly a word to say in regard to production within his economic commune. Production is indeed a sphere.in which robust facts are dealt with, and in which, consequently, "rational phantasy" should give but little scope to the winged soaring of its free soul, because the danger of making a blunder is too evident. It is quite otherwise with distribution—which in Herr Dühring's view has practically no connection with production and is determined not by production but by a pure act of the will—distribution is the predestined field of his "social alchemising."

To the equal obligation to produce corresponds the equal right to consume, organised in the economic commune and in the trading commune embracing a large number of economic communes. "Labour ... is here offered in exchange against other labour on the basis of equal valuation. ... Service and counter-service represent here real equality between quantities of labour." And there is still this "equalisation of human energies, whether the individuals have in fact done more or less, or perhaps *even nothing at all*"; for all activities, in so far as they involve time and energy, can be regarded as labour performed—therefore even playing skittles or going for a walk. This exchange, however, does not take place between individuals as the collective group is the owner of all means of production and consequently also of all products; but on the one hand between each economic commune and its individual members, and on the other between the various economic and trading communes themselves. "The individual economic communes, in particular, will replace retail trade within their own areas by completely planned sales." Wholesale trade will be organised on the same lines; "Hence the system of the free economic society ... remains a vast exchange institution, the operations within which are carried out through the medium of the basis provided by the precious metals. It is insight into the inevitable necessity of this fundamental property which distinguishes our scheme from all those nebulosities which cling even to the most rational forms of current socialist thought."

The economic commune, as the first appropriator of the social products, has to determine, with a view to this exchange, "for each type of articles, a single price," based on the average production costs. "The significance which the so-called natural costs of production ... have for value and price today, will be provided (in the socialitarian system) ... by the estimate of the quantity of labour required. This estimate, by virtue of the principle of equal rights for each individual also in the economic sphere, can be brought back, in the last analysis, to the number of persons participating in the labour; this estimate will give the relation of prices corresponding both to the natural conditions of production and to the social right of realisation. The output of the precious metal will continue, as now, to determine the value of money. . . . It can be seen from this that in the new constitution of society, the determining factor and measure in the first place of value, and with value, of the exchange relations between products, is not only not lost, but for the first time takes its rightful place." The famous "absolute value" is at last realised.

On the other hand, however, the commune must also put its individual members in a position to buy from it the articles produced, by paying out to each, in compensation for his labour, a certain sum of money, daily, weekly or monthly, but necessarily the same for all. "From the socialitarian standpoint it is consequently a matter of indifference whether we say that wages disappear, or, that they must become the exclusive form of economic income." Equal wages and equal prices, however, establish "quantitative, even if not qualitative equality of consumption," and thereby the "universal principle of justice" is realised in the economic sphere. As to how much this wage of the future is to be, Herr Dühring tells us only that here too, as in all other cases, there will be an exchange of "equal labour against equal labour." For six hours of labour, therefore, there will be a sum of money paid which also embodies in itself six hours of labour.

Nevertheless, the "universal principle of justice" must not in any way be confounded with that crude levelling down which makes the bourgeois so indignantly oppose all communism, and especially the instinctive communism of the workers. It is by no means so inexorable as it would like to appear. The "equality in principle of economic rights does not exclude the *voluntary* addition to what justice requires, of an expression of special recognition and honour. . . . Society *honours itself*, in distinguishing the higher types of work *by a moderate additional allocation* for consumption." And Herr Dühring, too, honours himself, when, combining the innocence of a dove with the wisdom of a serpent, he bestows such touching care on the moderate additional consumption of the Dührings of the future.

This will finally do away with the capitalist mode of distribution. For "supposing, under such conditions as we have outlined, someone actually had a surplus of private means at his disposal, he would not be able to find any use for it as capital. No individual and no group would take it from him for production, except by way of exchange or purchase, and interest or profit would never be paid to him." However, "inheritance conforming to the basic principle of justice" would be permissible. It cannot be done without, for "a certain measure of inheritance will always be the necessary accompaniment of the principle of the family." But even the right of inheritance "will not be able to lead to any amassing of considerable wealth, as the building up of property . . . can never aim at the creation of means of production and rent-receiving existences."

And with this the economic commune is fortunately complete. Let us now see how it works.

We assume that all of Herr Dühring's hypotheses are completely realised; we therefore take it for granted that the economic commune pays to each of its members, for six hours of labour a day, a sum of money in which also six hours of labour is embodied, let us say twelve shillings. We also assume that prices exactly correspond to values, and therefore, on our assumptions, cover only the costs of raw materials, the wear and tear of machinery and equipment and the wages paid. An economic commune of a hundred working members would then produce in a day commodities to the value of twelve hundred shillings, £60; and in a year of 300 working days, £18,000. It pays out the same sum to its members, each of whom does as he likes with his share, which is twelve shillings a day or £180 a year. At the end of a year, and at the end of a hundred years the commune is no richer than it was at the beginning. During this whole period it will never once be in a position to provide even the moderate additional allocation for Herr Dühring's consumption, unless it cares to take it from its stock of means of production. Accumulation is completely forgotten. Even worse: as accumulation is a social necessity, and the existence of money provides a convenient form of accumulation, the organisation of the economic commune directly impels its members to accumulate privately, and thereby it leads to its own destruction.

How can this contradiction in the nature of the economic commune be avoided? It might take refuge in his beloved "levy," the price surcharge, and sell its annual production for £24,000 instead of £18,000. But as all other economic communes are in the same position, and must therefore act in the same way, each of them, in its exchanges with the others, would have to pay just as much "levy" as it pockets itself, and the "tribute" would thus have to fall only on its own members.

Or the economic commune might settle the matter without more ado by paying to each member, for six hours of labour, the product of less than six hours of labour, let us say of four hours; that is to say, instead of twelve shillings only eight shillings a day, leaving the prices of commodities, however, at their former level. In this case it does directly and openly what it tried to do in a hidden and indirect way in the former case: it forms Marxian surplus value to the amount of £6,000 annually, by paying its members, on outright capitalist lines, less than the value of what they produce, while it sells them commodities, which they can only buy from it, at their full value. The economic commune can therefore only secure a reserve fund by revealing itself as an "ennobled" truck system * on the widest possible communist basis.

Of two alternatives, one: either the economic commune exchanges "equal labour against equal labour," and in this case it cannot accumulate a fund for the maintenance and extension of production, but only the individual members can do this; or, on the other hand, it forms such a fund, and in this case it does not exchange "equal labour against equal labour."

Such is the content of exchange in the economic commune. What of its form? The exchange is effected through the medium of metallic money, and Herr Dühring is not a little proud of the "human and historical import" of this reform. But in the trading between the commune and its members the money *is* not money at all, it does not in any way function as money. It serves as a mere labour certificate; to use Marx's phrase, it "is merely evidence of the part taken by the individual in the common labour, and of his right to a certain portion of the common produce destined for consumption," ** and in carrying out this function, it is "no more 'money' than a ticket for the theatre." *** It can therefore be replaced by any other token, just as Weitling replaces it by a "ledger," in which the labour hours worked are entered on one side and the enjoyments taken as compensation on the other. In a word, in the trading of the economic commune with its members it functions merely as Owen's "labour money," that "phantasy" which Herr Dühring looks down upon from such a height, but nevertheless is himself compelled to introduce in his economics of the future. Whether the token which certifies the measure of fulfilment of the "obligation to produce," and therewith of the "right to consume" that has been earned, is a piece of paper, a farthing or a gold coin is absolutely of no consequence for *this* purpose. For other purposes it is by no means immaterial, as we shall see.

* The truck system in England, also well known in Germany, is that system in which the manufacturers themselves run the shops and compel their workers to get their goods from them. [*Note by F. Engels.*]

** *Capital*, Vol. I, p. 106, footnote (Kerr edition).

*** *Ibid.*

If therefore, in the trading of an economic commune with its members, metallic money does not function as money but as a disguised labour certificate, it achieves its money function even to a less degree in exchange between the different economic communes. In this exchange, on the assumptions made by Herr Dühring, metallic money is totally superfluous. In fact, mere bookkeeping would suffice, which would effect the exchange of products of equal labour against products of equal labour far more simply if it used the actual measure of labour—time, with the labour hour as unit— than if it first converted the labour hours into money. The exchange is in reality simple exchange in kind; all balances are easily and simply settled by drafts on other communes. But if a commune should really have a deficit in its dealings with other communes, all "the gold present in the universe," "natural money" though it be, could not save this commune from the fate of having to make good this deficit by increasing the quantity of its own labour, if it does not want to fall into a position of dependence on other communes through its debt. And the reader should always bear in mind that we are not ourselves constructing any edifice of the future; we are merely accepting Herr Dühring's assumptions and drawing from them the inevitable conclusions.

So that neither in exchange between the economic commune and its members, nor in exchange between the different communes, can gold, which is "natural money," succeed in realising its nature. Nevertheless, Herr Dühring assigns to it the function of money, even in the socialitarian system. We must therefore see if there is any other field in which its money function can be exercised. And this field exists. Herr Dühring certainly gives everyone a right to "quantitatively equal consumption," but he cannot compel anyone to exercise it. On the contrary, he prides himself that in the world he has created everyone can do what he likes with his money. He therefore cannot prevent some of them from setting aside a small money hoard, and others from not managing to live on the wage paid to them. He even makes this inevitable, by giving express recognition to the common property of the family in the right of inheritance, whence comes also the obligation of the parents to maintain their children. But this makes a wide breach in his quantitatively equal consumption. The bachelor lives in luxurious style on his eight or twelve shillings a day, while the widower with eight young children finds it very difficult to manage on this sum. On the other hand, by accepting money in payment without any question, the commune leaves open the possibility that this money may be obtained otherwise than by the individual's own labour. *Non olet.** The commune does not know whence it comes. But this brings in the conditions which permit metallic money, which hitherto played the role of a mere labour certificate, to exercise its real money function. Both the opportunity and the motive are present, on the one hand to the formation of a treasure, and on the other to running into debt. The needy individual borrows from the individual who builds up a hoard. The borrowed money, accepted by the commune in payment for means of subsistence, once more becomes what it is in existing society, the social incarnation of human labour, the real measure of labour, the general means of circulation. All the "laws and administrative regulations" in the world are just as powerless as against the laws of multiplication or of the chemical composition of water. And as the builder of the hoard is in a position to extort interest from people in need of money, along with metallic money functioning as money the usurer is also re-introduced.

Up to this point we have only considered the effects of existence of metallic money within the area of the Dühring economic commune. But outside this area the rest of the profligate world carries on contentedly along its old paths. On the world market gold and silver remain *world money*, a general means of purchase and payment, the absolute social embodiment of wealth. And this property of the precious metals gives the individual members of the economic communes a new motive to the accumulation of a hoard, to getting rich, to usury; the motive to act freely and independently of the commune outside its borders, and to realise on the world market the private wealth which they have accumulated. The usurers are transformed into dealers in the means of circulation, bankers, controllers of the means of circulation and of world money, and therefore into controllers of production, and therefore into controllers of the means of production, even though these may still for many years be regis-

* Money does not smell.—*Ed.*

tered nominally as the property of the economic communes and of the trading communes. And so the hoarders and usurers, transformed into bankers, become the masters also of the economic communes and the trading communes themselves. Herr Dühring's "socialitarian system" is indeed quite fundamentally different from the "nebulosities" of other socialists. It has no other purpose but the re-creation of high finance, under whose control and for whose purses it will work valiantly—if it should ever happen to be established and to hold together. Its one hope of salvation lies in the fact that the individual who amasses a hoard would prefer to make use of his world money and—get away from the commune as fast as possible.

Ignorance of earlier socialist thought is so widespread in Germany that an innocent youth might at this point raise the question whether, for example, Owen's labour certificates might not lead to a similar abuse. Although we are here not concerned with developing the significance of these labour certificates, the following may be said by way of contrasting Dühring's "comprehensive schematism" with the "crude, feeble and meagre ideas" of Owen: in the first place, such a misuse of Owen's labour certificates would require their conversion into real money, while Herr Dühring pre-supposes real money, though attempting to prohibit it from functioning otherwise than as mere labour certificates. While in Owen's scheme there would have to be a real abuse, in Dühring's scheme the immanent nature of money, independently of human volition, would assert itself; money would insist on its specific, correct use as against the misuse which Herr Dühring tries to impose on it owing to his own ignorance of the nature of money. Secondly, with Owen the labour certificates are only a transitional form to complete communism and the free utilisation of the resources of society; and incidentally at most only a means designed to make communism plausible to the British public. If therefore any form of misuse should compel Owen's society to do away with the labour certificates, the society would take a step forward towards its goal, entering upon a more complete stage of its development. But if the Dühring economic commune abolishes money, it at one blow destroys its "human and historical import," it puts an end to its peculiar beauty, ceases to

be the Dühring economic commune and sinks to the level of the
nebulosities to lift it from which Herr Dühring has devoted so much
of the hard labour of his rational phantasy.*

What then is the source of all the strange errors and entanglements amid which the Dühring economic commune moves? Simply
the nebulosity which, in Herr Dühring's mind, envelops the concepts of value and money, and finally drives him to attempt to discover the value of labour. But as Herr Dühring has not by any
means the monopoly for Germany of such haziness, but on the contrary meets with many competitors, we will "overcome our reluctance for a moment, and clear away the entanglements" which he
has erected here.

The only value known in economics is the value of commodities.
What are commodities? Products made in a society of private producers more or less separate from each other, and therefore in the
first place private products. These private products, however, become commodities only when they are made, not for use by their
producers, but for use by others, that is, for social use; they enter
into social use through exchange. The private producers therefore
stand in a social relation, constitute a society. Their products, although the private products of each individual, are therefore at the
same time, though unintentionally and as it were involuntarily, also
social products. In what, then, consists the social character of these
individual products? Evidently in two characteristics: first, that they
all satisfy some human want, have a use value not only for the
producers but also for others; and secondly, that although they are
products of the most varied individual labour, they are at the same
time products of human labour as such, of human labour in general.
In so far as they have use value also for other persons, they can
enter into exchange; in so far as in all of them is incorporated general human labour, the simple expenditure of human labour power,
they can be compared with each other in exchange, be said to be

---

* It may be noted in passing that the part played by labour certificates in
Owen's communist society is completely unknown to Herr Dühring. He knows
these certificates—from Sargant—only in so far as they figure in the Labour
Exchange Bazaars, which of course were failures—inasmuch as they were
attempts by means of the direct exchange of labour to pass from existing
society into communist society. [*Note by F. Engels.*]

equal or unequal, according to the quantity of this labour embodied in each. In two equal individual products, social conditions remaining equal, may be contained an unequal quantity of individual labour, but always only an equal quantity of general human labour. An unskilful smith may make five horseshoes in the time which a skilful smith may take to make ten. But society does not take into account the accident of the former's lack of skill; it recognises as general human labour only labour of a normal average degree of skill in each case. In exchange, therefore, one of the five horseshoes made by the first smith has not more value than one of the ten made by the other in an equal time: Individual labour contains general social labour only in so far as it is socially necessary.

Therefore when I say that a commodity has a particular value, I say (1) that it is a socially useful product; (2) that it has been produced by a private individual for private account; (3) that, although a product of individual labour, it is nevertheless at the same time and as it were unconsciously and involuntarily, also a product of social labour and indeed of a definite quantity of this labour, determined in a social way, through exchange; (4) I express this quantity not in labour itself, in such and such a number of labour hours, but *in another commodity*. If therefore I say that this clock is worth as much as this piece of cloth and each of these is worth fifty shillings, I say that in the clock, the cloth and the money there is contained an equal quantity of social labour. I therefore assert that the social labour time represented in them has been socially measured and found to be equal. But not directly, absolutely, as labour time is usually measured, in labour hours or days, etc., but in a roundabout way, relatively, through the medium of exchange. This is why I cannot express this definite quantity of labour time in labour hours—how many hours remain unknown to me—but also only in a roundabout way, relatively, in another commodity, which represents an equal quantity of social labour time. The clock is worth as much as the piece of cloth.

But the production and exchange of commodities, while compelling the society based on them to take this roundabout way, likewise compel it to make the detour as short as possible. They separate from the common crowd of commodities, one sovereign commodity in which the value of all other commodities can be expressed once for all; a commodity which serves as the direct incarnation of social labour, and is therefore directly and unconditionally exchangeable for all commodities—money. Money is already contained in embryo in the concept of value; it is value, only in developed form. But since the value of commodities, as opposed to the commodities themselves, makes itself independent in the form of money, a new factor appears in the society which produces and exchanges commodities, a factor with new social functions and effects. We need only state this point at the moment, without going more closely into it.

The economic science of commodity production is by no means the only science which has to deal with factors known only in a relative way. In physics also we do not know how many separate gas molecules there are in a given volume of gas, pressure and temperature being also given. But, so far as Boyle's law is correct, we know that such a given volume of any particular gas contains as many molecules as an equal volume of any other gas at the same pressure and temperature. We can therefore compare the molecular content of different volumes of different gases under different conditions of pressure and temperature; and if we take as the unit one litre of gas at 0° Cent. and 760 mm. pressure, we can measure the molecular content of each by this unity. In chemistry the absolute atomic weights of the various elements are also not known to us. But we know them relatively, in as much as we know their reciprocal relations. Just as commodity production and the economics of commodity production obtain a relative expression of the unknown quantity of labour contained in the various commodities, by comparing these commodities on the basis of their relative labour content, so chemistry obtains a relative expression for the magnitude of the unknown atomic weight by comparing the various elements on the basis of their atomic weights, expressing the atomic weight of one element in multiples or fractions of the other (sulphur, oxygen, hydrogen). And just as commodity production elevates gold into the absolute commodity, the general equivalent of all other commodities, the measure of all value, so chemistry promotes hydrogen to the rank of a chemical commodity money, by fixing its atomic weight at 1 and reducing the atomic weights of all other elements to hydrogen, expressed in multiples of its atomic weight.

Commodity production, however, is by no means the only form of social production. In the ancient Indian communities and in the family communities of the southern Slavs, products are not transformed into commodities. The members of the community are directly associated for production; the work is distributed on the basis of tradition and requirements, and likewise the products in so far as they are destined for consumption. Direct social production and direct distribution exclude all exchange of commodities, therefore also the transformation of the products into commodities (at any rate within the community) and consequently also their transformation into *values*.

From the moment when society enters into possession of the means of production and uses them in direct association for production, the labour of each individual, however varied its specifically useful character may be, is immediately and directly social labour. The quantity of social labour contained in a product has then no need to be established in a roundabout way; daily experience shows in a direct way how much of it is required on the average. Society can calculate simply how many hours of labour are contained in a steam-engine, a bushel of wheat of the last harvest, or a hundred square yards of cloth of a certain quality. It could therefore never occur to it still to express the quantity of labour put into the products, which it will then know directly and in its absolute amount in a third product, and moreover in a measure which is only relative, fluctuating, inadequate, though formerly unavoidable for lack of a better, and not in its natural, adequate and absolute measure, *time*. Just as little as it would occur to chemical science still to express atomic weights in a roundabout way, relatively, by means of the hydrogen atom if it was once able to express them absolutely, in their adequate measure, namely in actual weight, in billionths or quadrillionths of a gram. On the assumptions we made above, therefore, society will also not assign values to products. It will not express the simple fact that the hundred square yards of cloth have required for their production, let us say, a thousand hours of labour in the oblique and meaningless way, that they have the *value* of a thousand hours of labour. It is true that even then it will still be necessary for society to know how much labour each article of consumption requires for its production. It will have to arrange its plan of production in accordance with its means of production, which include, in particular, its labour forces. The useful effects of the various articles of consumption, compared with each other and with the quantity of labour required for their production, will in the last analysis determine the plan. People will be able to manage everything very simply, without the intervention of the famous "value." *

The concept of value is the most general and therefore the most comprehensive expression of the economic conditions of commodity production. Consequently, the concept of value contains the germ, not only of money, but also of all more developed forms of the production and exchange of commodities. The fact that value is the expression of the social labour contained in the individual products itself creates the possibility of a difference arising between this social labour and the individual labour contained in these same products. If therefore an individual producer continues to produce in the old way, while the social mode of production develops, this difference will become palpably evident to him. The same result follows when the aggregate of individual producers of a particular class of goods produces a quantity of them which exceeds the requirements of society. The fact that the value of a commodity is expressed only in terms of another commodity, and can only be realised in exchange against it, gives the possibility that the exchange may never take place, or at least may not realise the correct value. Finally, when the specific commodity labour power appears on the market, its value is determined, like that of any other commodity, by the labour time socially necessary for its production. The value form of products therefore already contains in embryo the whole capitalist form of production, the antagonism between capitalists and wage workers, the industrial reserve army, crises. To seek to abolish the

* As long ago as 1844 I stated that the above-mentioned balancing of useful effects and expenditure of labour would be all that would be left, in a communist society, of the concept of value as it appears in political economy (*Deutsch-Französische Jahrbücher*, p. 95). The scientific justification for this statement, however, as can be seen, was only made possible by Marx's *Capital*. [*Note by F. Engels.*]

capitalist form of production by establishing "true value" is therefore equivalent to attempting to abolish catholicism by establishing
the "true" Pope, or to set up a society in which at last the producers control their products by the logical application of an economic category which is the most comprehensive expression of the
subjection of the producers by their own product.

When the commodity-producing society has further developed
the value form, which is inherent in commodities as such, to the
money form, at this point many of the germs still hidden in value
break through to the light of day. The first and most essential effect
is the generalisation of the commodity form. Money forces the commodity form even on the objects which have hitherto been produced
for the producer's own use; it drags them into exchange. Thereby
the commodity form and money penetrate the internal economy of
the community directly associated for production, they break one
tie after another within the community, and dissolve the community
into a mass of private producers. At first, as can be seen in India,
money replaces joint tillage of the soil by individual tillage; at a
later stage it puts an end to the common ownership of the tillage
area, which still manifests itself in periodical redistribution, by a
final division (for example, in the peasant communities * on the
Moselle; and it is now beginning also in the Russian village communes); finally, it forces the dividing-up of whatever woodland and
grazing land still remains owned in common. Whatever other causes
arising in the development of production are also operating here,
money always remains the most powerful means through which influence is exerted on the communities. And, despite all "laws and
administrative regulations," with the same natural necessity money
would inevitably break up the Dühring economic commune, if it
ever came into existence.

We have already seen above (Political Economy VI) that it is
a self-contradiction to speak of the value of labour. As under certain social conditions labour produces not only products but also
value, and this value is measured by labour, it can as little have a
particular value as weight, as such, can have a special weight or
heat a special temperature. But it is the characteristic peculiarity

* Gehöferschaften.—*Ed.*

of all social confusion that ruminates on "true value" to imagine that in existing society the worker does not receive the full "value" of his labour, and that socialism is destined to remedy this; hence it is necessary in the first place to discover what is the value of labour, and this is done by attempting to measure labour, not by its adequate measure, time, but by its product. The worker should receive the "full proceeds of his labour." Not only the labour product, but labour itself must be directly exchangeable against products; one hour's labour against the product of another hour's labour. This, however, at once raises a very serious difficulty; *the whole product* is distributed. The function of society which is most important for progress, accumulation, is taken from society and put into the hands and the arbitrary discretion of individuals. The individuals can do what they like with their "proceeds" but society at best remains just as rich or as poor as it was. The means of production accumulated in the past have therefore been centralised in the hands of society, only in order that all means of production accumulated in the future may be once again dispersed in the hands of individuals. That is to strike a blow in the face at one's own presuppositions, and to arrive at a pure absurdity.

Fluid labour, active labour power, is to be exchanged for the product of labour. Then labour is a commodity, just like the product for which it is to be exchanged. Then the value of this labour is not in any sense determined by its product, but by the social labour embodied in it, and therefore by the present law of wages.

But it is precisely this which must not be. Fluid labour, labour power, should be exchangeable against its full product. That is to say, it should be exchangeable not against its *value,* but against its *use value;* the law of value is to apply for all other commodities, but must be suspended so far as labour power is concerned. Such is the self-destructive confusion that lies behind the "value of labour."

The "exchange of labour against labour on the principle of equal value," in so far as it has any meaning, that is to say, the exchangeability against each other of products of equal social labour, that is to say, the law of value, is precisely the fundamental law of commodity production, hence also of its highest form, capitalist production. It manifests itself in existing society in the only way in which economic laws can manifest themselves in a society of individual producers: as a law of Nature inherent in things and in external conditions, independent of the will or intentions of the producers, working blindly. By elevating this law into the basic law of his economic commune, and demanding that the commune should apply it with full consciousness, Herr Dühring makes the basic law of existing society into the basic law of his imaginary society. He wants existing society, but without its abuses. In this he is on the same ground as Proudhon. Like Proudhon, he wants to abolish the abuses which have arisen out of the evolution of commodity production into capitalist production, by applying to them the basic law of commodity production, precisely to the effects of which these abuses are due. Like Proudhon, Herr Dühring wants to abolish the real consequences of the law of value by means of imaginary ones.

Our modern Don Quixote, seated on his noble Rosinante "the universal principle of justice," and followed by his valiant Sancho Panza, Abraham Enss, rides out proudly on his knight errantry to win Mambrin's helmet, "the value of labour";—but we fear, we fear, he brings home nothing but the old familiar barber's basin.

V. STATE, FAMILY, EDUCATION

With the two last chapters we have now practically exhausted the economic content of Herr Dühring's "new socialitarian system." The only point we might add is that "the universal range of his historical survey" does not in any way prevent him from appreciating his own special interests, even apart from the moderate surplus consumption whose acquaintance we have already made. As the old division of labour continues to exist in the socialitarian system, the economic commune will have to reckon not only with architects and porters, but also with professional writers, and hence arises the question of how authors' rights will then be dealt with. This question is one which occupies Herr Dühring's attention more than any other. Everywhere, for example, in connection with Louis Blanc and Proudhon, the question of authors' rights keeps cropping up, and it is finally brought safely into the harbour of the "sociality," after nine full pages of the *Course*, in the form of a mysterious "remuneration of labour"—whether with or without moderate surplus consumption is not stated. A chapter on the position of fleas in the natural system of society would have been just as appropriate and in any case far less tedious.

The *Philosophy* gives detailed prescriptions for the organisation of the state of the future. Here Rousseau, although "the sole important forerunner" of Herr Dühring, nevertheless did not lay the foundations deep enough; his more profound successor puts this right, by completely watering down Rousseau and mixing in fragments of the Hegelian philosophy of law, also reduced to a watery mess. "The sovereignty of the individual" forms the basis of the Dühringian state of the future; it is not to be suppressed by the rule of the majority, but to find its real culmination in it. How does this work? Very simply. "If we presuppose reciprocal agreements between each individual and every other individual, and if the object of these agreements is mutual aid against unjust violations—then only the force destined for the maintenance of right is strengthened, and right is not deduced from the mere superior strength of the many over an individual or of the majority over the minority." Such is the ease with which the living force of the philosophy of reality hocus-pocus surmounts the most impassable obstacles; and if the reader thinks that after that he is no wiser than he was before, Herr Dühring replies that he really must not think it is such a simple matter, for "*the slightest error* in the conception of the role of the collective will would *destroy* the sovereignty of the individual, and it is from this sovereignty alone that real rights can be deduced." Herr Dühring treats his public as it deserves, when he makes game of it. He might have done so even more obviously: the disciples of the philosophy of reality would certaintly not have noticed it.

Now the sovereignty of the individual essentially consists in that "the individual is *subject to absolute compulsion* by the state"; this compulsion, however, can only be justified in so far as it "really serves natural justice." With this end in view there will be "legislative and judicial institutions," but they "must remain in the hands of the community"; and there will also be an alliance for defence, which will find expression in "association in the army or in an executive section for the maintenance of internal security"— that is to say, there will also be army, police, gendarmerie. Herr Dühring has indeed many times already shown that he is a good Prussian; here he shows himself a peer of that typical Prussian, who, as the late Minister von Rochow put it, "carries his gendarme in his breast." The gendarmerie of the future, however, will not be so dangerous as the *Zarucker* * of the present day. Whatever the sovereign individual may suffer at their hands, he will always have *one consolation:* "the right or wrong which, according to the circumstances, may then befall him at the hands of the free society can never be *any worse* than that which the *state of nature* would have brought with it"! And then, after Herr Dühring has once more tripped us up on those authors' rights of his which are always getting in the way, he assures us that in his world of the future there will be "of course, an absolutely free body of barristers available to all." "The free society as it is conceived today" gets steadily more

* *Zarucker.* A term applied to the police in Austria.—*Ed.*

and more of a mixture. Architects, porters, professional writers, gendarmes, and now also barristers! This "world of sober and critical thought" and the various heavenly kingdoms of the different religions, in which the believer always finds in transfigured form the things which have sweetened his earthly existence, are as like as two peas. And Herr Dühring is a citizen of the state where "everyone can be happy in his own way." What more do we want?

But it does not matter what *we* want. What matters is what Herr Dühring wants. And he distinguishes himself from Frederick II by the fact that in the Dühringian future state everyone will certainly not be able to be happy in his own way. The constitution of this future state provides: "In the free society there can be no religious cults; *for* each of its members has got beyond the primitive childish superstition that there is some Being, behind Nature or above it, who can be influenced by sacrifices or prayers." A "socialitarian system, rightly conceived, *has* therefore ... *to abolish* all the paraphernalia of religious magic, and therewith all the essential elements of religious cults." Religion will be prohibited.

All religion, however, is nothing but the phantastic reflection in men's minds of those external forces which control their daily life, a reflection in which the terrestrial forces assume the form of supernatural forces. In the beginnings of history it was the forces of Nature which were at first so reflected, and in the course of further evolution they underwent the most manifold and varied personifications among the various peoples. Comparative mythology has traced back this first process, at least in the case of the Indo-European nations, to its origin in the Indian Vedas, and has shown its detailed evolution among the Indians, Persians, Greeks, Romans, Germans and, so far as material is available, also among the Celts, Lithuanians and Slavs. But it is not long before, side by side with the forces of Nature, social forces begin to be active; forces which present themselves to man as equally extraneous and at first equally inexplicable, dominating them with the same apparent necessity, as the forces of Nature themselves. The phantastic personifications, which at first only reflected the mysterious forces of Nature, at this point acquire social attributes, become representatives of the forces of history.* At a still further stage of evolution, all the natural and social attributes of the innumerable gods are transferred to one almighty god, who himself once more is only the reflex of the abstract man. Such was the origin of monotheism, which was historically the last product of the vulgarised philosophy of the later Greeks and found its incarnation in the exclusively national god of the Jews, Jehovah. In this convenient, handy and readily adaptable form, religion can continue to exist as the immediate, that is, the sentimental form of men's relation to the extraneous natural and social forces which dominate them, so long as men remain under the control of these forces. We have already seen, more than once, that in existing bourgeois society men are dominated by the economic conditions created by themselves, by the means of production which they themselves have produced, as if by an extraneous force. The actual basis of religious reflex action therefore continues to exist, and with it the religious reflex itself. And although bourgeois political economy has given a certain insight into the causal basis of this domination by extraneous forces, this makes no essential difference. Bourgeois economics can neither prevent crises in general, nor protect the individual capitalists from losses, bad debts and bankruptcy, nor secure the individual workers against unemployment and destitution. It is still true that man proposes and God (that is, the extraneous force of the capitalist mode of production) disposes. Mere knowledge, even if it went much further and deeper than that of bourgeois economic science, is not enough to bring social forces under the control of society. What is above all necessary for this, is a social *act*. And when this act has been accomplished, when society, by taking possession of all means of production and using them on a planned basis, has freed itself and all its members from the bondage in which they are at present

* Comparative mythology overlooks this twofold character assumed at a later stage by the gods; it continues to pay exclusive attention to their character as reflexes of the forces of Nature, although it is this twofold character which is the basis of the confusion of mythologies which subsequently creeps in. Thus in some Germanic tribes the ancient Nordic war-god, Tyr, in Old High German Zio, corresponds to the Greek Zeus, Latin Jupiter for Dui-piter; in other Germanic tribes, Er, Eor, corresponds to the Greek Ares, Latin Mars. [*Note by F. Engels.*]

held by these means of production which they themselves have produced but which now confront them as an irresistible extraneous force; when therefore man no longer merely proposes, but also disposes—only then will the last extraneous force which is still reflected in religion vanish; and with it will also vanish the religious reflection itself, for the simple reason that then there will be nothing left to reflect.

Herr Dühring, however, cannot wait until religion dies this natural death. He proceeds in more deep-rooted fashion. He out-Bismarcks Bismarck; he decrees sharper May laws * not merely against catholicism, but against all religion whatsoever; he incites his gendarmes of the future to attack religion, and thereby helps it to martyrdom and a prolonged lease of life. Wherever we turn, we find that his socialism is specifically Prussian.

After Herr Dühring has so happily destroyed religion, "man, relying only on himself and Nature, and mature in the knowledge of his collective powers, can intrepidly enter on all the roads which the course of things and his own nature open to him." By way of a diversion let us consider what "course of things" the man relying on himself can intrepidly enter on, led by Herr Dühring.

The first course of things whereby man is made to rely on himself is: being born. Then, for the period of natural infancy, he remains committed to the "natural upbringer of children," his mother. "This period may last, as in ancient Roman law, until puberty, that is to say, until perhaps the fourteenth year." Only when badly brought up older boys do not pay proper respect to their mother's authority will recourse be necessary to the father's aid, and particularly to the public educational regulations, to remedy this. At puberty the child passes under "the natural guardianship of his father," if there is such a person "of real and uncontested paternity"; in other cases the community appoints a guardian.

Just as Herr Dühring at an earlier point imagined that the capitalist mode of production could be replaced by the social, without transforming production itself, so now he imagines that the modern bourgeois family can be torn from its whole economic foundations without thereby transforming its whole form. To him,

* The reference is to the German anti-Jesuit laws of May 1872.—*Ed.*

this form is so immutable that he even makes "ancient Roman law," though in a somewhat "ennobled" form, govern the family for all time; and he can only conceive a family as an "inheriting," which means a possessing, unit. Here the utopians are far in advance of Herr Dühring. They considered that the socialisation of education and, with this, real mutual freedom in the relations between members of a family, would necessarily follow from the free association of men and the transformation of private domestic work into a public industry. Marx also has already shown (*Capital,* Vol. I, p. 536) that "modern industry, by assigning as it does an important part in socially organised processes of production, outside the domestic sphere, to women, to young persons, and to children of both sexes, creates a new economic foundation for a higher form of the family and of the relations between the sexes."

"Every dreamer of social reforms," Herr Dühring says, "naturally has ready a pedagogy corresponding to his new social life." If we are to judge by this principle, Herr Dühring is a "veritable monster" among the dreamers of social reforms. For the school of the future occupies his attention at the very least as much as his author's rights, and this is really saying a great deal. He has his curricula for school and university all ready and complete, not only for the whole "predictable future" but for the transition period. But we will confine ourselves to what will be taught to the young people of both sexes in the final and ultimate socialitarian system.

The universal school will provide "everything which in itself and in principle can have any attraction for man," and therefore in particular "the foundations and principal conclusions of all sciences touching on the understanding of the world and of life." In the first place, therefore, it teaches mathematics, and indeed to such effect that the field of all fundamental concepts and methods, from simple enumeration and addition to the integral calculus, is "completely compassed." But this does not mean that in this school there will be anything really integrated or differentiated. On the contrary. What will be taught there will be, rather, absolutely new elements of mathematics as a whole, which contain in embryo both ordinary elementary and also higher mathematics. And although Herr Dühring asserts as regards himself that he already has in mind "the contents of the text-books," which the school of the future will use, "schematically, in their main lines," he has unfortunately not as yet succeeded in discovering these "elements of mathematics as a whole"; and what he cannot achieve "can only really be expected from the free and intensified forces of the new social order." But if the grapes of the mathematics of the future are still very sour, the astronomy, mechanics and physics of the future will present all the less difficulty and will "provide the kernel of all education," while "botany and zoology, which in spite of all theory, retain their mainly descriptive methods ... will serve rather as a light form of diversion." There it is, in black and white, in the *Philosophy*, page 417. Even to the present day Herr Dühring knows no other botany and zoology than that which is mainly descriptive. The whole of organic morphology, which embraces the comparative anatomy, embryology and palæontology of the organic world, is entirely unknown to him even by name. While in the sphere of biology totally new sciences are springing up, almost by dozens, behind his back, his puerile spirit still goes to Raff's *Natural History for Children* for "the eminently modern educative elements of natural science," and this constitution of the organic world he decrees likewise for the whole foreseeable future." Here too, as is his wont, he entirely forgets chemistry.

As for the æsthetic side of education, Herr Dühring will have to fashion it all anew. The poetry of the past is worthless. Where all religion is prohibited, it goes without saying that the "mythological or other religious trimmings" characteristic of poets in the past cannot be tolerated in this school. "Poetic mysticism," too, "such as, for example, Goethe practised to such an extent" is to be condemned. Herr Dühring will therefore have to make up his mind to produce for us those poetic masterpieces which "are in accord with the higher claims of an imagination which is reconciled with reason," and represent the pure ideal, which "denotes the perfection of the world." Let him not tarry with it! The economic commune can achieve the conquest of the world only when it comes in at the double in Alexandrine rhythm, reconciled with reason.

The young citizen of the future will not be much troubled with philology. "The dead languages will be entirely done away with ...

the foreign living languages, however ... will remain of secondary importance." Only where intercourse between nations extends to the movement of the masses of the peoples themselves would these languages be made accessible, according to needs and in an easy form. "Really educative study of language" will be provided by a kind of general grammar, and particularly by study of the "substance and form of one's own language."—Even the national narrow-mindedness of man at the present day is much too cosmopolitan for Herr Dühring. He wants also to do away with the two levers which in the world as it is today give at least the opportunity of rising above the narrow national standpoint: knowledge of the ancient languages, which opens a wider common horizon at least to those who have had a classical education; and knowledge of modern languages, through the medium of which alone the people of different nations can make themselves understood by one another and acquaint themselves with what is happening beyond their own frontiers. On the contrary, the grammar of the mother tongue is to be thoroughly taught. "Substance and form of one's own language," however, only become intelligible when their origin and gradual evolution are traced, and this cannot be done without taking into account, first, their own extinct forms, and secondly, allied languages, both living and dead. But this brings us back again to territory which has been expressly forbidden us. If Herr Dühring strikes out of his curriculum all modern historical grammar, there is nothing left for his language studies but the old-fashioned technical grammar, of the old classical philological type, with all its casuistry and arbitrariness, based on the lack of any historical basis. His hatred of the old philology makes him elevate the very worst product of the old philology into "the central point of the really educative study of language." It is clear that we have before us a linguist who has never heard a word of the wide and successful development of the historical science of language which had taken place during the last sixty years, and who therefore seeks "the eminently modern elements of education" in the science of language, not in Bopp, Grimm and Diez, but in Heyse and Becker of blessed memory.

But all this would still fall far short of making the young citizen of the future "rely on himself." To achieve this, it is necessary to lay a deeper foundation, by means of "the acquisition of ultimate philosophical principles." "Such a deepening of the foundations, however, will not be at all a gigantic task" now that Herr Dühring has cleared the ground. In fact, "if one purges of spurious scholastic excrescences those few strictly scientific truths of which the general schematics of being can boast, and determines to admit as valid only the reality which is well authenticated" (by Herr Dühring), elementary philosophy becomes perfectly accessible even to the youthful citizen of the future. "Recall to your mind the *extremely simple* processes by which we gave the idea of infinity and its critique a hitherto unknown import"—and then "you will not be able to see why the elements of the universal conception of space and time, which have been given such simple form through the present deepening and sharpening, should not eventually pass into the ranks of the elementary studies ... the most deep-rooted ideas" of Herr Dühring "should play no secondary role in the universal educational scheme of the new society." The identical state of matter and the numerated innumerable are on the contrary destined "not merely to put man on his own feet but also to make him realise of himself that he *is standing on the so-called absolute.*"

The people's school of the future, as we see, is nothing but a somewhat "ennobled" Prussian grammar school, in which Greek and Latin are replaced by a little more pure and applied mathematics and in particular by the elements of the philosophy of reality, and the teaching of German is brought back to Becker, that is, to about a third-form level. And in fact, now that we have demonstrated Herr Dühring's extremely scholarly "knowledge" in all the spheres on which he has touched, the reader will not be able to see why it, or rather, such of it as is left after preliminary thorough "purging," should not all "eventually pass into the ranks of the elementary studies"—since in reality they have never been anywhere else. It is true that Herr Dühring has heard something about the combination of work and instruction in socialist society, which is to ensure an all-round technical education, as well as a practical foundation for scientific training; and this point, too, is therefore brought in to help the socialitarian scheme in the usual way. But because, as we have seen, the old division of labour, in its essentials, is to continue to exist peacefully in the Dühringian production of the future, this technical training at school is deprived of any practical use later on in life, or any significance for production itself; it has only a purpose within the school; it is to replace gymnastics, which our deep-rooted revolutioniser wants to abolish altogether. He can therefore only offer us a few phrases, as for example, "young and old will work, in the full meaning of the word." This backboneless and meaningless effusion is really pitiful when we compare it with the passage in *Capital*, pages 529 to 536, in which Marx develops the thesis that "from the factory system budded, as Robert Owen has shown us in detail, the germ of the education of the future, an education that will, in the case of every child over a given age, combine productive labour with instruction and gymnastics, not only as one of the methods of adding to the efficiency of production, but as the only method of producing fully developed human beings."

We must pass over the university of the future, in which the philosophy of reality will be the kernel of all knowledge, and where, alongside of the Faculty of Medicine, the Faculty of Law will continue in full bloom; we must also omit the "special technical institutions"—about which all we learn is that they will be only "for a few subjects." Let us assume that the young citizen of the future has successfully passed through all his educational courses and has at last achieved such "self-reliance" that he is able to look round him for a wife. What is the course of things which Herr Dühring opens to him in this sphere?

"In view of the importance of propagation for the maintenance, elimination and blending, as well as even for the new formation and development of qualities, the ultimate roots of human and inhuman qualities must to a great extent be sought in sexual union and selection, and furthermore in the care taken for or against certain results of birth. We must leave it to a later epoch to pass judgment in practice on the brutality and stupidity now rife in this sphere. Nevertheless, from the outset we must at least make it clear, even in spite of the weight of prejudice, that far more important than the number of births is certainly whether their quality is good, thanks to Nature or human care, or bad. It is true that at all times and under all legal codes monstrosities have been destroyed; but there is a wide range of degrees between the normal human being and deformities which lack all resemblance to human being.... It is obviously an advantage to prevent the birth of a human being who would be only a defective creature." Another passage runs: "The idea of the right of the unborn to the best possible composition presents no difficulty to philosophic thought ... conception and also birth offer the opportunity for preventive, or in exceptional cases selective, care in this connection." Again: "Grecian art—the idealisation of man in marble—will not be able to retain its historical importance when the less artificial, and therefore, from the standpoint of the fate of millions, more important task of perfecting the human form in flesh and blood is taken in hand. This form of art does not merely deal with stone, and its æsthetic is not concerned with the consideration of dead forms"—and so on.

Our budding citizen of the future is brought to earth again. Even without Herr Dühring's help he certainly knew that marriage is not an art which merely deals with stone, or even with the consideration of dead forms; but after all Herr Dühring had promised him that he would be able to strike out along all roads which the course of things and his own nature opened to him, in order to discover a sympathetic female heart together with the body belonging to it. Now the "deeper and stricter morality" thunders to him that he must do nothing of the kind. The first thing that he must do is to cast off the brutality and stupidity now rife in the sphere of sexual union and selection, and bear in mind the right of the unborn to the best possible composition. At this solemn moment what matters for him is to perfect the human form in flesh and blood, to become a Phidias, so to speak, in flesh and blood. How is he to set about it? Herr Dühring's mysterious statements quoted above give him not the slightest indication, although Herr Dühring himself says it is an "art." Has Herr Dühring perhaps "in his mind's eye, schematically," a textbook also on this subject—of the kind of which, in sealed wrappers, German bookshops are now so full? Indeed, we are now no longer in the socialitarian society, but rather in the *Magic Flute*—the only difference being that Sarastro, the stout Masonic priest, would hardly rank as a "priest of the second order" in comparison with our deeper and stricter moralist. The tests to which Sarastro put his couple of love's adepts are mere child's play compared with the terrifying examination which Herr Dühring puts his two sovereign individuals through before he permits them to enter the state of "free and moral marriage." And so it may happen that our "self-reliant" Tamino of the future may indeed be standing on the so-called Absolute, but one of his feet may be a couple of degrees short of what it should be, so that evil tongues call him a club-foot. It is also within the sphere of the possible that his best-beloved Tamina of the future does not hold herself quite straight, owing to a slight deviation of her right shoulder which jealous tongues even call a little hump. What then? Will our deeper and stricter Sarastro forbid them to practise the art of perfecting humanity in flesh and blood; will he exercise his "preventive care" in conception, or his "selective care" at birth? Ten to one, things will happen otherwise; the pair of lovers will leave Sarastro-Dühring where he stands and will go off to the registry office.

Halt! Herr Dühring cries. This is not what was meant. Give me a chance to explain. In the "higher, really human motives of wholesome sexual unions ... the humanly ennobled form of sexual attraction, which in its intense manifestation is *passionate love,* when reciprocated is the best guarantee of a union which will be acceptable also in its result ... it is only an effect of the second order that from a relation which in itself is harmonious a harmoniously composed product should result. From this in turn it follows that any compulsion must have harmful effects" and so on. And thus all is for the best in the best of all possible socialitarian worlds: club-foot and hunch-back love each other passionately, and in their reciprocal relation therefore offer the best guarantee for a harmonious "effect of the second order"; it is all just like a novel— they love each other, they get each other, and all the deeper and stricter morality turns out as usual to be harmonious twaddle.

Herr Dühring's noble ideas on the female sex in general can be seen from the following indictment of existing society: "In this society of oppression based on the sale of human being to human being, prostitution is accepted as the natural complement of compulsory marriage ties in the husband's favour, and it is one of the most comprehensible but also *most significant* facts that *nothing of the kind is possible* for women." I would not care, for anything in the world, to have the thanks which should accrue to Herr Dühring from the women on account of this compliment. But has Herr Dühring never heard of the form of income known as a petticoat-pension, which is now no longer quite an exceptional thing? Herr Dühring himself was once a young barrister, and he lives in Berlin, where even in my day, thirty-six years ago, to say nothing of lieutenants, *Referendarius* * used often enough to rhyme with *Schürzenstipendarius!* **

The reader will permit us to take leave of our subject, which has often been dry and gloomy enough, on a note of raillery and reconciliation. So long as we were dealing with the separate issues raised, our judgment depended on objective, incontrovertible facts; and on the basis of these facts it was often enough necessarily sharp and even hard. Now, when philosophy, economics and socialitarian system all lie behind us; when we have before us the author's picture as a whole, which we had previously to judge in detail— now human consideration can come into the foreground; at this point we shall be permitted to trace back to personal causes many otherwise incomprehensible scientific errors and conceits, and to sum up our comprehensive judgment on Herr Dühring in the words: *mental incompetence due to megalomania.*

* The lowest grade in the state legal service.—*Ed.*
** Petticoat-pensioner.—*Ed.*

INDEX

INDEX

...Branch, Graham (1873-90), 368, 237 (?), ...
Bruce (?) of 78, 258, which came
371. ... ...

Bruce, Robert (1873?) 46, 46,
236.

59 William, Earl of Carrick

(1892?), ...

William, younger (?) ... circulate in the
... ...

Hugh Ludovic (1892?)